ACADEMIC LIBRARIES IN URBAN AND METROPOLITAN AREAS

Academic Libraries in Urban and Metropolitan Areas

A *Management Handbook*

EDITED BY

Gerard B. McCabe

THE GREENWOOD LIBRARY MANAGEMENT COLLECTION

Mary R. Sive, Series Adviser

Greenwood Press
NEW YORK • WESTPORT, CONNECTICUT • LONDON

Library of Congress Cataloging-in-Publication Data

Academic libraries in urban and metropolitan areas : a management
  handbook / edited by Gerard B. McCabe.
       p.   cm. — (The Greenwood library management collection, ISSN
  0894–2986)
     Includes bibliographical references and index.
     ISBN 0–313–27536–X (alk. paper)
     1. Libraries, University and college—United States.   2. Libraries
  and metropolitan areas.   I. McCabe, Gerard B.   II. Series.
  Z675.U5A338   1992
  027.7′0973—dc20   91–21182

British Library Cataloguing in Publication Data is available.

Library of Congress Catalog Card Number: 91–21182
ISBN: 0–313–27536–X
ISSN: 0894–2986

First published in 1992

Greenwood Press, 88 Post Road West, Westport, CT 06881
An imprint of Greenwood Publishing Group, Inc.

Printed in the United States of America

The paper used in this book complies with the
Permanent Paper Standard issued by the National
Information Standards Organization (Z39.48–1984).

10 9 8 7 6 5 4 3 2 1

Contents

PART IV: EXTENDED CAMPUS CONSIDERATIONS

PART V: SECURITY, SAFETY, AND PRESERVATION

PART VI: MANAGERIAL PERSPECTIVES

Introduction

Academic libraries in cities and their environs have unique concerns, missions, and expectations very different from those of their peers in the traditional university or college towns. Why is this so? Often it is because the urban school was started to fill a particular need; sometimes this need was to provide higher education for students who could not attend one of the traditional and often rural colleges or universities. In his chapter Dr. Delmus Williams addresses this and other reasons why these schools were begun. Some schools that started on the outskirts of a city, even several miles away from the city's center or its outer border, eventually found themselves surrounded by residential or even industrial areas and so had the needs of the city thrust upon them. Others even farther removed have found themselves providing library services for white-collar workers who commute to the city but live in the neighborhood of the school. Some of these people may actually be enrolled part-time in so-called downtown schools but expect the neighborhood college library to support their need for study materials. Others depend upon the academic library for their job-related reading or even for their leisure pursuits and believe that their needs cannot be met by a local public library. Voluntarily or not, these academic libraries have had the urban and metropolitan demands of everyday life thrust upon them and so have been forced to find direction for their role, which so often differs from the role of their peers in the traditional locales. For some libraries the concern for quality of service to their institution's students and faculty becomes critical as the demands of the general public seem to encroach upon available service time. In his very thoughtful essay, Dr. Fred Heath discusses the concern about this issue by his library, which serves a private institution. The resolution of the matter came only after serious consideration by staff and administrators, who reviewed every possible factor, including the role and good name of their institution in its metropolitan area and in the state and its participation in cooperative organizations. The result is preservation of high-quality service to the immediate academic community and favorable understanding by the public, which still has fair access to the library's services and resources. Other chapters discuss service to high school students, security for users, staff, and materials.

To arrive at subject material for this book, I prepared a survey with a long list of topics that appeared to be of interest to such libraries. Fifty of these survey forms were mailed to directors of libraries selected at random and located in standard metropolitan statistical areas. Of these surveys, each with a self-addressed, stamped envelope enclosed, 45 were returned. These were scored on an extra copy of the form. The chapters were then developed from the replies, and all written comments were considered in preparing these topics. After the chapter topics were prepared, they were mailed to a few library directors, including one public library director, for evaluation. After their evaluations were returned, the final draft of topics was finished, and a letter of explanation was prepared.

Two hundred invitations were mailed to library directors across the country. The letter asked the directors, in some cases specific individuals known to me, to alert their librarians to this opportunity. Prospective authors were asked to send me a chapter outline based on the chapter topics. People who thought they might have a better idea for a chapter were encouraged to do the same. The letter went to all types of libraries, serving all sizes of colleges and universities.

The concept of a book to meet the needs of these libraries had been lingering in my mind for several years. After all, I had been director of an urban university library system for 12 years prior to moving to Clarion University of Pennsylvania. In the winter of 1989, the time became available to devote some thought to the worthiness of this project. The conference of the Association of College and Research Libraries (ACRL) held in Cincinnati in April 1989 offered the opportunity to discuss this idea with several colleagues, all of them directors of such libraries. All were quite definite in their responses: there is a need, there are serious concerns, and such a book properly developed would be very useful. This response gave me the incentive to go on with the survey and attempt to identify precisely what was most needed.

The solicitation of authors was done in exactly the same way as the survey. Some invitations were sent to specific libraries where there was known interest; many others were sent at random. All of the chapter authors in this book volunteered for the assignment, and only a few were known to me prior to the solicitation.

The importance of the subject matter was reinforced when Dr. Rashelle Karp, author of the leadoff bibliographic essay, told me that her research uncovered few, if any, articles in the recent literature on some of the chapter topics. For that reason, the decision was made to open with her essay, which would serve as an additional introduction to the subject matter of the book.

Every effort was made to build a collection of chapters that would address many of the major concerns of these libraries. The resulting contents should be of great interest to those people who work in urban and metropolitan academic libraries and to those students of librarianship who will pursue their future careers in them.

Special thanks are due to Dr. Edward Garten of the University of Dayton and to Dr. Delmus Williams of the University of Alabama-Huntsville for their early encouragement of this project and their commitment to it. I sought their advice at the Cincinnati ACRL conference, and they were positive in their statement of need; both appear as chapter authors. Also reviewing the proposed content was Mr. Graham Sadler, Director of the County of Henrico Library System in suburban Richmond, Virginia; Mr. Sadler and I were colleagues in the Richmond Area Library Cooperative when I was director of an academic library system in Richmond. Cooperative efforts among libraries of all types are especially important in metropolitan areas. My appreciation is also due to Mrs. Peggy Postlewait, Carlson Library's administrative secretary, for her assistance with this project.

The Urban Academic Library: Opportunity Spawned of Pressure

A Bibliographic Essay

Rashelle S. Karp

As the introduction to this excellent reference on the issues and solutions to problems of the urban academic library, this bibliographic essay reinforces the need for such information. A comprehensive search of the literature over the past two years (judged to be most relevant to the timely content of the articles presented in this volume) yields almost nothing devoted entirely to the urban academic library. The institution's incidence in the United States far exceeds the incidence of articles about it. Some of the major issues facing today's urban academic library are identified in the literature but there are other (and there are many) issues that are not documented in the literature.

THE ISSUES

Issues Not Significantly Visible in the Literature

Urban academic library issues that are most visible in the literature include the impact of new technology, bibliographic instruction, and the pressures on administrators. Other issues, not as visible in the literature but of critical import, are dealt with more extensively in the chapters within this volume. They include

1. Access to academic library collections by nonaffiliated users. Ralph Russell et al. provide some of the only research-based data on this topic. Their chapter is based on their own recent survey of 26 large urban universities.

2. Circulation policies for nonaffiliated users. The most recent survey data prior to Eugene Mitchell's chapter in this volume are from 1986 (Dubois), and most of the literature dealing with circulation policies seems to focus on policies for affiliates (Intner 1987). For this volume, Mitchell undertook a survey of 68 publicly controlled four-year colleges and universities located in major metropolitan areas in the United States.

3. Service to international students. Harriet Pastor and Lia Hemphill's chapter highlights an innovative approach to breaking down cultural barriers by employing international students in the library. Based on their survey results, they provide the first data regarding this technique.

4. Security of library materials and legal ramifications. Carolyn Robison et al. provide a detailed examination of the legal precedents and consequences of protecting a library's collections.

5. Use of government documents in academic libraries. The literature indicates that a significant issue regarding government documents in academic libraries is their under-utilization by faculty (Fraser and Fisher 1987; McClure and Hernon 1989). Catherine Dwyer's chapter provides a detailed examination of the most valuable government documents in the areas of demographics, business statistics, government finance, climate, and environment, all of which have particular importance for urban library patrons.

6. Extension and cooperative library services. Although much of the literature examines the importance of library services to extension students, little has been written on the ways to implement such service. Yvonne Ralston and Adele Oldenburg's chapter provides a complete plan. including a philosophy statement and concrete suggestions for facility planning, document delivery, and operations. Susan Anderson's chapter on networking complements and enhances Ralston and Oldenburg's vision of distance library services with her concise and thorough review of innovative networking arrangements among academic libraries.

7. Reference service in an urban academic setting. Although much is written about reference services in general, Carolyn Sheehy's chapter on their provision in an urban setting provides a unique perspective on the types of services which are most commonly provided in urban academic settings as contrasted to those provided in nonurban environments.

Impact of New Technology

It is not within the purview of this essay to detail all of the new technology with which academic librarians work; that purpose is well achieved by John Head in this volume. Certain trends and innovations, however, that put much pressure on the urban academic library to adapt quickly to change seem to be foremost in the recent literature and therefore deserve mention. Much of the literature speculates on the academic library's increasing dependence upon electronic publishing. One author projects an increase in electronic publishing from ''less than one percent of acquisitions . . . in 1989 to possibly ten percent in 1995 and to 25–30 percent by 1998'' (Downes 1990, 59). This dependence is resulting in (1) an increased need for more sustained vendor training focused on greater numbers of library professionals, as well as greater attention to training requirements spelled out in a library's Request for Proposal (RFP) (Litchfield 1990); (2) an imperative to exploit nontraditional formats before they follow the path of encyclopedias and textbooks, which are marketed not to libraries, but rather directly to end users (Rumsey 1990); and (3) continuing, vigorous attention to preservation policies that focus on an item's internal integrity rather than its artifact value (Hazen 1990).

Along with electronic publishing, academic librarians are also relying most heavily on electronic databases, bibliographic utilities, internal automation of library processes, and the integration of all of these into one usable system. This emphasis on technology has given birth to new and sometimes unreasonable pressures upon the "systems librarian," whose job is becoming harder to define and even harder to limit. Today's academic librarians must carefully distinguish between responsibilities appropriate for a systems librarian, a data-processing professional, or a technician, even as they look, often in vain, for an automation expert who can manage the automation project from design to installation and maintenance and at the same time serve as a "software engineer, a hardware specialist, a systems programmer, a telecommunications expert, and an electrical engineer" (Chu 1990, 101).

In part because of electronic technologies, the core of academic library service seems to be changing from one of "ownership" of materials to one of "access" to materials. This shift from "predemand stockpiling" to "on-demand delivery" (Hacken 1988) is especially putting pressure on technical services staff, whose traditionally defined positions assumed ownership of documents. Technical services staff now need to be familiar with several bibliographic utilities, as well as local utilities (Lowell 1990), as they gradually become database managers (Dwyer 1988) who must develop intelligent interfaces between access systems (Graham 1990). Other traditional library staff functions have also been dramatically changed as a result of new technology. With the advent of expert systems, many library functions are becoming automated: acquisitions (approval plans, selective dissemination of information); cataloging (assignation of main entries, descriptive cataloging based on semiotic study of title pages, selection of name access points); classification and indexing (Cavanagh 1989); library orientation (Fadell and Myers 1989); instruction on online public access catalog use (Ercegovac 1989; Travis 1989); humanized (Smith 1989) reference (via machine-readable, full text files and sophisticated "user models"); bibliographic instruction; training of new reference librarians (Parrott 1989); and end user online database searching (Trautman and von Flittner 1989). It is also becoming more common to use off-the-shelf software packages (i.e., Q and A by Symantec) to produce these expert systems in-house (Butkovich et al. 1989). The urban academic library, with its human resources, which reach far beyond the university employees into a large external community, possesses unique opportunity creatively to exploit and manipulate new technologies. The same resources that provide the opportunity, however, also exert tremendous pressure on urban academic librarians to seize the opportunity or lose credibility.

With every benefit provided by the computer, there are consequences, which some of the literature decries. Particularly debated are the status and operation of bibliographic instruction.

Bibliographic Instruction

Since bibliographic instruction became a visible part of the academic library in the late 1970s, it has changed from being considered a nontraditional service and candidate for curtailment in times of budgetary constraint to a well-recognized core service (Chandley and Gavryck 1989). Current major structures for academic library bibliographic instruction include orientation (Arp and Wilson 1989); course-related instruction (Maloney 1989); course-integrated instruction (Blystone 1989); independent courses (Allen 1989); curriculum-integrated instruction, especially into the general education requirements (Blandy 1989; Reynolds 1989; Spitzer 1989); an "each one teach one" approach in which nonlibrary faculty orient new faculty to the library (Werking and Ford 1989); and integration across the curriculum modeled after the "Writing Across the Curriculum" movement (Elliot 1989). Techniques of bibliographic instruction are increasingly making use of new technology (Baker and Steffen 1989) to reduce the labor intensiveness of this and other public services (Martin 1990). The content of bibliographic instruction is also changing to include an electronic information literacy component (Lowry 1990) and to better apply learning theory to electronic instructional aids (Frick 1989). Even as bibliographic instruction becomes more computer-assisted and more efficient, however, a growing number of public service academic librarians are becoming uncomfortable with its importance as they perceive the provision of library instruction as substituting for library service (Pinzelik 1990). They advocate a shift away from a focus on bibliographic instruction and toward service that more specifically satisfies user requests and is more closely aligned with the special library service philosophy (Bessler 1990). Finally, E. Ray Hall's chapter in this volume creatively suggests ways in which adult students can be more appropriately accommodated into innovative bibliographic instruction strategies.

Administration

The pressures of change are probably most keenly felt by urban academic library administrators, who must manage many conflicts that arise from many different fronts.

The need to supply extensive document delivery has led to a dependence on networking and local cooperative agreements. The members of cooperative systems, however, often accuse each other of not contributing enough to the cooperative effort, especially in terms of cataloging utilities (Lowry 1990). In an era of cost consciousness, the benefits of consortia are no longer argued on a philosophical level but rather are argued on the basis of cost benefit analysis. Programs are evaluated on their ability to reduce costs, especially materials and collection maintenance costs (Dowd 1990), and on their efficient maximization of value to members (Simpson 1990). Cost consciousness is especially true in urban areas, where many local cooperative agreements are possible because of the availability of many local resource collections. As the availability of resources increases because of networking, however, the local focus on access and access technologies, rather than collections, brings about much more labor-intensive, customized reference service and an orientation away from self-service in favor of more personalized, mediated service (Shaughnessy 1990). This change unfortunately comes at a time when current staff are already utilized to maximum capacity and money for additional staff is difficult to obtain. This situation demands vigilant and constant accountability and justification. The literature indicates that formulas previously used for budget allocation after a budget was in place are now being adapted to project and justify initial budget requests (Gregory 1990). In terms of collections, the scarcity of money is a constant frustration for urban academic library administrators, who are expected to maintain collections at a reasonable conspectus level but who must often fall below a research level except in very specialized and narrow subject areas (Hamaker and Grinell 1990) and who are expected to maintain collections broad enough to meet the nonacademic needs of a sizable external community, including provision of such materials as self-help manuals, travel guides, cookbooks, financial planning helps, and so on (Metz and Foltin 1990).

Serials and periodicals are still a source of major concern as their costs rise more quickly than do library budgets (Lynden 1990) and require sophisticated research techniques such as citation studies (Devin and Kellogg 1990) to facilitate cancellation decisions (Bustion and Treadwell 1990; Sapp and Watson 1989) and effect dramatic changes in the "scholarly information marketplace" (Byrd 1990) that will limit the proliferation of journal literature.

In terms of personnel management, administrators must encourage library faculty to become more involved in university service so the library will be more visible on campus (Gamble 1989); help library faculty to publish and perform more like teaching faculty so they will be promoted and tenured (Cosgriff, Kenney, and McMillan 1990; Hersberger 1989) even though they still do not have parity with classroom faculty (Meiseles 1990); facilitate the development of leadership skills among the staff (Jurow 1990); provide nonthreatening, creative in-house educational opportunities that will improve professional skills for immediate positions (Arthur 1990; Cevallos and Kratz 1990; Mushrush 1990); combat the lack of communication between public service and technical service librarians in innovative ways (Gossen et al. 1990); and organize the library in new ways that are more flexible and more quickly able to adapt to change (Hay 1990).

Strategic planning is still a paramount function of the urban academic library director, with new planning processes like readiness, planning, training, implementation, maintenance (RPTIM) that include staff development as a prime element (Weaver-Meyers 1990) and analysis of the values and belief systems of employees as a foundation upon which to ensure the success of the plan (Forsman 1990). The national trend away from narrowly defined personnel directors and toward human resource directors with diverse responsibilities has been embraced by many academic libraries (Rooks 1989), and the debate on faculty status for librarians continues, with the recent appointment of a task force by the ACRL to study in the issue in Association for Research Libraries (ARL) institutions as well as colleges and community colleges ("Librarian Status Study," 1989).

It is no wonder that recent articles in the literature have discussed burnout among academic library administrators. Cited as factors contributing to burnout are frequent changes in university presidencies; the addition of an echelon of vice presidents between the library director and the president (which has downgraded the library director's status); the changing nature of administrative structures in general, related to enrollment patterns at the university (Schwartz 1988); increasing controls by state boards (MacAnally and Downs 1989); lack of upward mobility; and the lack of a peer group on campus (Woodsworth 1989).

Other

Issues not highly visible in the literature but represented include facilities, service to special groups, the charging of fees, dealing with international or English as a Second Language (ESL) students, and security.

Facilities seem to be a concern primarily in terms of (1) ways to most effectively determine use patterns in the library so that renovations and additions will have maximum benefit (Potthoff and Montanelli 1990; Schloman 1990); (2) the need to move away from architectural tradition and toward architectural principle in the design of new library buildings that will attract patrons (Oringdulph 1990); (3) recent concern about environmental disability, or the "sick building syndrome" (Simon 1990); and (4) special concerns about air pollution in industrialized urban areas and its effects on library collections (see James Gwin's chapter in this volume) and the differences between perceptions and uses of the physical facility when it is located in an urban environment (see Ruth Person and Joan Rapp's chapter in this volume).

Urban academic librarians must, more than other academic librarians, deal with issues regarding service to special groups. Services to special groups that have been recently documented in the literature follow.

1. "Partnerships" with librarians at other institutions whose students use the urban academic library, where the nonaffiliated librarian provides instruction and orientation for nonaffiliated students, but at the urban academic library (Hammond 1989).

2. Information and referral services that can be used by the entire community, including nonaffiliated patrons (Demo and McClure 1988; Leavy and Moore 1988).

3. Bibliographic instruction, summer institutions, guides and handouts written specifically for young adults, and orientation for high school students; Egbers and Giesecke 1989; Kenney 1989; Nofsinger 1989); and free academic library cards for high school seniors (LeClercq 1989). Policies regarding such services and the services that can be provided are discussed at length in the chapters by Kathleen Tiller and by Jay McNamara and Delmus Williams in this volume.

4. Provision of the online academic library catalog in local school libraries (Craver 1988).

5. Academic library orientation for elementary students in order to minimize interruptions caused when young people use the urban academic library as a baby-sitting service after school (Hammond 1989b).

6. Provision of document processing services for primary schools in the area (Bennett 1989).

7. Development of an automated "Faculty Research Profile" to facilitate selective dissemination of information and also to provide information services about the university faculty (Richardson 1990).

8. Extended service and off-campus service via telephone, fax, document delivery, photocopying, and agreements with off-campus libraries not affiliated with the university (Wittucke 1990) to serve the needs of older and returning students who often commute and who constitute "an important segment of enrollment on most college campuses" (Moran 1989, 28). Guidelines for off-campus extended service are currently being finalized by ACRL (Pickett 1990).

9. "Peer information counseling," by which successful minority undergraduates are recruited to teach incoming minority undergraduates about the library (MacAdam and Nichols 1989).

10. Innovative approaches to bibliographic instruction for international students (Jacobson 1988; Koehler and Swanson 1988) that focus on workshops (Ball and Mahony 1987) to increase librarians' understanding of the cultural background of each international student (Wayman 1984), the ability to adjust language patterns to accommodate the specific needs of each international student (MacDonald and Sarkodie-Mensah 1988), and specifically tailored course-integrated instruction (Ormondroyd 1989).

11. In-house education to familiarize librarians with the necessary accommodations and specific needs of disabled students (Rude and Hauptman 1990), especially in terms of reference services (Huang 1989).

To provide some of these services (in particular, those to nonaffiliated groups), university libraries have adopted fee schedules beyond traditional membership fees, especially for services rendered to business and industry (Marvin 1988). Recently, issues surrounding fees have focused on a librarian's accountability for information provided (Murphy 1990); document delivery; the range of services to be provided; staffing; legalities such as copyright (Caren 1988) and claims of unfair competition from the private sector (Josephine and Renecker 1989); how to advertise and market the service without unfairly competing with the private sector ("Cornell Library Services," 1986); and philosophical and ethical considerations (Budd 1989; Nielson 1989). Issues aside, Linda Simons and Edward Garten's chapter in this volume presents a core collection of business reference materials that should meet the majority of urban demands for information in this area.

Internal security is also an issue, not only in terms of the maintenance and protection of collections from vandalism, theft (Dubois 1986; Mitchell 1988; Pederson 1990); and arson (Goldberg 1990), but also in terms of the safety of staff (O'Brien 1989) and patrons (Barsumyan 1988).

SUMMARY

Information gleaned from the literature indicates that the state of being for urban academic libraries is pressure spawned of opportunity.

Unlike the public library, whose responsibility is to serve the diverse and fragmented interests (Shavit 1989) of the varied clientele in a diverse and increasingly complex and amorphous community, the academic library's overriding responsibility is to a diverse and increasingly complex but well-defined community of its own students, staff, and faculty. Because of its location, however, the urban academic library is also called upon to serve the much more expansive community within which it geographically and socially operates (Ford and Likness 1988/1989).

The presence of a large external community presents immeasurable opportunity in the form of diverse human resources, many local collections of document resources, and an available population to whom education about academe and academic libraries can be provided (Rettig 1988/1989). But, with every strong opportunity that presents itself, an equally strong pressure to seize the opportunity is exerted. The pressure mounts as urban university librarians try, within a milieu where both resources and time are never sufficient (Dunlap 1988/1989), to provide necessary resources and services for their affiliated community, while simultaneously, and because of principle, trying to satisfy the exigencies of an increasingly demanding nonaffiliated community.

Opportunity spawned of pressure is overwhelming but will prove positive as urban academic librarians continue to rise to the challenges presented in innovative ways that will lead the rest of the profession.

REFERENCES

Allen, Mary Beth. 1989. Focusing the one-shot lecture. *Research Strategies* 1, no. 3 (Summer): 100–105.

Arp, Lori, and Wilson, Lizabeth A. 1989. Structures of bibliographic instruction programs: A continuum for planning. *Reference Librarian* 24: 25–35.

Arthur, Gwen. 1990. Peer coaching in a university reference department. *College and Research Libraries* 51 (July): 367–73.

Baker, Betsy, and Steffen, Susan Swords. 1989. Microcomputers and bibliographic instruction. *Reference Librarian* 24: 223–32.

Ball, Mary Alice, and Mahony, Molly. 1987. Foreign students, libraries, and culture. *College and Research Libraries* 48 no. 1: 160–66.

Barsumyan, S. E. 1988. Premises liability. *New Jersey Libraries* 21: 9–10.

Bennett, Peg. 1989. An ANGEL (Adventist Network of General Education Libraries) in the southeast: Private small school networking (college involvement in a processing center for elementary schools). *Southeastern Librarian* 39 (Summer): 55–56.

Bessler, Joanne. 1990. Do library patrons know what's good for them? *Journal of Academic Librarianship* 16 (May): 76–85.

Blandy, Susan Griswold. 1989. Building alliances: General education and library skills in a community college. *Reference Librarian* 24: 57–73.

Blystone, Robert V. 1989. Enhancing science courses with bibliographic instruction: Three approaches. *Research Strategies* 7 no. 2 (Spring): 55–60.

Bodi, Sonia. 1990. Teaching effectiveness and bibliographic instruction: The relevance of learning styles. *College and Research Libraries* 51 (March): 113–19.

Budd, John. 1989. It's not the principle, it's the money of the thing. *Journal of Academic Librarianship* 15 (September): 218–22.

Bustion, Marifran, and Treadwell, Jane. 1990. Reported relative value of journals versus use: A comparison. *College and Research Libraries* 51 (March): 142–51.

Butkovich, Nancy J.; Taylor, Kathryn L.; Dent, Sharon H.; and Moore, Ann S. 1989. An expert system at the reference desk: Impressions from users. *Reference Librarian* 23: 61–74.

Byrd, Gary D. 1990. An economic "commons" tragedy for research libraries: Scholarly journal publishing and pricing trends. *College and Research Libraries* 51 (May): 184–96.

Caren, Loretta. 1988. Issues facing private academic libraries considering fee-based programs. *Reference Librarian* 22: 37–47.

Cavanagh, Joseph M. A. 1989. Library applications of knowledge-based systems. *Reference Librarian* 23: 1–19. (This is an excellent overview of the entire field.)

Cevallos, Elena E., and Kratz, Charles E. 1990. Training for public services. *Journal of Library Administration* 12: 27–45.

Chandley, Otis, and Gavryck, Jacquelyn. 1989. Bibliographic instruction trends in research libraries. *Research Strategies* 1, no. 3 (Summer): 106–13.

Chu, Felix T. 1990. Evaluating the skills of the systems librarian. *Journal of Library Administration* 12: 91–102.

Cornell library services marketed to a wider public. 1986. *Library Journal* 111 (July): 22.

Cosgriff, John; Kenney, Donald; and McMillan, Gail. 1990. *Journal of Academic Librarianship* 16 (May): 94–97.

Craver, Kathleen. 1988. The influence of online catalogs on academic library use by college-bound high school seniors (access to the online catalog of the University of Illinois at Urbana-Champaign Library encourages local high school students to use the university library). *RQ* 28 (Winter): 220–31.

———. 1989. The impact on the school library of online access to academic libraries: Implications for the future (study at the Laboratory School, University of Illinois). *Catholic Library World* 60 (January/February): 164–68.

Demo, Teresa L., and McClure, Charles R. 1988. Information and referral in the academic library. *Reference Librarian* 21: 95–108.

Devin, Robin B., and Kellogg, Martha. 1990. The serial/monograph ratio in research libraries: Budgeting in light of citation studies. *College and Research Libraries* 51 (January): 46–54.

Dowd, Sheila T. 1990. Library cooperation: Methods, models to aid information access. *Journal of Library Administration* 12: 63–81.

Downes, Robin N. 1990. Electronic technology and access to information. *Journal of Library Administration* 12: 51–61.

Dubois, Henry. 1986. From leniency to lockout. *College and Research Libraries News* 47 (December): 698–702.

Dunlap, Barbara. 1988/1989. The essence of urban academic librarianship. *Urban Academic Librarian* 6/7, nos. 2/1 (Fall/Spring): 25–29.

Dwyer, James R. 1988. The evolutionary role of technical services. *Journal of Library Administration* 9: 13–26.

Egbers, Gail, and Giesecke, Joan. 1989. SPICE (Summer Pre-college Instruction and Career Experience). *College and Research Libraries News* 9 (October): 840–43.

Elliot, Paula. 1989. The view from square one: Librarian and teaching faculty collaboration on a new interdisciplinary course in world civilizations. *Reference Librarian* 24: 87–112.

Ercegovac, Zorana. 1989. Augmented assistance in online catalog subject searching. *Reference Librarian* 23: 21–40.

Fadell, Jeff, and Myers, Judy E. 1989. The information machine: A microcomputer-based reference service. *Reference Librarian* 23: 75–112.

Ford, Barbara J., and Likness, Craig S. 1988/1989. Varied clientele, service objectives and limited resources. *Urban Academic Librarian* 6/7, nos. 2/1 (Fall/Spring): 20–24.

Forsman, Rick B. 1990. Incorporating organizational values into the strategic planning process. *Journal of Academic Librarianship* 16 (July): 150–53.

Fraser, Emily Joan, and Fisher, William H. 1987. Use of federal government documents by science and engineering faculty. *Government Publications Review* 14, no. 1: 33–44.

Frick, Elizabeth. 1989. Theories of learning and their impact on OPAC instruction. *Research Strategies* 7, no. 2 (Spring): 67–68.

Gamble, Lynne E. 1989. University service: New implications for academic librarians. *Journal of Academic Librarianship* 14 (January): 344–47.

Goldberg, B. 1990. Arson in Asheville; medical library recovering. *American Libraries* 21 (March): 182.

Gossen, Eleanor; Reynolds, Frances; Ricker, Karina; and Smirenski, Helen. 1990. Forging new communication links in an academic library: A cross-training experience. *Journal of Academic Librarianship* 16 (March): 18–21.

Graham, Peter S. 1990. Electronic information and research library technical services. *College and Research Libraries* 51 (May): 241–50.

Gregory, Vicki L. 1990. Development of academic library budgets in selected states with emphasis on the utilization of formulas. *Journal of Library Administration* 12: 23–45.

Hacken, Richard. 1988. Tomorrow's research library: Vigor or rigor mortis? *College and Research Libraries* 49 (November): 485–93.

Hamaker, Charles A., and Grinell, Stuart. 1990. Cost analysis of monographs and serials. *Journal of Library Administration* 12: 41–49.

Hammond, Carol Burroughs. 1989a. Aliens in the house: Those other students who use your library. *Research Strategies* 7, no. 3 (Summer): 134–37.

————. 1989b. Kids, the academic library and the schools (Arizona State University West Campus Library offers tours as an alternative approach to correct behavior problems from local students). *College and Research Libraries News* 4 (April): 264–66.

Hay, Fred. 1990. The subject specialist in the academic library: A review article. *Journal of Academic Librarianship* 16 (March): 11–17.

Hazen, Dan C. 1990. Preservation in poverty and plenty: Policy issues for the 1990s. *Journal of Academic Librarianship* 15 (January): 344–51.

Hersberger, Rodney M. 1989. The challenges of leading and managing faculty status librarians. *Journal of Academic Librarianship* 14 (January): 361–65.

Huang, Samuel T. 1989. Reference services for disabled individuals in academic libraries. *Reference Librarian* 25/26: 527–39.

Intner, Sheila. 1987. *Circulation policy in academic, public and school libraries.* Westport, CT: Greenwood Press.

Jacobson, F. F. 1988. Bibliographic instruction and international students. *Illinois Libraries* 70 (December): 628–33.

Josephine, Jelen B., and Renecker, Maxine H. 1989. In defense of FIRST and freedom of access to information. *College and Research Libraries News* 50 (May): 377–79.

Jurow, Susan. 1990. Preparing for library leadership. *Journal of Library Administration* 12: 57–73.

Kenney, Donald J. 1989. Teens in academe. *School Library Journal* 35 (September): 181.

Koehler, Boyd, and Swanson, Kathryn. 1988. ESL students and bibliographic instruction: Learning yet another language. *Research Strategies* 6, no. 4 (Fall): 148–60.

Leavy, Marvin D., and Moore, Elaine E. 1988. I & R in an academic library. *Reference Librarian* 21: 109–19.

LeClercq, Angie. 1989. High school library access to an academic library. In *Reaching and teaching diverse library groups*, ed. Teresa B. Mensching, 11–17. Ann Arbor, MI: Pierian Press.

Librarian status study. 1989. *College and Research Library News* 8 (September): 677.

Litchfield, Charles A. 1990. Vendor training: A question of commitment to user success. *Journal of Library Administration* 12: 3–12.

Lowell, Gerald R. 1990. Local systems and bibliographic utilities in 1992: A large research library perspective. *Journal of Academic Librarianship* 16 (July): 140–44.

Lowry, Anita Kay. 1990. Beyond BI: Information literacy in the electronic age. *Research Strategies* 8, no. 1 (Winter): 22–27.

Lowry, Charles B. 1990. Resource sharing or cost shifting? *College and Research Libraries* 51 (January): 11–19.

Lynden, Frederick C. 1990. Cost analysis of monographs and serials. *Journal of Library Administration* 12: 19–40.

MacAdam, Barbara, and Nichols, Darlene. 1989. Peer information counseling: An academic library program for minority students. *Journal of Academic Librarianship* 15 (September): 204.

McAnally, A. M., and Downs, R. B. 1989. The changing role of directors of university libraries. *College and Research Libraries* 50 (May): 307–27.

McClure, Charles R., and Hernon, Peter. 1989. *Users of academic and public GPO depository libraries*. Washington, DC: U.S. Government Printing Office.

MacDonald, G., and Sarkodie-Mensah, E. 1988. ESL students and American libraries. *College and Research Libraries* 49 (September): 425–31.

Maloney, Yolanda. 1989. Bibliographic instruction for foreign language classes: A pilot project. *Research Strategies* 7, no. 2 (Spring): 61–66.

Martin, Rebecca R. 1990. The paradox of public service: Where do we draw the line? *College and Research Libraries* 51 (January): 20–26.

Marvin, Stephen. 1988. ExeLS: Executive library services. *Reference Librarian* 22: 145–60.

Meiseles, Linda. 1990. Faculty status for librarians: The City University of New York's experience. *Urban Academic Librarian* 7, no. 2 (Winter): 57–65.

Metz, Paul, and Foltin, Bela. 1990. A social history of madness. *College and Research Libraries* 51 (January): 33–40.

Mitchell, W. Bede. 1988. On the use of positive reinforcement to minimize the problem of overdue library materials. *Journal of Library Administration* 9, no. 3: 87–101.

Moran, B. B. 1989. The unintended revolution in academic libraries: 1939 to 1989 and beyond. *College and Research Libraries* 50 (January): 25–41.

Murphy, Marcy. 1990. Evaluating public service. *Journal of Library Administration* 12: 63–90.

Mushrush, Janel L. 1990. Options in learning instructor led and computer based training. *Journal of Library Administration* 12: 47–55.

Nielson, Brian. 1989. Allocating costs, thinking about values: The fee-or-free debate revisited. *Journal of Academic Librarianship* 15 (September): 211–17.

Nofsinger, Mary M. 1989. Library use skills for college-bound high school students: A survey (of academic library user education services provided to high school students in Washington State). *Reference Librarian* 24: 35–56.

O'Brien, M. J. 1989. ABA 1989: Security in the wake of the Rushdie death threat. *Publisher's Weekly* 235 (June 30): 33–34.

Oringdulph, Robert E. 1990. Thoughts on library buildings and their parts. *Library Administration and Management* 4, no. 2 (Spring): 71–76.

Ormondroyd, Joan. 1989. The international student and course-integrated instruction: The librarian's perspective. *Research Strategies* 7 (Fall): 148–58.

Parrott, James R. 1989. Simulation of the reference process, Part II: REFSIM, an implementation with Expert system and ICAI modes. *Reference Librarian* 23: 153–76.

Pederson, Terri L. 1990. Theft and mutilation of library materials. *College and Research Libraries* 51 (March): 120–28.

Pickett, Mary Joyce. 1990. ACRL guidelines for extended campus library services. *College and Research Library News* 51, no. 4 (April): 353–55.

Pinzelik, Barbara P. 1990. An unreasonable burden. *Journal of Academic Librarianship* 16 (May): 83–85.

Potthoff, Joy K., and Montanelli, Dale S. 1990. Use of library facilities: Behavioral research as a tool for library space planning. *Journal of Library Administration* 12: 47–61.

Rettig, James. 1988/1989. Cakes and ale in the city. *Urban Academic Libraries* 6/7, nos. 2/1 (Fall/Spring): 14–20.

Reynolds, Judy. 1989. University approval of library research skills as part of the general education curriculum requirements. *Reference Librarian* 24: 75–86.

Richardson, Jeanne M. 1990. Faculty research profile created for use in a university library. *Journal of Academic Librarianship* 16 (July): 154–57.

Rooks, D. C. 1989. The technicolor coat of the academic library personnel officer: The evolution from paper-pusher to policy maker. *Journal of Library Administration* 10, no. 4 (March): 99–113.

Rude, R., and Hauptman, R. 1990. To serve the unserved: Social responsibility in the academy. *Journal of Academic Librarianship* 15 (January): 364–65.

Rumsey, Eric. 1990. The power of the new microcomputers: Challenge and opportunity. *College and Research Libraries* 51 (March): 95–99.

Sapp, Gregg, and Watson, Peter G. 1989. Librarian-faculty relations during a period of journals cancellations. *Journal of Academic Librarianship* 15 (September): 285–89.

Schloman, Barbara F. 1990. Multifaceted assessment of facility needs in an academic library. *Journal of Library Administration* 12: 9–21.

Schwartz, R. 1988. *Multicampus libraries: Organization and administration case studies.* Metuchen, NJ: Scarecrow Press.

Shaughnessy, Thomas W. 1990. The library as information center: Wishful thinking or realistic role? *Journal of Library Administration* 12: 3–18.

Shavit, David. 1989. Urban political trends. In *Trends in urban library management,* ed. Mohammed Aman and Donald Sager. Metuchen, NJ: Scarecrow Press.

Simon, Matthew J. 1990. The sick (library) building syndrome. *Library Administration and Management* 4, no. 2 (Spring): 87–91.

Simpson, Donald B. 1990. Library consortia and access to information: Costs and cost justification. *Journal of Library Administration* 12: 83–98.

Smith, Dana E. 1989. Reference expert systems: Humanizing depersonalized service. *Reference Librarian* 23: 177–90.

Spitzer, Alice M. 1989. Bringing an interdisciplinary world view to English 101—the library's involvement. *Reference Librarian* 24: 113–21.

Trautman, Rodes, and Flittner, Sara von. 1989. An expert system for microcomputers to aid selection of online databases. *Reference Librarian* 23: 207–38.

Travis, Irene L. 1989. Knowledge-based systems in information work: A view of the future. *Reference Librarian* 23: 41–60.

Wayman, Sally A. 1984. The international student in the academic library. *Journal of Academic Librarianship* 9, no. 6 (January): 336–41.

Weaver-Meyers, Pat. 1990. ARL libraries and staff development: A suggested model for success. *College and Research Libraries* 51 (May): 251–65.

Werking, Richard Hume, and Ford, Barbara J. 1989. From the users: Faculty introduce new faculty to library services. *Research Strategies* 7, no. 2 (Spring): 52.

Wittucke, Virginia. 1990. Off-campus library services: Leading the way. *College and Research Library News* 51, no. 3 (March): 252–56.

Woodsworth, Anne. 1989. Getting off the library merry-go-round: McAnally and Downs revisited. *Library Journal* 114, no. 8 (May 1): 35–38.

PART I

The Mission of the Urban Academic Library

1

Defining the Mission of the Urban University and Its Library: The Beginnings of a Typology

Delmus E. Williams

When one begins to look at the urban university library and its role within both the university and the larger community, it is important to understand, first, that the mission of the library can be defined only within the context of the university and, second, that the role of the university is defined by its relation to the community surrounding it. The purpose of this chapter will be to begin to develop a definition of those contexts and to consider ways in which they can shape the library programs of institutions operating in cities.

UNIVERSITIES IN THE UNITED STATES

One of the strengths of higher education in the United States has always been its diversity. When American colleges were established, they were based on different traditions. While these traditions have now been integrated into the common fabric of higher education, the emphasis that is placed on them contributes to the distinctiveness of individual colleges and universities. Leonard Veysey (1965) contends that American universities began primarily as institutions that were designed to instill discipline and culture in their students in keeping with the model of the English universities upon which they were patterned. Veysey also feels that the primary functions of these institutions have since become spreading liberal culture, doing research, and providing useful services to the greater community. In his view, these three missions are incorporated into virtually every institution to varying degrees and can be used to explain both the similarities and the differences that exist within the community of higher education.

Halls of Liberal Culture

The role of universities and colleges in the spreading of liberal culture probably relates most closely to the original mission of higher education in this country. Colleges are expected to produce educated men and women who conform to the traditions of civilized behavior within their culture, who can read, write, and reason effectively, and who can provide leadership to the society in which they live. This view is an elitist view of higher education that values schooling in the intangibles rather than focusing on the employment opportunities that might await a new college graduate. While those who stress this mission de-emphasize the kind of rote learning that characterized the nineteenth-century college, they seek to carry on the traditions of American culture and give students the basic tools that will fit them for any challenge that might confront them. Persons with this view see higher education as a preprofessional program designed to provide the students with basic skills and a general sense of how individuals might fit into society. This part of higher education's mission is reflected most clearly in the universities' core curricula, in the general organization of colleges of arts and sciences within those universities, and in the educational program of small, freestanding liberal arts colleges.

The University and Research

The second mission that is generally assigned to institutions of higher education comes from the German university tradition that was imported into this country after the Civil War. This mission emphasizes a requirement for scholars to contribute to the base of knowledge available to society through their own research and through the education of the next generation of scholars. Universities are havens for those who are objectively searching for new levels of truth in all disciplines, and these institutions have pulled together impressive communities of scholars, laboratory facilities, computer networks, and libraries to ensure that the efforts of these individuals can be supported.

Universities and the Service Mission

The third major focus of universities and colleges has to do with those activities that are designed to provide services to the community. This mission, as defined by Veysey, is distinctly American and contrasts sharply with the other missions assigned to institutions of higher education. The spread of liberal culture implies that there are arbiters who know what parts of culture are appropriate and fosters a kind of social elitism. Research emphasizes the need for the development of an intellectual elite. The service mission emphasizes the more democratic principle that communities of talent should contribute directly to the betterment of the life of individual citizens by developing a mechanism for social mobility, by providing men and women with the special skills needed by society, by developing programs that exploit the talents of those who work and study in the university for the good of society, and by applying research directly to society's problems.

This concept developed as America's population expanded into the midwest and western United States, as the country industrialized, and as its population became more diverse. As society became more complex, people began to ask more of higher education. The need for schoolteachers led to the establishment of normal schools and then of colleges of education. To meet the needs of the farmer, the Morrill Act of 1862 required that state universities be established to provide education and research for the improvement of agriculture and led to the development of farm extension services. Polytechnics and engineering schools were established to provide both manpower and applied research in engineering and science, and business schools were developed as the structure of the financial community became more complex. David Starr Jordan, then president of Stanford University, argued in the early 1900s that "the college has ceased to be a cloister and has become a workshop" (1903, 46), and that sentiment has become increasingly important as ever larger numbers of people have availed themselves of a college education.

As the concept that universities should provide service to the larger society gained acceptance, advocates of this position began to stress the importance of democracy in higher education, with equal emphasis on the idea that any area of study that was appropriately rigorous should be given equal value in the university curriculum and that any students who studied there should be given equal treatment no matter what their social background or their course of study. This position is perhaps best stated by Lloyd Morey, who contended that the university serves the aims and wishes of the people based on the principle that its doors are open to all who can meet its minimum requirements for so long as they can measure up to its minimum standards of performance (1961, 22).

THE PLACE OF URBAN UNIVERSITIES WITHIN HIGHER EDUCATION

Every institution in higher education has developed a mission that includes some elements of all of these ideals with varying degrees of emphasis, but urban universities have developed as perhaps the purest form of a university devoted to the service ideal. These institutions were established specifically to meet the needs of the city and its population, and while they have developed significant research programs, they have remained true to this purpose. They were designed to provide opportunity for people within the city, services to the city, research to solve the problems of the city, and an intellectual center that could enrich and revitalize city life. As Edward G. Holley noted, the question for the urban universities "was not whether they would be committed to community action and service but how and in what ways" (1972, 179). The urban universities in this country were expected by those who established and nurtured them to become as significant to the development of the city as the land-grant schools had been to agriculture (Jencks and Riesman 1968).

The concept of the urban university grew out of a need for educational opportunities and services to newly arrived immigrants and to others living in the city. Many of the early universities were established by church groups that saw large numbers of their coreligionists entering the country or congregating in the city. Temple University was established by the Baptists to "provide meaningful education for the workingmen of Philadelphia" (Rudolph 1962) as a result of a strong sense that something had to be done to provide opportunities for those employed in the city to rise above their situation. Catholic colleges were set up in the areas populated by Irish, Italian, German, or other newcomers to ensure that these people could be educated in a way that would allow them to integrate successfully into American life without abandoning their religious and social traditions (Gleason 1967). By the end of World War II, city and state universities had been established all over the United States to provide opportunity to the people of the city, teachers for its schools, continuing education and advanced degrees for its work force, and laboratories for social work, medicine, and other professions. These institutions have been growing in importance ever since. At their best, these universities are institutions "of" the city rather than schools that are merely located within them, and, as such, they occupy a unique niche in American higher education (Rudnick 1983).

THE CHARACTER OF URBAN UNIVERSITIES

Urban universities share with other residents of the city both the benefits of urban living and the difficulties that are associated with city life. The world of the urban university is not the world of a self-contained college town that is isolated from the world. It connects directly with its environment. These institutions are frequently surrounded by museums and other cultural activities and provide ready access to the performing arts. They are also close to business communities that can provide employment for students and graduates, research and consulting opportunities for faculty, part-time faculty, learning experiences for students, and financial assistance for programs. They are often served by large public libraries with substantial collections that do not need to be duplicated in the university or that can supplement university resources. Above all, the ability of faculty and students to connect directly with the community beyond the university provides attractive opportunities for faculty to pursue their personal interests, to expose their students to a larger world, and to develop personal contacts.

Living and working in an urban university do, however, present problems. These institutions are designed to serve the city and those who live and work in them and must by their nature locate at the heart of the city. While this location may be convenient to those who wish to avail themselves of its services, it is not always the easiest place to conduct business. City universities are often beset by the high cost of urban real estate and the high cost of doing business in these areas, as well as the kinds of environmental and security problems that affect others who live and work there. While mass transit may be available, parking problems for commuting students lead to congestion. Unionization also presents a challenge that must be dealt with. Universities located in cities find it difficult to develop community among students and faculty members who must commute 30 minutes to an hour or more to get to and from the campus.

The traditions of the urban university also present certain kinds of problems. For the most part these institutions are relatively new, and they lack the kind of prestige and the loyal alumni that undergird more traditional institutions. Even when they are older, their clientele is likely to be less affluent than those of other schools. While some of their graduates have done well, these schools are less likely than older, more traditional institutions to have built well-established fund-raising efforts or be in a position to exert political influence.

In addition, their capacity to provide the kind of support services needed to foster research is often limited by their age and their relative poverty. Many of these institutions began either as teachers' colleges or as extension campuses of state universities, and throughout their existence, many have tried to be inexpensive alternatives for students. As the schools have grown, they have become dependent on community resources to support their curricula and concentrated their efforts on staffing the classroom. In many cases, both community dependency and emphasis on teaching have proved to be sufficient since most of their curricula have been aimed toward undergraduate and master's programs with particular emphases on education, law, business, and professional fields, and much of their clientele has been more likely to draw library and other resources from places nearer to their home than the university campus. While some urban universities have developed fine campuses with good facilities, few compare with other universities of the same class in the state in which they reside (Grobman 1988).

The urban university has also been given a very special challenge in the students whom it is being asked to educate. These universities are likely to be open admissions institutions that accept everyone who has graduated from high school, and they are sitting at the top of school systems that serve some of the poorest Americans and that have often been castigated for their failures. Many good, academic-minded students are drawn off to residential campuses, and the results are predictable. According to Arnold B. Grobman (1988), the average student in the urban university will have a Scholastic Aptitude Test (SAT) score that is 100 points lower than his or her counterpart in other universities, and a teacher is five times more likely to find a National Merit Scholar in his or her classroom in a nonurban university than in an urban one. Many of the students who go to urban universities will be returning to college after time in the work force, and the average student there will be four years older than his or her counterpart at a nonurban campus. A third of the students will be taking night courses and working full-time or part-time, and even more of the graduate students will be completing programs one or two courses at a time. As a result, it is likely that urban students will take longer to complete their academic programs.

Urban universities are relatively inexpensive, and they do not generally compete for the best and the brightest with Ivy League schools. But they often provide the only affordable option for the factory worker who is studying at night so that he or she might leave the assembly line. Robert Hassenger referred to these colleges as "decompression chambers for those edging their way out of the ghetto" (1967, 4), and they are viewed by many of those who live in the city as paths for the brightest and most ambitious to rise to the middle class. Many of those who matriculate at these institutions as undergraduates are the first members of their family to go to college, and they often come to college with a very practical agenda. These students are likely to be very pragmatic in their approach to higher education and are less likely to respect knowledge in the abstract or have a broad exposure to books and other cultural artifacts than are students in more traditional universities.

Grobman (1988) also found that there are likely to be almost twice as many minority students on an urban campus as there are at other universities, and almost three-quarters of all students enrolled in these schools will live within 20 miles of the campus. These students are likely to be more diverse in terms of their cultural background, and far more of them will come to the university with a first language that is not English. As a result of all of these circumstances, these urban universities are being asked to serve unsophisticated client groups who may not be well prepared for traditional college life and who have special needs. To help these students survive in this environment, these urban universities need to tailor their services to address the needs of these students.

TYPES OF PUBLIC URBAN UNIVERSITIES

In the final analysis, urban universities are different from other universities. But it must also be understood that not all urban universities are alike, and the differences between them are significant. Grobman (1988) divides state-supported, urban universities into two sets, namely, primary urban universities and secondary urban universities. The first set includes new urban universities established specifically to meet the needs of the city. Grobman included institutions like Wright State University and the University of Illinois at Chicago in this category. He defined secondary urban universities as institutions that had once functioned either as private or municipal colleges or as teacher training institutes that have been converted into more comprehensive universities by the state. This group included institutions like Virginia Commonwealth University, Memphis State, and the University of Nebraska at Omaha. While he saw specific distinctions between these two types of schools, he concluded that they were more alike than different and served similar functions within the city (13–18).

While Grobman's distinction might be helpful, it may be more reasonable to distinguish between urban universities that have become research universities and those that are primarily teaching institutions. In many cases, comparing programs at the University of California, Los Angeles, to a distinctly nonurban institution like the University of Illinois will be more useful than comparisons to a crosstown institution serving city students like the California State University at Los Angeles. In any case, the special needs and capabilities of research institutions and teaching colleges and of the different clienteles that they serve must be considered in any reasonable discussion, whether in the context of the city or in another setting.

When considering urban universities, one should make some distinction between the older institutions that are located in the largest cities in this country and those institutions that might be viewed as either new urban or suburban universities. For instance, George Mason University in Virginia, the University of Colorado in Colorado Springs, and Kennesaw College in Georgia have many of the attributes of urban universities in that they are commuter schools that cater to a working clientele employed in a city. But all are quite different from the traditional model of the urban university. These institutions cater to a wealthier clientele that has a different set of expectations and a different set of priorities than does the clientele of inner-city universities.

They do, however, serve many of the same purposes for newer cities that older urban universities serve in old ones. Each of these universities serves a new city that has not yet fully developed in its own right. For the most part, universities of this type are new, having typically been established after 1970 and after federal spending for universities in general and for libraries in particular had become less plentiful. These universities lack access to the kind of resources that are available in older cities, and they are just beginning to define themselves after having been driven by the growth of the areas that surround them. Their constituencies are more affluent than those of their older cousins and frequently better prepared for college. But, at the same time, these institutions have not had the time to amass the resources needed to meet the needs of their students. As noted earlier, these new urban universities are quite different from other universities, but they represent a segment of the higher education community that is becoming increasingly important.

PRIVATE URBAN UNIVERSITIES

Beyond these groups of state universities, one must also recognize that there are a number of private colleges that were set up to meet the needs of urban populations. As noted earlier, these institutions pioneered the concept of urban higher education, and many of the Catholic colleges in the United States are still located close to what were once the enclaves of immigrants who had need for their services. These universities have always provided reasonable educational opportunities to new Americans who were either discouraged from entering other institutions or who might have been uncomfortable in more traditional colleges. Schools like DePaul and Fordham have developed an environment in which working men and women can get the kind of education that will lead to economic opportunity while keeping in touch with the values of the Catholic community, and they have a long tradition of service in producing leaders for their communities. Beyond the community of religious schools, specialized colleges like the Illinois Institute of Technology, Stevens Institute, and the National College of Education have also been established to provide engineers, businessmen, teachers, and other professionals for the developing cities, and these colleges have become important parts of their educational establishments.

NONURBAN UNIVERSITIES IN THE CITY

Not all universities that are located within cities can be considered urban universities. The fact that Columbia University is in New York or that Yale is in New Haven does not make them urban universities. While these institutions do enjoy the benefits of the city and have to cope with problems as a result of their location, they are national universities that must be viewed as being "in" but not "of" the city (Rudnick 1983).

THE URBAN UNIVERSITY, ITS LIBRARY, AND THE CITY

Having described urban universities in some detail, one must raise the question of what exactly that description means in terms of what the mission of both the university and its library should be. It is suggested here that the primary differences between the emphases within the mission that might be assigned to an urban university and those of other schools relate primarily to the demographics of the students within the university and the need for sensitivity for community needs in this environment.

THE URBAN UNIVERSITY LIBRARY AND THE STUDENTS IT SERVES

This chapter spoke earlier of the diversity of the student body within urban universities. It is particularly important that libraries stress the development of new approaches to service when dealing with students who come to the university from ethnic and social groups that do not have long histories of involvement with higher education. It is difficult, in any case, for teachers or librarians to convince students that the process of seeking information is important to them. This problem is compounded when one is dealing with students who are economically or educationally disadvantaged. Children of working-class families are often not comfortable using libraries regularly or well to meet information needs, and they may well have limited exposure to books and literature. Those from immigrant or ethnic families have additional cultural barriers to overcome before they can reap the rewards of an association with a university. As Ellen Broidy (1989) pointed out, it is particularly difficult to involve students in this process when they have difficulty speaking English, may not understand their assignments, are hesitant about asking for help, and are unprepared to handle rudimentary library research. Many of the students have come to the university because they are intelligent, they are focused on finding a better future, and they have overcome the obstacles set for them by the educational system. They may be well motivated to learn and willing to do what is required to get the information they need, but it is imperative that libraries in the universities that they attend develop services that deal with their problems with compassion and raise skill levels to a point where they can reasonably be expected to compete with better-prepared students. The only alternatives are to de-emphasize the library in the curriculum or lose these students, and these options are not acceptable.

These students are not the only nontraditional students present in this environment. Older than average students attend urban universities in large numbers, and when dealing with this constituency, service agencies within the university like the library must be sensitive to additional problems. Older students do not approach their studies as other students do. While they may share many of the frustrations and limitations of their younger colleagues, they see learning within the context of their lives (Carr 1989). They come to the university with rusty study skills, an unfamiliarity with how libraries operate, a fear of seeming to fail and of appearing foolish, and a strong sense of purpose that is ready to question the relevance of what they are being taught. They frequently work under severe time constraints as they juggle jobs, families, and studies, and making time for things like library research can be very difficult. These clients are also accustomed to being treated as adults. They are people with responsibilities who are making sacrifices for an education, and the library must deal with them with sensitivity. To be effective, it must provide good service that does not threaten them at those odd hours when they can come to the library. The librarian must be prepared to ensure that a user leaves the point of service with a feeling of having been dealt with as a peer who needs specific knowledge but who is competent to find it in most cases. Assistance must be proactive and must reinforce rather than threaten. While librarians prefer to view themselves as teachers, this author's contention is that, at least in this context, the model of a shoe salesman helping to satisfy a customer's need for good fitting shoes reflects more accurately how the information needs of this clientele might be met, and affecting this attitude requires a major change in attitude for many of those who work in the library.

There is little evidence in the literature that librarians have been concerned with the special needs of the clients who come to urban university libraries. Edward Holley found little evidence in his 1972 study of the organization of urban universities and their services that they were trying to be anything other than generic academic libraries. More recently, Broidy described an interview in which candidates were asked to confront the changing human face of the library (meaning the different kinds of clients who were coming to it and their needs) as opposed to its technological face. The general response she received was that the candidates had not "given that one much thought" (1989, 4), and it is suspected that she would have gotten a similar answer had she questioned most of those who are now being asked to lead urban university libraries. Patricia Breivik (1977, 11) called the academic library in open admissions institutions a "twentieth-century cop-out" that was unconcerned by its clients' lack of interest in using its resources, and, while that criticism might be severe, it quite clearly is not far enough from the truth to give comfort to those who lead and work in these organizations. If this situation is to change, librarians and the teaching faculty members with whom they work must find a way to make the importance of information-seeking strategies obvious to students who do not come to the university with an established commitment to the concept.

LIBRARIES AND THE SERVICE MISSION OF THE UNIVERSITY

Urban universities, which cannot be considered outside of the context of the city, were established particularly to serve the needs of the city, and in many cases their programs have long been dependent on the resources of the city to meet the demands of their academic programs. While the universities' services that are most obvious focus on providing traditional educational opportunities for working-class students to prepare them for professional life, they are also in a unique position to provide services to the business community, to city government, and to others who have need for the special skills and services that they bring to the community. The library should be a key part of this service program.

Many of the library resources that are required so that a university can train businesspeople, scientists, engineers, and other professionals and can support the research of its faculty can also be important to entrepreneurs starting new businesses, other businesspeople, lawyers, health professionals, and those engaged in research and development enterprises. In some cases, libraries will develop special services to meet these needs, but, even when these are not present, the universities' library collections are a special bonus that comes to taxpayers with the establishment of a university close to their home or work. While serving these clients may be taxing, reaching out to serve the community can provide a linkage to members of the community who may never take a course in the university or send their children there and, as a result, is an important part of the effort to develop acceptance within the community for the university and to increase its political clout in the city and state.

A key component of this service to the community should be a linkage forged with local schools. The urban university serves as a mentor for city school systems that are being tasked with the education of a difficult student population. These school systems are often handicapped by inadequate resources and a number of other problems. Given that urban universities can expect to get most of their students directly from these systems, will educate a large percentage of the teachers who will work in their classrooms, will place most of their student teachers in city schools, and will provide continuing education for the teachers and administrators, it is important that they relate directly to secondary and even to primary schools in their area. In addition to the obvious educational benefits that can be derived from this kind of cooperation and their capacity to prepare more and better students for entry into the university, these programs can serve as a mechanism for building goodwill within the community.

In this area the library can play a key role. Many urban universities began their lives with a heavy dependence on city libraries. But in many cases, city library systems have now come to be more interested in developing branch libraries located close to their users. These libraries are often helpful in that they encourage reading; however, they are often too small to handle the needs of students writing term papers, preparing science projects, or doing other kinds of assignments. This point is particularly true when one is dealing with the better students who are more likely to go to college. The literature indicates that these students will go to academic libraries unless they are denied entry, and special efforts should be made to design programs that cope with and capitalize on this reality. While this subject will be discussed in greater detail elsewhere in this volume, it is important to acknowledge that service to high school students is becoming a more readily apparent challenge than ever before and that it will not be ignored.

CONCLUSION

Urban universities are unique institutions with very special clienteles. They require those who lead them and those who work within them to develop a clear understanding of how they differ from other college libraries and what specific services will be required to meet the particular needs of their clients. For the librarian, understanding this role presents a very special challenge. Too often, the library has tended to view itself as a generic academic library burdened with the additional inconvenience of being in a city rather than as an institution that needed to develop in its own way. That view must change, and those who lead these kinds of institutions and those who avail themselves of their services must see to it. The uniqueness of the urban academic library and the uniqueness of individual institutions must be taken into account as libraries plan for their future. Only in this way can they expect to cope with the changing needs of urban America.

14 The Mission of the Urban Academic Library

REFERENCES

Breivik, Patricia. 1977. *Open admissions and the academic library*. Chicago: American Library Association.
Broidy, Ellen. 1989. Celebrating diversity: Teaching library skills as if people matter. In *Reaching and teaching diverse library user groups*, ed. Teresa B. Mensching. Ann Arbor, MI: Pierian.
Cafferty, Pastora San Juan, and Spangenburg, Gail. 1983. *Backs against the wall: Urban-oriented colleges and universities and the urban poor and disadvantaged*. New York: Ford Foundation.
Carr, David. 1989. The situation of the adult lender in the library. In *Reaching and teaching diverse library user groups*, ed. Teresa B. Mensching. Ann Arbor, MI: Pierian.
Gleason, Philip. 1967. American Catholic higher education: A historical perspective. In *The shape of Catholic higher education*, ed. Robert Hassenger, 15–53. Chicago: University of Chicago Press.
Grobman, Arnold B. 1988. *Urban state universities: An unfinished national agenda*. New York: Praeger.
Hassenger, Robert, ed. 1967. Colleges and Catholics: An introduction. In *The shape of Catholic higher education*, 3–14. Chicago: University of Chicago Press.
Holley, Edward G. 1972. Organization and administration of urban university libraries. *College and Research Libraries* 32: 175–89.
Jencks, Christopher, and Riesman, David. 1968. *The academic revolution*. Garden City, NY: Doubleday.
Jordan, David Starr. 1903. *The voice of the scholar*. San Francisco: Paul Elder.
Morey, Lloyd. 1961. *The state-supported university*. Carbondale: Southern Illinois Press.
Rudnick, Andrew J. 1983. *The American university in the urban context*. Washington, DC: National Association of State Universities and Land-Grant Colleges.
Rudolph, Frederick. 1962. *The American college and university*. New York: Knopf.
Veysey, Leonard. 1965. *The emergence of the American university*. Chicago: University of Chicago Press.

2

Conflict of Mission: The Midsize Private University in an Urban Environment

Fred Heath

Among librarians, there is an almost universal commitment to the ideals of cooperation and resource sharing. In metropolitan areas, the close proximity of libraries, which has always made cooperation more practical than elsewhere, has been joined by the emergence of new technologies to make interlibrary cooperation part of the everyday landscape. Every major urban area boasts library consortia, within which all types of libraries contribute to common social purposes. In some quarters, however, the time and energy allotted to the cooperative endeavor have begun to raise questions about costs and benefits. The purpose of this chapter is to suggest that, in some circumstances, there may develop situations where the opportunities for cooperation and resource sharing exceed the resources that some libraries can commit to them without compromising support of their primary clientele. I offer that observation from my perspective as director of a private university library and suggest that it may have applications in some other instances as well.

One does not enter the social services without a commitment to sharing. I remember a time almost 20 years ago when, as director of public services in a resource-constrained public university and only recently out of library school, I was an enthusiastic supporter of the concept of resource sharing and unrestricted access to all libraries by the population at large. I recall rising early one day to drive to Charlottesville from my southwestern Virginia campus for a meeting on some aspects of library cooperation. As that day's session meandered toward some conclusion that has long since escaped recollection, I can still recall my surprise at the attitude of the director of one private university library whom I had previously regarded as one of the more forward-thinking practitioners in our profession. There, at a meeting on interlibrary resource sharing and cooperation, my would-be mentor coolly questioned some of the notions his colleagues advanced. He talked about denying access to his institutional library by students from a nearby public college and even aired the possibility of having to limit interlibrary loan privileges to public libraries and out-of-state colleges.

We left that meeting poles apart on those service issues, and I suppose for the remainder of my stay in that state, my estimation of him was somewhat diminished. Today, I am library director at Texas Christian University (TCU), a private school supporting 6,000 students and doctoral-level research in Dallas-Fort Worth, one of the nation's largest metropolitan areas. Today, the TCU library

- restricts access to the library during evening hours and on Sundays to all but the university community and recognized cardholder categories;
- controls in some instances use of certain materials and services by nonuniversity traffic;
- actively engages in consortia arrangements, the purpose of which is to provide preferential benefits to those in the consortia; and
- provides more limited interlibrary loan services to those outside preferential compacts.

Not only have I undergone this philosophical transformation, but I find myself the apologist for what many would interpret as an elitist profile. The following paragraphs attempt to reconcile the conflict between a personal commitment to cooperative effort and responsibilities to a private university community that has purchased enhanced library services at a premium. For me, the reconciliation began with acceptance of the high costs of the services my organization is called upon to provide.

LIBRARIES AS A "FREE" GOOD

Public Libraries

From our education in graduate schools of library and information services, we are exposed to the American ideal of the "free" library and the right of the people to unimpeded access to information. To the credit of our educators, we emerge as uncompromising advocates of free and unrestricted access to information in a democratic society. Somehow, all too often, we translate that view into the notion that information itself is free. Only later, perhaps when we prepare our first budget for review by some higher level of bureaucracy, do we begin to acknowledge just how "soft" a social good libraries can become. Even in this affluent age skyrocketing costs of other social services—public health, security, and the like—have had a corrosive effect on many urban public libraries.

Here in Dallas-Fort Worth, public libraries must look upon the 1980s as a time of decline, with diminished hours of operation, reduced staff, and significant cuts in materials budgets. To many city planners, the costs of library operations are all too real. Their significant costs have placed libraries at a disadvantage in the competition for public revenues.

Alternatives to Public Libraries

Where public libraries have been unable to answer growing public demands for services, the need for information and the issue of access have impacted other types of libraries. Here in Dallas–Fort Worth, the segments of the population whose access to library service has been impacted are huge: K-12 students needing evening study spaces, community college enrollees depending on the large circulating collections of downtown central libraries, and the general reading public desiring access to a panoply of reference and information services. When public libraries curtail hours or fail to build new branches to respond to population shifts, those information-deprived constituencies exert their pressure for access elsewhere.

Some institutions are better able to respond to, or deflect, these pressures than others. Many valuable collections in an urban area—corporate and special libraries—remain inaccessible to the general public. The restricted and specialized missions of medical, scientific, and industrial libraries are generally respected by the public at large, and there is little pressure for access, even through interlibrary loan channels. Corporate libraries remain almost entirely aloof from access issues and concentrate their energies on service to their primary clientele.

For the state-supported universities, the issue of access has been somewhat more difficult to resolve. In Dallas–Fort Worth, most library directors and campus administrators in the tax-supported universities seem to accept the idea that their public status implies an obligation to permit the citizenry to use their library collections. While there are some exceptions, most admit the general public to their libraries at all times and permit them to charge resources. Costs to the public, if any, are generally minimal. Without this admirable response from many of the state-supported universities, the limitations of public library service would be far more severely felt.

Where I live, there are three large private universities: TCU, Southern Methodist, and Baylor. All belong to the Association for Higher Education (AHE) of North Texas, whose members also include the public universities and community colleges, some smaller private colleges, and one of the larger public libraries. While AHE is distinguished by its efforts to open access to all area libraries, the three private university libraries have elected to impose some restrictions on the general public. There are differences among them in the nature of their individual access policies, but each has more rigorous regulations than the public institutions. The following section conveys the rationale behind those decisions to restrict access at Texas Christian University.

THE DECISION TO RESTRICT ACCESS

The Dallas–Fort Worth metroplex has several large academic libraries. Nine libraries belong to the Research Libraries Interest Group (RLIG), a component of AHE whose purpose is to provide a forum for the discussion of issues common to its larger members. While there are no members of the Association of Research Libraries (ARL) in the membership, most of the institutions have materials budgets in excess of $1 million, and collectively they constitute a significant regional research resource. Within that group, the holdings of Texas Christian University fall into the midrange of membership. Protection of collections was not a compelling factor in the TCU decision to restrict access and services. The major considerations were security and maintenance of the quality of service.

Security

Shocking events such as the serial murders of students in Gainesville, Florida, have served to remind us that universities, too, are subject to the vagaries of urban life. By my public library colleagues, the Texas Christian University library would be viewed as a placid place. While it is largely untroubled by problem patrons, its location adjacent to a major swath of urban green space does mean a steady stream of transients and minor problems with petty theft, purses stolen from inattentive patrons, and the like. Two years ago, at about the time the *Chronicle of Higher Education* ran a series of articles on crime on the urban campus, the university administration took steps to ensure the security of the TCU student body.

Turnstiles with magnetic card readers were installed in the library foyer. An access policy was devised that permitted admission to the library by the general public during the workday, when the library was staffed at full complement; however, during the evening and weekends, when the number of employees in the building fell sharply, access by the general public was denied. To be sure, a number of exemptions were defined and, subsequently, some weekend hours were restored to community patrons. (Those exemptions and changes are explained in some detail in the following section.) Nevertheless, with the installation of the turnstiles there occurred a fundamental change in the relationship between the Texas Christian University library and the information-consuming component of the metroplex population.

Access

As we devised the access policy, it became clear that in erecting a barrier to keep out those elements that might constitute a threat to security, we were also denying access to large segments of the community with legitimate information needs, specifically those K-12, community college, and the general reading public enumerated above, as well as those undergraduate students enrolled at the state-supported senior colleges. As a staff we debated these issues, and slowly, as the policy coalesced, we became more comfortable with the notion of exclusion.

Our metropolitan area is shaped like a large ellipse, and TCU is the only large institution in the western quadrant. Citizens living in that part of the metroplex who opt for public higher education must drive 40 to 60 minutes to avail themselves of the opportunity. To make the trip to class and return can be as much as a two-hour commute; to return for an evening's library work doubles the time spent in travel. All other things being equal, the optimal economic arrangement for a commuter would be to enroll in classes at one of the state schools and use the TCU library for course-related assignments.

Within that context, the notion of restricted access clarified itself and took final form. The student body at a private institution pays a considerable premium to attend—in Texas the difference is almost 10 times the amount paid at a state-supported university. For that premium, students tend to expect certain emollients, such as smaller class sizes and the presence of senior professors in the classroom. One of the attendant benefits within the library is the amount of quality time that can be expected from the professional staff.

Technologies

Imposition of restricted access coincided with a quantum change in the provision of information services within the library. A major grant had permitted installation of state-of-the art information technologies, including microcomputer laboratories, large arrays of CD-ROM (Compact Disk—Read Only Memory) workstations, and a modern, new integrated system with menu-driven connections to external libraries and databases. Already attracted to campus by the pleasant surroundings of a recently constructed (and award-winning) library annex, the stream of visitors thickened, drawn by the new technologies.

In the evenings and on weekends, the library was almost overrun. TCU students and faculty frequently were unable to find quality seating in their own facility. All too often they had to compete with visitors for the time of the professional librarians, whose service as intermediaries in an automated environment was suddenly more highly prized. Turning away on nights and weekends the high school student, the other undergraduates, and the general public ensured the local students the quality sessions with librarians that they have come to expect as a perquisite.

Other Restrictions

Concerns with maintaining the service profile for the local population eventually prompted other decisions to restrict access to selected library services. The library's CD-ROM databases are probably the most extensive of any in the metropolitan area and are potentially as useful to the external population as they are to local students and faculty. The university's size, however, permits certain economies of scale, and most databases are purchased in single copy. As soon as CD-ROM services grew to significant size, it became apparent that access to the databases would have to be restricted, and they are currently available to external users only on Saturday mornings or by permission of the public services coordinator.

Similarly, the local integrated system was introduced with menu-driven access to attractive external databases, including major university library collections and text databases. Inasmuch as those databases were accessible via modem as well as by campus networks, limited modems and switching mechanisms were soon overwhelmed by external users navigating through our system to gain access to the other sources. To make certain that lines were available to the local community, we found it necessary to link access to the external menu with positive identification in the local patron database, and effectively we excluded the external community.

Interlibrary Loan

Finally, there have been growing pressures on interlibrary loan. The new integrated system has eliminated backlog in library processing; new materials appear in the Online Computer Library Center (OCLC) system as rapidly as they are received. This availability, plus the reality that our holdings symbol appears first in the Texas OCLC string, has led to a steady and inexorable rise in the number of incoming interlibrary loan requests. At the same time, the new finding aids have raised the level of outgoing requests from our community. Yet, the throughput capacity, defined by staffing levels, has remained largely unchanged. To process requests promptly and accord priority to our growing number of local requests, we have found it necessary to deny an ever increasing number of incoming requests.

Concerns

Is this stance elitist? How does a library staff, schooled in the tradition of free and open access to information, reconcile those values with the practices of the private urban university library where they work? The concluding section of this essay attempts to answer that question.

CONFLICT OF MISSION: A RECONCILIATION

Fundamentally, the dilemma in which we find ourselves can be resolved through market segmentation. Instead of overreaching our capabilities, we must focus on a segment of the market and aggressively establish our niche there. With regard to both the local area and the state, we have attempted to do just that, focusing on the concepts of quality and speed. We have set out to determine the organic units with which we can identify a necessary or desirable relationship. With those units we seek to establish compacts for service that are the highest upon which we can mutually agree.

As individuals, as librarians, we content ourselves with the knowledge that controls on the number of patrons we see over the public service desk mean that we are able to do a better job with each. The information superhighway is exciting, and undergraduates grasp its possibilities as fully as do seasoned researchers. Users and librarians alike recognize that to fully realize its potentials, to navigate efficiently among the databases, we must spend time on sharpening the skills of inquiry. When we restrict access, patron and professional alike find the reference transaction a satisfactory process. This generality aside, it is also important to take some space to emphasize that the TCU library continues to concern itself with its responsibilities to the metropolitan community.

Means of Access

While it is true that access to the library is now restricted, high levels of service and support are available to broad categories of the population. Honoring standing agreements with all members of the metropolitan consortium, the North Texas AHE, we offer graduate students and faculty of AHE schools unrestricted access to the our library as well as circulation privileges. Similarly, a reciprocal arrangement exists with an area seminary and permits its students to have comparable privileges. Undergraduates of AHE institutions are admitted on the strength of an AHE card on weekdays and Saturday. Within the larger community, employees of area K-12 school systems and government employees are issued access cards. The public at large may purchase unlimited access privileges. If a purchase applicant is approved, the cost of library access is less than one-half of the fee paid by a TCU student for a single credit hour. Further, as government depository, all citizens are permitted unrestricted access to federal and Texas documents. Finally, onetime access cards are available to individuals at no charge. Save for the area undergraduates, cardholders may use the library at any time. A CD-ROM tower, permitting multiple users, is now in implementation, and as licensing questions are resolved, we hope to make those discs fully accessible to all patrons. Once that distinction is erased, there will be no substantial difference in the in-building services available to TCU students as compared with others permitted under the terms of the access policy.

By this tiered approach, Texas Christian University Library has reserved access to its library information professionals, its collections, and its seating to a selected universe of potential users during times of peak demands. For all other visitors, including undergraduates at other institutions, access can still be obtained during the regular 8 A.M.–5 P.M. workweek, when the library is fully staffed and TCU students are still engaged in class work and other priorities. Subsequent observation of light use of the facility has permitted us to reopen the facility to external users on Saturday as well, a popular move that has largely defused community reservations about the access policy.

Cooperation

As an urban private university library, TCU Library has over time elected not to participate in certain resource-sharing ventures in the state and region. Those decisions were made after calculating the resources that would have to be diverted from serving the primary population to serving the information needs of the external community. For example, TCU is currently an interlibrary loan net lender by a ratio of approximately 2.5 to 1. The demand is such that if sufficient resources were directed to that service, the ratio could easily approach 5 to 1. In today's educational environment, TCU is not in a position to make that service self-supporting. Until our major utilities can assist us with the accounting superstructure necessary to compensate net lenders on a nationwide basis, there is little hope of placing interlibrary loan on a cost recovery basis. For now, lending remains something of a library service that institutions provide each other in the interest of scholarship. Given staffing realities, we have determined that a 2.5 to 1 ratio is as much as we choose to contribute to the general welfare. Moreover, in the library's planning documents, additional staffing for interlibrary loan is considerably down the list of staffing priorities assembled by the library's management group.

To stay within that ratio, the library has committed itself to a limited number of cooperative efforts, which it supports unstintingly. Top priority is given to three groups: (1) AHE, (2) the "quintessentials," and (3) individual institutions with which reciprocal relationships exist. For these groups, interlibrary loan staff endeavor to pull requests the day of their appearance on OCLC, process them, and put them into the proper delivery system before the lapse of 24 hours. Telefacsimile requests are almost always honored.

The AHE group refers to the several institutions that are members of the Association of Higher Education of North Texas. In addition to telefacsimile, a courier makes daily rounds to speed interlibrary loans among sites. The "quintessentials" is the whimsical sobriquet accorded an informal association of the five largest private institutional libraries in Texas. For this group, the emphasis is on speed; the requestor determines the mode of delivery at the time of request, including telefacsimile or UPS options. Still in its formative stages, the organization shows promise of reducing turnaround time among institutions. The third group refers to other institutions around the country with which a special relationship has evolved over time, interlibrary staff according each other priorities and courtesies that usually translate themselves into speedy response. Outside of these arrangements revolve concentric circles of other would-be borrowers, defined more by custom than by policy, who compete for borrowing privileges based on the processing capacity of the interlibrary loan unit at that moment. While no borrowers are excluded by name, each day many requests are denied as the unit assesses its priorities and capacity. It is the unit's practice to deny loans as early in the request cycle as possible rather than to allow them to linger until defaulting to the next borrower in the chain. From one perspective, timely denial is a service of sorts.

SUMMARY: THE VALUE OF ORGANIC COMPACTS

In short, we have determined that there is a net benefit to the education community when we segment and concentrate our energies. Private urban universities generally lack a mandate to serve the entire community. Rather, the reverse may be the case; the local mandate is to provide preferential services to those who have elected to pay a premium to attain them. To discharge those service obligations to the broader community acknowledged by the university administration and the library, the universities focus their energies on certain organic compacts where there is a recognition of special relationships or mutual interests. Thus, K-12 educators in the various metroplex systems are accorded access and borrowing privileges whereas other categories of borrowers must accommodate themselves to some restrictions. Similarly, the libraries of AHE and the larger private universities in Texas are accorded preferential library treatment in terms of speed, mode of delivery, and other matters.

To conclude, those of us who have hammered out these policies of TCU have never forgotten the lessons of library school. The service philosophy remains at the fore. Never comfortable with the conflict of mission, we are slowly acclimating ourselves to the solution that we have devised: to keep the quality of service high and to provide as much service to the external community as resources will allow. It is my belief that we have succeeded in doing that. If I ever see that gentleman with whom I clashed on these very ideas 20 years ago, I must tell him how much wiser he has become over the years.

PART II

Services to External Population Groups

3

External User Access to Academic Libraries in Urban/Metropolitan Areas

Ralph E. Russell, Carolyn L. Robison, James E. Prather, and Christina E. Carlson

The subject of this chapter is the academic library in the urban/metropolitan area. Academic libraries in metropolitan areas have unique service requirements, and the issues faced by these libraries can differ markedly from those encountered in rural college towns. This chapter will look at the issues of external user access to libraries in the urban/metropolitan environment.

Urban academic libraries have often become victims of their own success. Compared to public libraries, their collections are strong; their facilities are usually accessible to handicapped individuals; their online bibliographic databases are accessible to many who have no affiliation with the institution; and the public perceives libraries as free for everyone to use. Yet these assets may prove to be liabilities when they attract large numbers of external library users who are not considered in funding formulas driven by student enrollment figures.

External users, defined as individuals with no affiliation with the institution, are generally more diverse than typical institutional users and in some instances lack academic backgrounds. They may request different types of information and unusual services that are outside of those most frequently used by the academic library's primary clientele. Frequent external users of metropolitan academic libraries are students and faculty from other colleges and universities. These students and faculty use urban academic libraries because of the convenient location, extended hours, better collections, or greater accessibility in terms of transportation and service. Many persons not enrolled at any institution may need a foreign language newspaper, information on an investment, or even consumer information to guide an imminent purchase. Business and government employees, as well as high school students, are frequent users of many urban academic libraries.

As part of their mission, many large urban university libraries attempt to serve the diverse needs of broad-based metropolitan populations. Yet this desire—and its additional costs—has increasingly come into conflict with university administrations that do not take a library's total number of users into account when making budgetary allocations. In other words the library's funding is based on the number of students enrolled. There is no income specifically provided to support the services and collections granted to external users. Static library budgets simply cannot cope with the rising costs of books and serials, personnel, equipment, and supplies; the stagnant nature of library financing has created a climate in which library administrators are forced to evaluate all expenditures and constantly to seek ways of cost containment and reduction.

Are the commitments of urban academic libraries and the public's expectations and demands outstripping resources? The purpose of this study is to determine access for external users provided by academic libraries in major, public, doctoral-granting universities in large metropolitan areas nationwide. This includes access to various levels and types of staff assistance, to electronic information, to automated local and remote information files, to special collections and facilities, and to borrowing privileges.

The literature on external access to academic libraries reflects a variety of approaches. There are little hard data, but many opinions and viewpoints. While some warn that university and college libraries must avoid the image of an "elitist fortress" (Dumbleton 1984, 7), the question most often addressed is how to clarify the issue of access by external users.

One possible response is to charge fees for external use. Fees are usually a reflection of economic necessity, though some librarians are "philosophically opposed to fees" (Donnellan and Rasmussen 1983, 70). Some institutions have found it difficult to maintain external access for large, diverse populations and have withdrawn from "information broker" activity altogether (1983, 72).

B. L. Johnson summarized the arguments for closing the library to external users as (1) increased seating space, (2) reduced wear and tear, (3) better security, and (4) increased support for internal users (1984, 405). The reasons for offering access to external users include (1) philosophical commitment to the public by public institutions, (2) good public relations, and (3) access to special collections and government documents (1984, 405).

A survey of University Center in Georgia member libraries was conducted in 1989 (Russell, Robison, and Prather) to ascertain the policies of members regarding external user access in the Atlanta metropolitan area. The authors found that most of these libraries provided open access to their collections and

Table 3.1
The Urban University Respondents

Name	Metropolitan Area
University of Alabama-Birmingham	Birmingham, Alabama
Arizona State University	Phoenix, Arizona (Tempe)
University of South Florida-Tampa	Tampa, Florida
Georgia State University	Atlanta, Georgia
Wayne State University	Detroit, Michigan
University of Missouri-Kansas City	Kansas City, Missouri
State University of New York-Albany	Albany, New York
State University of New York-Buffalo	Buffalo, New York
University of Akron	Akron, Ohio
Cleveland State University	Cleveland, Ohio
University of Toledo	Toledo, Ohio
Portland State University	Portland, Oregon
Memphis State University	Memphis, Tennessee
University of Texas at Dallas	Dallas, Texas
University of Houston	Houston, Texas
Old Dominion University	Norfolk, Virginia
Virginia Commonwealth University	Richmond, Virginia
University of Wisconsin-Milwaukee	Milwaukee, Wisconsin

services but generally did not extend checkout privileges to the public. The fees charged to external users varied widely, apparently as a result of professional uncertainty regarding the relative worth of the services provided.

METHODS

In September 1989, a survey was mailed to 26 large, comprehensive urban universities with a self-declared urban mission. The survey was designed to determine the variety, depth, and types of access accorded by each library to external users. External users are defined as having no affiliation with the institution as students, faculty, staff, alumni, or members of the governing board or are affiliated with an institution having a consortium agreement with the host institution for reciprocal borrowing.

When separated by the Carnegie Commission's classification system, 2 universities fall into the Research Universities I category, 6 into Research Universities II, 9 into Doctorate-Granting Universities I, and 9 into Doctorate-Granting Universities II. The 18 schools that responded are listed in Table 3.1. Of the respondents, 5 are Research Universities II, 7 are Doctoral-Granting Universities I, and 6 are Doctoral-Granting Universities II (*Chronicle of Higher Education*, July 6, 1988.) The response rate was 69 percent.

FINDINGS

Responses are summarized following the format of the survey. Negative replies to questions are not included in the summaries; therefore, the number of published responses does not always add up to 18. All of the institutions responding to the survey are publicly funded. Enrollments of the respondent institutions vary from 7,300 to more than 43,000, with a median enrollment of 21,536.

Checkout privileges

Of those institutions that specified the fees charged for checkout privileges, the amounts ranged from $25 to $125.

General public: 9 charge a fee, 5 allow without charges or restrictions, and 1 allows with limitations.

Government employees: 7 charge a fee, 7 allow, and 2 allow with limitations.

State legislators: 6 charge a fee, 9 allow, and 1 allows with limitations.

Private employees: 9 charge a fee, 5 allow, and 2 allow with limitations. One institution charges a $150 corporate fee.

Nonprofit employees: 8 charge a fee, 6 allow, and 2 allow with limitations.

High school students: 5 charge a fee, 4 allow, and 4 allow with limitations. This category is more likely to be restricted from checkout privileges and library services in general than any other group, although one institution does receive a fee from the local school system to cover the cost of serving its high school students.

High school teachers: 8 charge a fee, 5 allow, and 2 allow with limitations.

Local college students: 4 charge a fee, 7 allow, and 6 allow with limitations.

Local college teachers: 4 charge a fee, 9 allow, and 4 allow with limitations.

Visiting scholars: 2 charge a fee, 12 allow, and 1 allows with limitations.

Students in external degree programs: 6 charge a fee, 8 allow, and 1 allows with limitations.

Family members of primary users: 5 charge a fee, and 10 allow.

College students on holiday: 7 charge a fee, 5 allow, and 4 allow with limitations.

In-house Use of Materials

One institution does not allow any external access to its collection. One institution limits access to high school students. One institution does not allow access to visiting scholars, students in external degree programs, and family members.

Reference Assistance

One institution places limitations on high school students' use of reference assistance. The remainder of the respondents provide reference assistance to external users.

Library Services

Access to special collections: 1 charges a fee, 4 allow without charges or restrictions, 9 allow with limitations, and 2 did not respond. Access to and use of these collections are more likely to be restricted than other services in this category.

Access to media collections: 3 charge a fee, 2 allow, 4 allow with limitations, and 3 did not respond.

Access to microforms: 1 charges a fee, 10 allow, 2 allow with limitations, and 2 did not respond.

Online searching of commercial databases: 15 charge a fee, and 1 did not respond.

Interlibrary loans: 2 charge a fee, 1 allows with limitations, and 1 did not respond.

Use of CD-ROM products: 2 charge a fee, 7 allow, 1 allows with limitations, 2 did not respond, and the question was not applicable for 2 institutions.

Use of special facilities: 2 charge a fee, 2 allow, 3 allow with limitations, 2 did not respond, and the question was not applicable for 1 institution.

Use of photocopiers: 13 allow, 2 did not respond, and the question was not applicable for 1 institution.

Do you have an online catalog? 15 do.

If yes, is dial access possible for primary users? Possible at 13 institutions.

If dial access is possible, is it available to external users? Available at 11 and available with limitations at 1 institution.

Type of shelving arrangement: 15 have open stacks, 1 has open stacks that are closed to external users, and 2 have both open and closed stacks.

Are there branch libraries? 15 have branch libraries. Of the 8 institutions with law libraries, 6 administer these branches separately. One institution has a medical library that is administered separately, and 1 institution has four branch libraries at branch campuses, which are separately administered.

CONCLUSION

The libraries of major, public, doctoral-granting universities in large metropolitan areas with self-declared urban missions are faced with unique demands on their collections and personnel by unaffiliated external users. Because these public institutions are predominantly funded based upon the number of students enrolled, the fiscal drains experienced by these urban libraries due to the demands of external users are often not recompensed.

The purpose of this chapter was to survey these libraries to ascertain their policies and practices toward accommodating external users. Of the 26 institutions surveyed, 18 responded. They ranged in enrollments from 7,300 to 43,000.

As a group, these institutions showed a strong commitment to meeting the needs of external users whenever possible. For instance, only 1 institution did not allow any external access to its collection. All libraries allowed external access to their reference services. Nine of the 18 charged a fee to the general public for circulation privileges, but 5 did not. High school students were the most likely of the categories of external users to be restricted from circulation and services. Fifteen institutions charged fees for searches performed on online, commercial databases. For access to information located on compact disk (CD-ROM), 8 provided access for no charge. This finding is particularly significant because of the demand for such information and potential queues waiting to use CD-ROM products. Of the 15 institutions that indicated they had an online catalog, 13 had dial access to the catalog, and 11 had unrestricted dial access. Fifteen of the institutions had open stacks, and 1 closed access to external users.

Since we have just completed a decade during which libraries have been buffeted by burgeoning prices and weakened by static or declining budgets, it is commendable that most members of this subset of metropolitan academic libraries continue to provide access to materials and services for a broad range of users. The problem is clear: how to obtain adequate funding to continue and expand such access. From the results of this survey, it is evident that an adequate picture of these libraries' contributions to their cities, regions, and the nation must be conveyed to funding authorities and academic administrators.

REFERENCES

Chronicle of Higher Education. July 6, 1988.

Donnellan, A. M., and Rasmussen, L. 1983. Fee-based services in academic libraries: Preliminary results of a survey. *Drexel Library Quarterly* 19 (Fall): 68–79.

Dumbleton, N. 1984. Town and gown. *SLA News* 183 (September/October): 7–9.

Johnson, B. L. 1984. A case study in closing the university library to the public. *College & Research Libraries News* 45 (September): 404–7.

Russell, R.; Robison, C. R., and Prather, J. E. 1989. External user access to academic libraries. *Southeastern Librarian* 39 (Winter): 135–38.

4

General Circulation Policies for Private Citizens: The Practices of Publicly Supported Academic Libraries

Eugene S. Mitchell

As society's needs for information increase, the demands upon academic libraries to share their resources with a community wider than their individual campuses may increase also. Of course, all academic libraries circulate materials to their affiliated patrons, the most common being the faculty, staff, and students of the parent institution. This affiliation often also includes alumni, retired faculty and staff, and faculty and staff families. Affiliation may be extended to faculty and staff of other, sometimes neighboring, colleges and universities. Often, this group is included in reciprocal arrangements resulting from consortial or local agreements.

What about the faculty and students who fall outside the scope of such arrangements? What about private citizens who have no direct affiliation with the institution? This chapter is concerned with the group at this fuzzier end of the spectrum, the persons who have no affiliation with the institution.

The purpose of the circulation function and circulation policies is to provide maximum availability of information. Ideally, this access should not be restricted in any way; realistically, circulation is usually limited to a primary clientele. Often, however, a private citizen wants to make use of an academic library's collection. The reasons may be varied: the collection may be better than that of the public library, the individual may need access to more scholarly information, the academic library may be easier to get to or more comfortable, or the individual may feel he or she has a taxpayer's right to use any institution supported by public funds.

This chapter examines the circulation policies regarding nonaffiliated patrons at publicly supported academic libraries to determine how those libraries are facing the pressures being placed on them by private citizens.

LITERATURE REVIEW

A review of the literature reveals that little information is available on circulation policies in general, let alone those for nonaffiliated patrons in urban and metropolitan areas.

In 1965, an Ad Hoc Committee on Community Use of Academic Libraries was formed by the College Library Section of the Association of College and Research Libraries (ACRL) to study the problems faced by academic libraries serving the general public. Questionnaires were sent to 1,100 academic libraries across the country. The major findings showed that 94 percent of the libraries permitted some building use of materials by nonaffiliated patrons and that 85 percent of them extended circulation privileges (Josey 1967).

In 1968, the Circulation Services Section of the Library Administration Division, American Library Association (ALA) conducted a survey "to summarize practices of charges, frequency of notices, collection policies, and related information" for academic libraries throughout the United States (Circulation Control Committee 1970). Although 430 usable responses were examined, respondents were asked only to identify the number of faculty, undergraduates, and graduate students among the populations they served. An attempt was made to distinguish between rural and urban institutions but was abandoned as being too subjective. As a result, no determination was made of the impact of outside users on urban institutions.

Also in 1968, the ACRL Ad Hoc Committee on Community Use of Academic Libraries surveyed 308 junior colleges in the United States to determine the extent to which library service was given to community users (Josey 1970). A total of 91 percent of the respondents allowed in-building use of materials, while 70 percent permitted borrowing privileges. Fewer than 20 percent charged a fee for this service. Of the various categories of users considered, high school students appeared to be the least welcome. Very little demand appeared to be placed on the libraries by nonaffiliated patrons.

Bill Isom (1982) reviewed the written circulation policies of libraries at 15 state-supported universities in the western and midwestern regions of the United States. With respect to nonaffiliated patrons, he found that all but three libraries lent materials to local, county, or state residents. Other groups that were provided borrowing privileges included Friends of the Library, high school students, students and faculty at other universities and colleges, visiting scholars, federal and state government employees who had need of material while working in an official capacity, and other individuals who secured special permission.

In 1985, Naomi Paul conducted a telephone survey of circulation policies at

11 state-supported universities in Texas. All of the libraries issued library cards to adult residents of the area with certain restrictions in an attempt to limit the use of these cards to responsible persons. The restrictions included an age requirement, possession of a driver's license, statement of a valid need, and the payment of a fee. Seven of the libraries placed a limit on the number of items to be borrowed at any one time. The majority of them did not lend to high school students or restricted such lending to academically superior students in special programs.

In a review of lending policies and procedures (DuBois 1986), a committee at California State University, Long Beach, mailed a survey questionnaire to a group of 46 academic libraries comprised of the other 18 campuses in the California State University system, branches of the University of California, and 21 other institutions nationwide with characteristics similar to its own. The survey "often revealed a good deal of consensus." Nonaffiliated patrons and alumni had the most restrictions placed on them of any of the user groups identified, but they were generally allowed the same borrowing privileges as undergraduate students. The majority had no renewal limit.

THE CIRCULATION POLICIES SURVEY

In an attempt to broaden our knowledge of nonaffiliated patron loan policies, a letter with a five-page questionnaire was addressed to 68 library directors in February 1990. This survey solicited information on loan policies and practices for nonaffiliated patrons, who were defined as "patrons who wish to use the library, but are not affiliated with the library's parent institution."

This request was directed to publicly controlled four-year colleges and universities located in major metropolitan areas in the United States. Although they were also sent questionnaires, institutions with specialized interests, such as medical schools and art institutes, were eventually excluded from consideration.

The questionnaire was designed to elicit information regarding the specific groups to which the library circulated materials or granted library use privileges. Participants were asked to identify the types of material circulated and the types of circulation services (recalls, traces, renewals, and so forth) offered to nonaffiliated patrons. They were also asked if and for what reason circulation was blocked or restricted. Standard loan and renewal periods were identified, as were the fees for overdue and lost materials. Information on the application and record-keeping processes was also solicited. Participants were asked to describe their policy or recourse for delinquent patrons. They were encouraged to comment freely on their policies and experiences. Finally, they were requested to send any documents pertaining to nonaffiliated patron circulation policies.

Results

By the deadline for responses at the end of March 1990, 49 usable replies had been received for a response rate of 72 percent. These replies formed the basis for analysis.

The respondent libraries were located at colleges and universities in 24 states. Although all were located in urban or metropolitan areas, they were quite diverse. Their enrollments ranged from almost 4,000 to over 53,000 students. The size of their collections ranged from 23,000 to 5.8 million volumes. Forty-three (88 percent) of them had automated circulation systems. Their reported annual circulation ranged from 30,000 to 1,900,000.

Nonaffiliated Use

The first two questions of the survey were designed to determine the extent to which academic libraries in metropolitan areas circulate library materials or grant library use privileges to any of nine specified groups, namely, any member of the general public, adults only (persons over 18 years of age), high school students, applicants who must demonstrate a "valid need," Friends of the Library, families of Friends of the Library, faculty and staff of other colleges or universities, students of other colleges or universities, and others.

Responses to these questions showed that virtually all of the libraries granted library use privileges to nonaffiliated patrons. Only one library indicated that it did not allow use by the general public.

With respect to circulating materials, the libraries were less generous. Only 27 (55 percent) circulated materials to the general public, and only 22 (45 percent) of them circulated materials to high school students.

The largest group of nonaffiliated patrons who could borrow materials was the faculty (92 percent) and students (88 percent) of other colleges and universities. Several comments suggested that the faculty and staff of other institutions received reciprocal borrowing privileges as a result of consortial agreements. The second largest group was Friends of the Library; 35 (71 percent) of the respondent libraries indicated that they had such organizations and loaned materials to their members. The smallest group to receive circulation privileges was family members of Friends. Only 13 (27 percent) of the libraries extended privileges to them.

Types of Materials Circulated

One question was asked to determine what types of materials were circulated to nonaffiliated patrons. The specific types listed were general stack books, bound periodicals, unbound periodicals, reserve materials, newspapers, vertical file materials, government documents, microforms, instructional materials, juvenile books, theses and dissertations, nonprint materials, rare books, special collections, and others. In addition to identifying whether these items circulated, respondents were asked to indicate whether their policies were the same as or different than those for affiliated patrons.

The materials that the greatest proportion of libraries allowed nonaffiliated patrons to borrow were, as expected, books from the general stacks. The least circulated, also as expected, were rare books. Other materials that were circulated to nonaffiliated patrons by more than 50 percent of the respondents were government documents, theses and dissertations, and juvenile books.

Reserve materials, the sixth most circulated type of material (as reported by 39 percent of the respondents), are also the materials for which there is the least policy similarity between affiliated and nonaffiliated patrons. Only 47 percent of the libraries responded that their policy for circulating reserve materials to both groups was the same, probably the result of the need for greater access by affiliated patrons. This level of policy diversion did not occur with any other type of material. All other materials were circulated to nonaffiliated patrons according to policies that were the same for affiliated patrons in 70 percent of the libraries or more.

Controls

Questions were asked to determine the standard loan and renewal periods for nonaffiliated patrons, the fines and charges for overdue and lost materials, and the limits on the number of items nonaffiliated patrons could borrow.

Participants were also asked if they restricted or blocked circulation to nonaffiliated patrons for any of the following reasons: too many books currently charged out, too many overdue books, fines beyond a certain threshold, value of items currently charged beyond a certain threshold, an excessive number or value of items lost and not paid, renewals beyond a certain limit, and others. As before, participants were asked to indicate if these policies were the same as those for their affiliated patrons. Finally, participants were asked to describe briefly their policy or recourse for delinquent nonaffiliated patrons.

The three major loan periods reported were 21 days (39 percent), 28 days (33 percent), and 14 days (12 percent). Two libraries (4 percent) had 30-day loan periods, and two more (4 percent) reported ranges of 21 to 49 days and 28 to 42 days, respectively. Four libraries reported that they did not circulate materials to nonaffiliated patrons.

With respect to renewals, the most common loan periods once again were 21 days (37 percent), 28 days (26 percent), and 14 days (14 percent). One library allowed a 30-day renewal, and two libraries allowed the ranges stated above: 21 to 49 days and 28 to 48 days. In addition to the four libraries above that did not allow any loans, four more reported they did not allow renewals to nonaffiliated patrons.

Over 91 percent of the libraries indicated that their standard loan period was the same for both affiliated and nonaffiliated patrons. Respondents appeared to be slightly less generous with respect to renewals. In that case, 89 percent reported that their renewal policy was the same for both groups.

It should be noted that the affiliated patrons used as the standard by most of the respondents were undergraduate students. Although graduate students and faculty members appeared to get more liberal loan periods in most cases, the libraries preferred to equate their nonaffiliated patrons with the group that had the most restrictive loan period.

The most common reason cited for restricting or blocking circulation to non-affiliated patrons was that an excessive number or value of items were lost and not paid for. Forty-one libraries (84 percent) listed this problem as the main reason. Thirty-five (71 percent) indicated that they also blocked circulation when a fine threshold was exceeded or when a patron had too many items overdue. The next most common reason for blocking circulation, although it was cited by only 23 (47 percent) of the respondents, was that the patron had too many books currently charged out. Circulation was blocked by 19 (39 percent) when a renewal limit was exceeded and by 11 (23 percent) when the value of the items currently charged out exceeded a specific threshold. Overall, 82 percent of those responding indicated that their policies for restricting or blocking circulation were the same for both types of patrons.

One of the most consistent applications of policy for both types of patrons was in the area of charging overdue fines. Only 1 library responded that its policy for charging overdue fines was different for each group. The most common daily fine was $.25 per day. Sixteen respondents (36 percent) who answered this question charged that amount. The next most common amounts were $.10 per day (18 percent), $.15 per day (7 percent), and $1.00 per day (7 percent). Other amounts charged by 1 or 2 libraries were $.05 per day, $.20 per day, $.30 per day, and $.50 per day. Three libraries charged a flat rate of $5.00 after 20 or 30 days had elapsed, and one library reported that its fines varied according to the holding branch. Four libraries reported that they charged no overdue fines of their nonaffiliated patrons.

The most common approach to charging for lost materials was to assess the patron for the cost of the book plus a fee, usually for processing. Twenty (42 percent) of the libraries that answered this question used that approach. Eleven more (23 percent) charged the cost of the book, a processing fee, and whatever fines had accrued. Nine (19 percent) charged a flat rate ranging from $35.00 to $67.50. Two libraries reported that the fee varied by material, subject, or format. One library charged a processing fee only, one charged the cost only, and one charged cost plus fines accrued. Charging for lost materials showed the most consistent application of policy in the entire survey. All of the libraries reported that they assessed their charges for lost materials in the same way for both affiliated and nonaffiliated patrons.

The greatest degree of policy difference occurred in the area of borrowing limits. Only 60 percent of the respondents indicated that their policy for non-affiliated patrons was the same as that for affiliated patrons. Twenty-one (44

percent) of the respondents who answered this question indicated that they had
no limit on the amount of items nonaffiliated patrons could borrow. Of the 22
respondents (46 percent) who did specify a limit for nonaffiliated patrons, however, 17 (77 percent) indicated that the limit was different from that for affiliated
patrons. This finding suggests that the libraries held nonaffiliated patrons to a
different standard when it came to the number of items they could take out.

The limits on borrowing appeared to be quite arbitrary, and no pattern existed
among the responses. One library each reported that its borrowing limits were
2, 3, 6, 25, 35, and 50 items. Two libraries placed a limit of 4 items, five placed
a limit of 10 items, and seven placed a limit of 5. Two libraries reported their
borrowing limit was 255 items (this figure probably was a default amount established by their automated circulation systems).

Forty-five respondents offered comments when asked to describe their policy
or recourse for delinquent nonaffiliated patrons. The most common recourse
reported was blocking circulation privileges until the delinquency was cleared.
Some libraries went to further lengths. Ten respondents indicated that an unsettled
obligation would be referred to a collection agency. Five reported that unpaid
debts were submitted to the state for collection through a state income tax
encumbrance or offset program in which the patron's income tax refund was
garnisheed. One library reported a very thorough string of communication: "Send
overdue notice, one final notice, one bill, one letter from Director, one letter
from VP for Business Affairs, finally turn over to the University's Office of
General Counsel who threatens legal action." Two libraries reported that they
would bill the patron's home institution for materials not returned.

In general, libraries did not appear to be taking the patron's responsibility
lightly. Perhaps because they did not have the same type or amount of control
that they had over their affiliated patrons, the libraries were even more resolute
when it came to the delinquent nonaffiliated patron.

Circulation Services

To determine the types of specific circulation services provided, the survey
asked participants if they offered any of the following services to nonaffiliated
patrons and if the policy was the same as or different from the one for affiliated
patrons: renewals, traces, recalls, holds, and checks to determine if the item was
in circulation or on the shelf.

With respect to renewals, 39 (81 percent) of the respondents who answered
the question said they offered renewals to nonaffiliated patrons. Virtually all
who offered this service also offered the same renewal privileges to their affiliated
patrons; only two libraries reported that their renewal policy for nonaffiliated
patrons was different. Nine libraries (19 percent) did not offer renewals to
nonaffiliated patrons. They indicated that their policy was different from that
for affiliated patrons.

Most libraries, therefore, were willing to offer the same circulation and renewal services to both types of patrons. As the services became more complicated or time-consuming, however, it appeared that the libraries were less willing to provide them to their nonaffiliated patrons.

A total of 37 libraries (76 percent) were willing to provide traces for both their affiliated and nonaffiliated patrons. Of the 12 (24 percent) that did not provide this service for nonaffiliated patrons, 9 indicated that their policy was different for affiliated patrons. Fewer libraries would hold materials for nonaffiliated patrons; only 31 (63 percent) were willing to do so. Libraries were even less willing to recall materials for their nonaffiliated patrons, as evidenced by the more even split among responses: 25 said they provided recall services, and 24 said they did not.

Recall and hold policies showed the least similarity for affiliated and nonaffiliated patrons. Only 24 (55 percent) of the respondents indicated that their recall policy was the same for both types of patrons; 29 (66 percent) indicated their hold policy was the same.

Virtually all of the libraries said that they would check for their nonaffiliated patrons to see if an item was in circulation. Their willingness may be the result of the ease with which the status of an item can be checked in an automated system. When it came to checking to see if an item was actually on the shelf, however, only 13 (27 percent) said they offered this service to their nonaffiliated patrons.

Upon closer examination, of all the libraries that said they would not check to see if an item was on the shelf for nonaffiliated patrons, only one indicated that it did so for affiliated patrons. It appears, then, that almost all the patrons were treated alike. If a library checked the shelves for its affiliated patrons, it would also check for its nonaffiliated patrons. If it did not check for its affiliated patrons, it did not check for anyone.

In conclusion it appeared that the nonaffiliated patron can expect the same treatment as affiliated patrons when it comes to loan and renewal periods. The nonaffiliated patron, however, will find less cooperation if he or she expects the library to trace items not found on the shelves, hold materials for later pickup, or recall items from circulation.

Application Policies and Procedures

Forty-two (89 percent) of the libraries issued special cards to nonaffiliated patrons. Thirty-nine (81 percent) responded that nonaffiliated patrons must make a special request or application; of these, 30 (77 percent) indicated that it must be made in writing.

The information requested of nonaffiliated patrons was fairly straightforward. Name, address, Social Security number, and telephone numbers were the most commonly requested items. Some requested school affiliation, place of employment, or driver's license number. Eight libraries indicated that they required a photo ID. One library each requested a credit card or a voter registration card as proof of identification. Interestingly, only one requested a statement of need, and only one asked for the names and addresses of references.

One comment worthy of note was received that suggested the value that some nonaffiliated patrons place on their access to an academic library. A library located in a popular resort area reported that the area receives a large number of seasonal visitors who do not possess the appropriate identification to qualify for a library card, namely, a driver's license or a voter's registration card. They are so intent on using the library that "they will often bring in rent receipts, newspaper clippings, letters from friends as testimonials." Such determination, while unsuccessful, is encouraging.

When respondents were asked about who makes the final decision to approve an application, it appeared that the decision-making responsibility most often rested in the circulation area. The head of circulation was the person most often involved in granting approval (64 percent of the time), either alone or in conjunction with others, such as the director or members of the circulation staff. Eighty-two percent of the time, someone from the circulation staff made the decision.

Almost 18 percent of the time, the director or someone from that office staff, either alone or with others, made the decision. A little over 11 percent of the respondents indicated that some other member of the library administration, such as the head of public services or access services, was involved.

Fees

Thirty (63 percent) of the libraries that answered the question regarding fees reported that they did charge their nonaffiliated patrons. The most common pattern was to charge an annual fee for each individual borrower. The fee charged most often was $25 per year; 11 libraries charged that much. Nine others charged $50, three charged $20, and two charged $30. One library charged $10, and one charged $500.

Regarding other fees and patterns, two libraries charged quarterly fees of $10 and $25 each, and three libraries had six-month fees, two of $25 and one of $250. One library had a one-time charge of $5. Finally, two libraries added a $25 deposit onto their basic fees.

These charges were for individuals who desired borrowing privileges. Some libraries charged less if the patron was interested in access only and not in borrowing materials. Some also charged less if the individual was an alumnus. (Libraries were not asked specifically about their circulation policies for corporate groups. Although some sent information regarding these policies, there was an insufficient amount to make a general analysis.)

General Experiences

Participants were asked to describe any major problems they experienced with their circulation policies for nonaffiliated patrons and to indicate whether they were satisfied with their policies.

Thirty-seven (77 percent) of the responding libraries indicated that they were generally satisfied with their circulation policies for nonaffiliated patrons. Of course, not everyone was so pleased. Comments received from some of the libraries indicated dissatisfaction with their policies:

- Cost of serving patrons greatly outweighs fee. Unclear if "goodwill" gained is worth inconvenience to primary borrowers.
- Constant source of irritation.
- Difficult to enforce; creates bureaucratic records; many volumes have been lost over the years from the collection as a result; causes confusion with staff turnover; many privileges are requested and never used.
- The public relations and financial benefits do not offset the staff cost and material loss. We raise approximately $10,000 a year through Friends of the Library, but we lose in terms of staff time and lost materials.

Only one librarian who was dissatisfied with the policies for nonaffiliated patrons felt that they should be extended: "The benefits to the great majority far outweigh most potential threats to the participating libraries."

When asked to describe any major problems they have experienced with their circulation policies for nonaffiliated patrons, respondents showed a strong feeling of general satisfaction in approximately one-third of the responses by such comments as "not a major problem," "virtually none," and "no more or less than with affiliated patrons." One library even admitted that its nonaffiliated patrons "tend to handle themselves better than our regular patrons"!

The major problem commented on by a third of the respondents was, as expected, the failure of patrons to return books when due. Even with the various types of recourse described above, these libraries still appear frustrated with their lack of success. Although some had the ability to collect money from delinquent patrons, their comments suggested that this recourse was not a satisfying alternative to retrieving the materials:

- If a nonaffiliated patron does not return books, it is difficult to retrieve them. At this time, we only have the power to block them from further borrowing.
- The use of the tax offset program for bill collection requires a great deal of staff time and only works if a state tax refund is due to the patron.
- We have had several patrons refuse to return materials because our billing amount is not high enough to be an effective deterrent.

Some of the problems fell into the general category of public relations in that libraries had difficulty explaining their policies or did not offer services desired by nonaffiliated patrons. For example:

- Sometimes taxpayers have a hard time realizing that we are not funded adequately to serve as an alternative to the public library.
- Some verbal abuse on how "their library lets them do this."

- Sometimes there are complaints about the restrictions.
- Major problem is explaining why we don't issue a "corporate card," that is, one card that can be used by everyone in a company.

A few comments expressed dissatisfaction with the lack of cooperation the libraries received from the patron's home institution:

- When home institutions are billed, they occasionally have trouble getting their institutions to make payments.
- Institution fails to take responsibility previously agreed to and either will not pay for loss or assist with retrieval.

CONCLUSION

Although responses were received from a variety of diverse institutions, it is clear that there is a great amount of similarity in the ways affiliated and non-affiliated patrons are treated with respect to circulation policies.

The greatest similarity was in the area of charging for lost materials. In every case, respondents indicated that the charge to nonaffiliated patrons for lost materials was the same as the charge to affiliated borrowers. Similarly, the charge for overdue materials for both types of patrons was the same in almost 98 percent of the cases.

The greatest dissimilarity occurred with respect to borrowing limits. Forty percent of the respondents indicated that the borrowing limit was different for affiliated patrons. It could not be determined whether affiliated patrons had borrowing limits in all cases, but the fact remains that the situation is quite different for nonaffiliated patrons. This may be a reflection of the fear that nonaffiliated patrons might drain the collection of those resources needed by the library's primary clientele.

In those responses to questions related to the types of material circulated, the circulation services offered, and the bases for restricting circulation, only 82 percent of the respondents indicated similar policies for both types of patrons. There appears to be more willingness to consider patrons equals when it comes to charging them but not when it comes to offering them services.

What, then, can typical nonaffiliated patrons expect when they enter an academic library in a metropolitan area and seek circulation privileges?

Virtually all libraries will allow patrons not affiliated with the parent institution to use the materials within the building. Unless the patrons are faculty members or students at another academic institution that participates in the same consortium, however, they will find it somewhat more difficult to borrow materials. They have little more than a 50 percent chance of obtaining borrowing privileges. If they are high school students, they have even less than a 50 percent chance.

If they do find a library willing to circulate materials to them, they will have to pay a price. More often than not, they will either have to join a Friends group or pay a general fee, probably between $10 and $50 per year.

Once they have borrowing privileges, they will find that they will be treated quite the same as the typical undergraduate student at that institution. They will most likely be able to borrow the same materials, although they will have less access to reserve materials and will be more limited in the amount of materials they can take out.

Their loan periods will probably be the same as those for affiliated patrons. They may have slightly less of a chance to renew materials, but if they do, their privileges will once again be the same as those for affiliated patrons. They have a better than 75 percent chance of being in a library that will trace books for them if they cannot find them on the shelves. They will, however, be less likely to receive the same types of other circulation services. It becomes more difficult to find a library that will recall a book for them from circulation or hold it for them when it returns.

If their books become overdue, they will once again most likely be treated as affiliated patrons. Their privileges will be blocked for most of the same reasons, and they will be fined the same. If they lose materials, they will also be charged the same fees. Once they become seriously delinquent, the libraries will pursue them more tenaciously. It appears that libraries are more willing than with affiliated patrons to resort to such measures as collection agencies and state income tax encumbrances.

In general, however, the nonaffiliated borrower is as welcome as the typical undergraduate. Although there is some dissatisfaction with the difficulty of retrieving overdue materials, more than three-quarters of the libraries are generally satisfied with their policies.

In conclusion, it appears that academic libraries are facing the issue of demands by the public for borrowing privileges in positive ways that support the general philosophy of providing information to all who seek it.

REFERENCES

Circulation Control Committee, LAD Section on Circulation Services. 1970. *Circulation policies of academic libraries in the United States, 1968*. Chicago: Library Administration Division, American Library Association.

DuBois, Henry J. 1986. From leniency to lockout. *College and Research Libraries News* 56 (December): 698–702.

Isom, Bill V. 1982. Circulation policies of some state-supported academic libraries in Idaho, Illinois, Indiana, Iowa, Montana, South Dakota and Washington. ERIC Document Reproduction Service, No. ED 239 621.

Josey, E. J. 1967. Community use of academic libraries: A symposium. *College and Research Libraries* 28 (May): 184–202.

———. 1970. Community use of junior college libraries—A symposium. *College and Research Libraries* 31 (May): 185–98.

Paul, Naomi R. 1985. A survey of circulation policies: Eleven Texas universities. ERIC Document Reproduction Service, No. ED 255 214.

5

Urban University Library Services to Business and Industry

Linda Keir Simons and
Edward D. Garten

Prior to the Civil War, American colleges were largely founded in small towns or rural areas. Following the passage of the Morrill Land Grant Act of 1863, many of the land grant universities were founded in small towns as well. American higher education as a more urban phenomenon was to parallel the growth of cities, which were fed by immigration and urban and industrial development.

The development of the urban and, more specifically, the municipal university came about through both a belief in the extension of educational opportunities to the masses and in the secularization of education and the need of rapidly expanding business and industry for more technically trained employees.

While some notable private, nonsectarian and private, church-related colleges and universities were very early founded in America's larger urban areas, it was not until the advent of what was called the municipal university movement, and then later the urban state university or metropolitan university movement, that urban higher education become massive in sheer enrollment and range of programs.

In R. H. Eckelberry's *The History of the Municipal University in the United States* (1932), the extension of higher education to serve the emerging needs of early twentieth-century business and industry is clearly documented. Such universities as the University of Louisville, the University of Cincinnati, the College of the City of New York, the University of Toledo, the University of Akron, and the Municipal Colleges of Detroit (later to become Wayne State University) were among the first actively to reach out into their communities to establish linkages with business and industry. Northwestern University and the University of Cincinnati, for example, were the first universities to establish cooperative education programs as early as 1909 and 1906, respectively (Nash 1973, 2). In the 1960s a number of writers, including Charles Dobbins (1964), William Carlson (1962), and J. Martin Klotsche (1966), continued to stress the mission of both the urban and the municipal university in supporting local economic development, urban renewal, and technical development. All stressed the stakeholder role played by local business and industry in an urban university's development and vice-versa. Words like "partnership," "stockholder," and "interdependence" were often stressed in these works, and others, when discussing the urban university's interplay with its environment. As Beadle Moore noted in *The Urban University: Present and Future*, "Urban universities have carved out their own mission and their own style of offering the massive store of knowledge and human talent they possess to city residents and institutions" (1981, 32).

Private and public universities located in urban areas, over time, initiated numerous community outreach programs, many directly related to the support of the business and industrial community. Among the many programs that such universities have supported are urban fellows programs, which have related scholars and researchers to local industries and municipal governments; social science research centers, which have conducted applied research for urban businesses; business and economic development centers, which have provided market and economic forecast information to the business and industrial community; university research institute contractual arrangements with industry to perform applied research and related experimentation; technology and innovation transfer initiatives with local industry; regional development partnerships; and as noted earlier, cooperative education agreements with local business and industry, many of which date to the early part of this century.

Academic libraries at urban and municipal universities have had a long record of involvement with local businesses and industries; they have served their own students who are involved in co-op programs in the community, answered reference questions from area businesses and industries, and conducted more in-depth research investigations requiring substantial commitments of time and personnel. Larger research libraries located in urban areas have, in more recent years, tended to have business librarians and collections that can offer more specialized and tailored services and resources to local business. A few of the larger such universities have branch business libraries located in their schools or colleges of business administration, which maintain close working relationships with area business. Often these branch or business school libraries serve not only the primary needs of the business schools to which they are attached but many of the needs of the surrounding industrial community. Others are part of business and economic research centers. More moderately sized academic libraries located in urban areas tend not to have specialized personnel in a separate business library or collection; rather, all information service librarians are charged with addressing reference and information queries from area businesses and industries.

TYPES OF INFORMATION PROVIDED TO LOCAL BUSINESS AND INDUSTRY BY CONTEMPORARY URBAN UNIVERSITY LIBRARIES

Information services requested by businesses tend to fall into several categories. The first of these is the traditional information request made at the reference desk. Frequently called for is directory information, such as an address, a telephone number, or an officer's name. Perhaps reflecting the increasing internationalization of business, clients need more names and addresses of foreign businesses and associations than they did 10 years ago. Since many business schools are also more concerned with global business than previously, university libraries need to purchase directories of foreign enterprises in greater numbers than before.

Often businesses request information on competitors. Most helpful here are files of annual reports and/or a subscription to a product like *Compact Disclosure*. This disc provides corporate information for over 14,000 publicly held companies and solves the problem of where to house annual reports. Other sources of competitor information include the reports issued by Moody's, Standard and Poor, and Dun & Bradstreet; *Value Line Investment Survey*; articles found through periodical indexes; and industry publications.

Another type of information often requested is economic or demographic statistics. When a company is deciding whether or not to enter a particular market or to locate a plant in a community, it needs information about that place. Thus, the statistics published by the U.S. Department of Commerce are vitally important. Two supplements of the *Statistical Abstract of the United States*, the *State and Metropolitan Area Data Book* and the *County and City Data Book*, provide starting points for community research. Since the statistical tables in these books cite their sources, further research is often possible by consulting the original source. Other series that may be useful include the various Current Population Reports and *County Business Patterns*, both issued by the Bureau of the Census. The *Sales and Marketing Management Survey of Buying Power* provides marketers with additional information on consumer markets in the United States. Of course, referrals can be made in this area, as well. Good possibilities include a local chamber of commerce; the Census Bureau document users centers; and professional marketing organizations.

Finally, executives sometimes request general information that is not available in the corporate library. The topic could be one the executive must address in a speech, or it could be a new area of interest to a corporate researcher. A university library, because of its breadth, will usually excel in providing this type of information. Because of the wide variety of topics, it is impossible to generalize further about this type of request.

If the library does not have the information requested, a referral is helpful. Gale's *Directory of Directories*, Lorna Daniells's *Business Information Sources*, Michael R. Lavin's *Business Information; How to Find It, How to Use It*, and Diane Wheeler Strauss's *Handbook of Business Information; A Guide for Librarians, Students, and Researchers* are helpful in determining the correct source to use. It can then be located using the Online Computer Library Center (OCLC) or another network.

A second broad category of information requested is computer searchers. Either the business client will know that computerized databases exist and will request a search, or a librarian may suggest a computer search after consultation. Often requests for searches are made by former students who used search results while in school. Requests for computer searches generally come from smaller businesses that do not have a corporate library to use. The most common areas to search are technical (engineering, chemistry, computer science, artificial intelligence, and so on) and commercial (new products, industry information, current trends in marketing, and so on).

When providing computer searches to nonuniversity clients, the library should have a written statement of fees and other policies. For example, the library may require the client to complete an information form stating exactly what information is needed. If a minimum time to complete the search is needed, that should be stated. Before starting a computer search, the librarian should discuss the search topic and the fee structure thoroughly with the client, and after the search is completed, the librarian should go over the results with the client. Because of the consultation and searching time involved, libraries often attach a surcharge representing the librarian's salary and overhead to the actual online costs. If the library can provide a billing mechanism, it will be appreciated by businesses. The ability to handle purchase orders and to provide invoices simplifies payment for businesses. With the arrival of compact disc technology, many business people prefer to conduct their own searches, especially if use of the compact disc workstation is free and online searching is fee-based. Databases such as *Disclosure*, *ABI/INFORM*, *Compendex*, and even Information Access Corporation's *General Periodicals Index* are used heavily by business people in their compact disc format. Online searches are now more likely to be on specialized topics requiring *Inspec*, *PTS PROMPT*, and other expensive, less common databases.

A third general category of service businesses ask for is document delivery. Most business people are more concerned with timeliness than with cost and look to the bottom line—delivery of the actual information they need. They inquire about photocopy reproduction services, interlibrary loan, and commercial document delivery services. The academic library is faced with a dilemma. If it chooses to do the work of ordering books and photocopies for a local business, is it spending time that could be used ordering materials for students and faculty? If it refuses to obtain materials for businesses, is it angering a potential supporter of the school? Because of the high cost of interlibrary loan (Miller and Tegler

[1988, 365] reported cost estimates between $1 and $18, depending on what costs are measured, but a figure near the high end seems more likely), some libraries have opted to refer business clients to the commercial suppliers who accept orders by telephone or telefacsimile, accept credit cards for payment, and deliver at least as rapidly as traditional interlibrary loan services.

COLLECTION AND STAFFING IMPLICATIONS

As noted in the preceding section, some universities support separate business and/or engineering libraries while others incorporate all fields of study into one central library. Whatever the arrangement, however, service to the business community requires looking at collection development and staffing issues.

Collection Development

Although business users have some impact on university library collections, the primary influence remains the curriculum. Certainly, academic libraries will rarely, if ever, purchase expensive reference books and periodical subscriptions unless the librarians feel the materials will be used for student assignments or faculty research. Quite often, however, materials needed for the curriculum are also useful to the business community. Some examples include business directories; marketing reference sources, such as the *Standard Directory of Advertisers* and the *Standard Directory of Advertising Agencies*; stock evaluation guides, such as *Value Line Investment Survey*; and tax services. Also, of course, periodical indexes and computer databases are intended for corporate users as well as students.

There are some materials that are either so expensive or so specialized that academic libraries seldom have them. One example is Dun & Bradstreet's "Business Information Reports," informally known as its credit reports. Although these reports are available on over 5 million American companies, they are expensive, and, as Michael Lavin (1987, 75) points out, they are not sold to libraries. An alternative is the DIALOG database *Duns Financial Records* (File 519), but it contains many fewer records, and it is also expensive to use. Specialized industry reports are better obtained from the industry association rather than the library, although the librarian can supply the address and telephone number of the association. Sometimes a library keeps publications such as *Leading National Advertisers* or *Standard Rate and Data Service* only in outdated editions as examples for students. These editions will not be useful to corporate clients.

Occasionally a library will buy an item that is primarily used by outsiders, although the implication is that university people might use it as well. An example might be an expensive set such as the American Society for Testing and Materials (ASTM) standards. At the University of Dayton, faculty and students use it occasionally. Outsiders, however, make heavy use of it, and until recently it was the only set in the area's libraries. In supporting the area's leading engineering school, the University of Dayton library accepts a responsibility to maintain the ASTM standards not just for on-campus users but for the industrial community as well. If possible, it is important for libraries to cooperate with other libraries in the community on large purchases and to remember to include public and community college libraries as well as other university libraries. It is a good idea to know what the other libraries in the area hold in terms of expensive business and technical materials.

Government documents are a special case of materials both because of their special requirements in collection, classification, and use and because of their invisibility in many libraries. Yet government documents offer some of the best materials available to answer business information needs. The Commerce Department issues scores of useful documents, including the *Censuses of Manufacturing; Wholesale; Trade; Retail Trade; Transportation; Agriculture; Service Industries; Mineral Industries; and Construction.* The International Trade Administration issues reports helpful to exporters, including the "Foreign Economic Trends" series, the "Country Market Surveys," and the "Overseas Business Reports." The State Department's "Post Reports" and "Background Notes" are also useful to anyone going overseas on business. The many reports derived from the decennial censuses of population and housing as well as ongoing census surveys are helpful to those who need to forecast demographic trends. The Bureau of Labor Statistics publications, especially the *Monthly Labor Review*, report on hours of work, wages, and other labor issues that influence business. Through the National Technical Information Service (NTIS) and its publication *Government Reports Announcements & Index*, businesses can access much of the research conducted by government agencies and their contractors. Having the *Announcements* available online on both DIALOG and BRS makes the information even easier to find. Many business and industry users should be familiar with government publications, yet many are not. Any academic library that wishes to serve this clientele well needs to hire a knowledgeable and enthusiastic documents librarian to publicize and promote the use of these publications. More detail is given in another chapter.

Staffing Implications

The most difficult staffing issue, of course, is in deciding how much help business clients should receive in light of other service demands. Should the librarians distinguish among students, faculty, and nonuniversity persons when deciding the level of help to offer? The question is complicated by other considerations, some of which have little to do with the library. For example, should a company that donates generously to the university receive preferential treatment from the library? Local businesses are often owned or managed by alumni. Should they be able to claim extra service by virtue of their alumni status? How does the librarian separate a graduate student's request for information needed for a class assignment from that needed for a problem at work? Indeed, in a university that offers graduate business courses, it is often hard to separate the graduate business students from nonuniversity business people. Much of the information needed to decide on a help level will have to be obtained from the reference interview. Some libraries have written policies about how much time to spend with a non-university patron. At Drexel University, for example, the limit is 15 minutes (Marvin 1988, 147). After that time, the client must work independently or, where available, switch to a payment situation. In fact, one would suspect that if a library has initiated a fee-based business information service, it is more likely to have a strict policy regarding the amount of help offered free, partly because it will help the fee-based service and partly because fee-based services have tended to be developed in libraries where the amount of outside requests was large and increasing. Strict policies have been necessary to keep the nonuniversity clients from overwhelming the library staff.

The question of whether a public university should operate in a different fashion from a private university also arises. Private universities may feel free to bar or limit nonuniversity users on the grounds that the tuition-paying students are their primary clientele. Public institutions, conversely, face the political reality that much of their activity is tax-supported, making for a broader mandate to serve a wider constituency. They may feel a greater responsibility to offer their collections and staff to the general public, including the business community. In general, most university libraries will admit that their primary clientele is students and faculty, and other clients are secondary. Although there may be some exceptions, libraries are not likely to add staff to serve nonuniversity clients unless the position is expected to be self-supporting.

FEE-BASED SERVICES

When it comes to serving the business community, academic librarians seem to have decided in favor of fees, at least after a certain point of service or time is passed. Public libraries, which are supported by taxes, have wrestled with their consciences longer and harder than those serving the academy. James Govan (1988, 36), university librarian at the University of North Carolina at Chapel Hill, has pointed out that first photocopy machines and then computer searches opened the door to user fees. As Harry Kibirige (1983, 95) states, the library's choice is often between charging for the service or not offering it. If the library does not offer the service, a business will find some other institution or person who does. The business is also likely to gain an unfavorable impression of the library as uncooperative or ineffective. Charging a fee, on the other hand, rarely causes a problem. Businesses expect to pay for information they need. It is not surprising, then, that many libraries opt for fee-based services, especially for interlibrary loan, computer searches, and photocopy services. Nevertheless, the concept of charging for any services has been criticized by a number of library leaders. Richard M. Dougherty (1987, 67) asserts that the very fact of charging for information affects the demand for it. Govan (1988, 37) worries that institutional support for academic libraries may be decreased if outside money is brought in. Both men are concerned with a domino effect, which could lead to user fees for other services and other groups of clients, including tuition-paying students. Despite these criticisms, however, the literature is filled with articles describing how fee-based business information centers have been implemented in many university libraries.

Some libraries have opted to establish a full-blown information center to serve the business community. When Kathleen Voigt surveyed 44 university libraries in Ohio, Michigan, and Indiana in 1987, the 3 she identified as having fee-based information centers were also 3 of the largest libraries studied—Ohio University, the University of Michigan, and Bowling Green State University. All three libraries identified business as the primary client of their fee-based services, which included searches, document delivery, and in-depth research as well as other services, such as records management and translation of technical materials (1988, 24). Stephen Marvin's description of the fee-based service at Drexel University describes the process Drexel went through to establish its "Executive Library Services" and gives practical advice on dealing with corporate clients and billing (1988, 145–60). Loretta Caren and Arleen Somerville, writing of the University of Rochester's experience with fee-based services (1988, 43–44), caution that many issues must be resolved before a library can successfully establish such a program. For example, is a staff member expected to drop other work to attend to a business request because it is being paid for and because the business needs the information quickly? Who will take care of the increased volume of searches, photocopying, and billing? This issue is especially troublesome during a start-up phase when there may not be enough money to pay a separate staff to do these jobs. Caren and Somerville also address legal questions such as the impact of a fee-based service on a university's non-profit status, liability problems, and copyright issues. Although these problems are not insurmountable, the authors rightly assert that the library should consult the university attorney before proceeding (44–46).

CONCLUSION

Today's academic librarians serving the business and industrial community must possess a strong sense of public relations. They are called upon to know many of the librarians and information specialists associated with corporate or business librarians in the area and to establish mutually beneficial relationships with those professionals. Urban academic librarians often cultivate area businesses and industries, not only to provide new and better services, thus serving a real need, but to place the university in a more desirable light when and if the business or industry desires to make a substantial financial contribution to the university. In all contacts, however, consistent and carefully conceived policies with respect to work done for business and industry must be established by academic librarians. Libraries need to publicize their external services through appropriate channels as well, ensuring that the community knows what their services are and how much they cost. Overall, and perhaps most importantly, librarians need to be constantly aware of a rapidly changing business and industrial environment that is increasingly information-dependent.

Librarians in urban academic settings cannot be all things to all people. Rather, they must carefully define how and to what extent they will provide specialized business information services, and they must balance this extension of service against their always present faculty and student clientele. Academic librarians serving surrounding business and industry will continue to face important choices in the future, but all of their service efforts will be logical expressions and extensions of services that have been provided to these communities ever since the large-scale growth of the urban university began after the turn of the century.

REFERENCES

Caren, Loretta, and Somerville, Arleen. 1988. Issues facing private academic libraries considering fee-based programs. *Reference Librarian* 22:37–49.

Carlson, William S. 1962. *The municipal university*. New York: Center for Applied Research in Education.

Dobbins, Charles G., ed. 1964. *The university, the city, and urban renewal*. Washington, DC: American Council on Education.

Dougherty, Richard M. 1987. Who is really willing to pay? *Journal of Academic Librarianship* 13 (May): 67.

Eckelberry, R. H. 1932. *The history of the municipal university in the United States*. Washington, DC: U.S. Department of the Interior, Office of Education, U.S. Government Printing Office.

Govan, James F. 1988. The creeping hand: Entrepreneurial librarianship. *Library Journal* 113 (January): 35–38.

Kibirige, Harry M. 1983. *The information dilemma: A critical analysis of information pricing and the fees controversy*. Westport, CT: Greenwood Press.

Klotsche, J. Martin. 1966. *The urban university and the future of our cities*. New York: Harper and Row.

Lavin, Michael R. 1987. *Business information: How to find it, how to use it*. Phoenix: Oryx Press.

Marvin, Stephen. 1988. Exels: Executive library services. *Reference Librarian*. 22: 145–60.

Miller, Connie, and Tegler, Patricia. 1988. An analysis of interlibrary loan and commercial document supply. *Library Quarterly* 59: 352–66.

Moore, Beadle. 1981. Introduction. In *The urban university: Present and future*. Little Rock, AR: University of Arkansas at Little Rock Monograph Series, Board of Trustees, University of Arkansas.

Nash, George. 1973. *The university and the city: Eight cases of involvement*. New York: McGraw-Hill.

Voigt, Kathleen. 1988. Computer search services and information brokering in academic libraries. *Reference Librarian* 22: 17–36.

6

High School Students and Libraries in Public Universities

Jay R. McNamara and
Delmus E. Williams

As urban high schools are placed under increasing pressure to upgrade their educational programs, their students are turning to academic libraries to meet their needs, requiring libraries to extend their service to the community. As a result, public universities in cities are being torn between an obligation to educate students and the requirements placed on them to serve the larger community. On the one hand, these institutions are oases that are designed to allow students to retreat from the world while they prepare themselves to deal with its rigors. On the other, the resources of the university provide unique opportunities to marshal intellectual resources for the good of the larger community. Urban universities set up specifically to serve as research centers for the city and as capstones to the city's educational establishment are particularly vulnerable to this increase in demand. While scholarly activity is encouraged in these institutions, their primary function is to provide students with the kind of opportunity that comes with a good education. While focusing on their own students, state-supported urban universities are often called upon to provide resources to support other levels within the educational enterprise.

In recent years, more and more has been written about the requirements that are being placed on academic libraries to support the service mission of universities located within cities. Academic libraries are designed specifically to support the education of young people and, as such, can provide useful research tools for students at both the high school and undergraduate level. At the same time, they are viewed by those in the academic community as the heart of the university and as havens for independent inquiry. Many of the scholars who depend on them are discomforted by the invasion of this haven by high school students and others who are not affiliated with the university. As a result, there is resistance to outside users within the academic community, and this resistance sparks conflict. The problem is universal, but the impact is especially telling in the state-supported urban university, and the questions raised about whether or not these people belong on the campus are difficult to address, given the historic mission of the university to serve the needs of the city.

Why do these students come? Most of those who have looked at the problem agree with a 1962 study conducted by Hardin Craig and Richard Perrine that students come because they find that high school libraries did not meet their research needs. LeClercq (1989) concluded that school libraries were busy places that were expected to meet the demands placed on students for research, to provide leisure reading, and to serve as a study hall for classes. In addition, these facilities serve a large and diverse curriculum with a small collection. Their clienteles consist of students ranging from freshmen in high school or even younger students to students who are taking college courses. These libraries tend to consist of relatively small collections made up primarily of monographs, even though juniors and seniors often need scholarly journals to support their research. In short, the collections may be sufficient to meet the needs of students at the beginning of their high school careers but are seldom adequate for students in the final stages of their secondary education as they prepare for college or work. In addition, the services offered by the library and the finding tools that are available in them are frequently not up to the demands of a challenging curriculum (LeClercq 1989). If teachers are expected to fulfill the charge given by Boyer in *High School: A Report on Secondary Education in America* to require "a written report that focuses on a significant social issue, and draws upon the various fields of study in the academic core" (1983, 305) it is clear that additional resources will be required to meet their needs.

In urban environments, it might be expected that resources other than the academic libraries of the city might be used to meet this need. From the nineteenth century onward, city libraries have been touted as universities of the people, places where anyone could come and find information on almost anything. But in many cases, at present, the public libraries that are available to most students are branch libraries of large systems with limited resources. Most of these systems will have headquarters libraries with larger collections; these, however, can be miles away, and, in the urban environment, there might be a college library between the student's home and these resource centers. As a result, the college library is often considered to be little more than a branch of the public library network that is available to the student.

In addition, students might actually prefer the services and collections offered by the college libraries. A 1987 study by Rosalind Miller and Ralph Russell also indicates that many young students find academic library services better suited to their needs than those available elsewhere. Online catalogs and a staff and library collections that are specifically designed to meet the needs of novice scholars are well suited to support their research. Even if the students are not aware of the differences in services that might be available, teachers sometimes steer their students into the college or university library. High school teachers frequently feel that their students are more likely to be challenged when they are given assignments that require them to use an academic library, or the teachers feel that using these kinds of resources can build confidence in bright students and so often direct them to the college campus (Miller and Russell 1987). It is also true that coming onto a college campus and using the same kind of resources as college students are alluring for high school students. As a result, college libraries can provide an excuse for their being on campus and give them the illusion that they are like college students at a time in their lives when this is important to them. While students might be able to find what they need in a public library, that institution might not have the same kind of cachet.

Whatever reason is given for high schoolers being attracted to an academic library, there is clear evidence that academic libraries are being confronted more and more with young people who want to use their collections. According to Kathleen Craver (1987), these students are, as a group, college-bound, grade-conscious, and highly motivated. Miller and Russell (1987) found that the majority of them are doing research for a junior or senior English project, with social science research being the next most popular. Most are in their last two years in high school, although some students will find the way to the academic library much earlier. Most come in the late afternoon, in the evenings, or on weekends, and most come to use reference tools, monographs, and journals, although some can be expected to use all of the library services that might be available to them. In short, the services that are most used and the materials most often required by high school students are precisely those that are most often sought by lower division students in the university.

THE CHALLENGE OF THE HIGH SCHOOL CLIENT

High school students pose a particular challenge to colleges and universities in cities. While some of these institutions have national constituencies, many of them are true urban universities that must be viewed as universities "of the city" as well as universities "in the cities" (Rudnick 1983). Most of their students are products of urban school systems, which, in turn, are often staffed with teachers trained by the same urban university. Many of the products of the university will remain as an educated elite in the city and can become the university's vocal supporters when funding questions arise. These universities were established precisely to serve the needs of the urban dweller, and it is important for them to maintain the best possible relationship with those in authority in the city and to do all that they can to ensure that students have every opportunity to prepare for college. According to Patricia Breivik (1977), many of the students who come to these institutions are first-generation college students who see college as a means rather an end. They are ambitious and hardworking, but they may not bring the kind of appreciation for abstract learning that might come from a more secure upbringing in a household with college-educated parents. Andrew Rudnick (1983) points out the need for partnerships between higher education in the city and local systems as one of the ways to ensure that appropriate bridges are built that can facilitate the transition of these students into higher education. At the same time, the state-supported university needs to provide services to a wide array of citizens in the city who may never take courses on campus if the university expects to maintain the kind of political base that will be required to ensure that funding levels keep pace with the needs of the institution.

Efforts to make students comfortable on the urban campus are an important element in the effort to make first-generation college students feel that higher education is possible for them, and access to campus facilities, including libraries, can provide a bridge for potential students to the campus as they are being recruited. This kind of access can also impress parents with the importance of having a university in their community, whether their children go to that university or not.

The library is in a particularly good position to help with this effort. Arnold Grobman (1988) contends that urban universities have a particular responsibility to support the non-traditional educational needs of the community, and library resources are designed precisely to support the kind of individual inquiry that is part and parcel of that experience. Materials bought to support the efforts of students enrolled in the university are precisely the kinds of materials that are needed by high school students for their projects. In theory, use of those materials can be extended to a wider group with little additional cost to the university, and the high school students who are likely to come to the academic library are precisely those kinds of motivated, inquisitive students most attractive to university recruiters. It is no wonder that many academic administrators see the library as a recruitment and public relations tool that can be used to advantage.

Ralph Russell, Carolyn Robison, and James Prather (1989) ask whether libraries are being oversold as a tool for outreach in general and as a vehicle for reaching high schoolers in particular. While university libraries are likely to buy materials in sufficient quantities to meet the needs of their students and faculty, they are seldom able to anticipate the needs of the 20, 30, or even 50 percent of their clientele that comes from the community. In dealing with high school users, this problem is particularly problematic in that the use of the library tends to focus on specific areas of the collection. For instance, Angie LeClercq (1989) cites the problem presented when a high school teacher assigned an essay on *Gulliver's Travels* to three classes that included 70 students who promptly checked out all of the materials on the subject. Shortly thereafter, seven sections of English 101 at the university were given a similar assignment, and the students in them found little on the shelf to support their work. Every library located in even a modest-sized city has its own collection of similar stories relating to materials about Shakespeare, Chaucer, or Poe, and each comes with an array of complaints from students and faculty. While libraries have been talking for the past 10 years about the need for multiple copies of heavily used materials, few have had the resources to provide those extra copies.

The bottom line is that the competition between students from the local high schools and students on the university campus often leaves library shelves depleted. At the same time, high school students who are desperate to find "five books and three articles for a paper" may take from the shelves sophisticated research tools that can be of little use for this kind of assignment. While some libraries find that many of their materials never circulate, materials in urban university libraries often circulate many times a year. In short order, the book stock wears out, leaving both groups of students with depleted resources.

High school students also compete with college students and faculty for the attention of the library staff. While younger students seem to have a less difficult time with computerized catalogs and other online services than do older students, they are not always prepared to search a large and sophisticated database effectively and to understand the results of that search. In addition, Craig and Perrine (1962) found that these students are not familiar with the tools that are routinely provided in academic libraries. In many cases, the urban university library will be the largest library that the student has ever used, and while it is easy to underestimate the sophistication of those who come to the library, it is fair to assume that high school students using an academic library will be no better than the average freshmen at the university, although frequently no worse. While the high school students may be eager to meet the requirements placed upon them by their teachers, they are likely to have no familiarity with indexes beyond the *Readers Guide to Periodical Literature*, no real understanding of scholarly documentation or the use of bibliographies, and a limited understanding of how classification systems work, beyond a rudimentary understanding of the Dewey decimal system. Most reference departments are staffed to provide service to an array of students, many of whom know their way in the library, and the appearance of large numbers of students who know little about how libraries operate or how one performs scholarly research can be daunting. The additional time required to make novices comfortable and to help them develop strategies for research often demands more staff than might otherwise be needed. Failure to provide that level of staffing can lead to a degradation of service to all patrons. To serve high school students well, the library staff must be prepared to provide additional attention to patrons and to provide a level of one-on-one instruction that is not otherwise required of the librarians.

Another problem that must be dealt with if the library expects to serve the high school student well has to do with the lack of communication between high school teachers and librarians. Every librarian is familiar with the complaint that teaching faculty in the university will not give librarians notice when library-related projects are assigned. This situation is only a small frustration compared to the arrival of 30 high school students who have been assigned a critical essay on an esoteric short story and who have specific instructions from the high school teacher to come to the academic library for help. Typically, the group will arrive when staffing at the reference desk is leanest, and no effort will have been made to ensure that materials on the topic are available. At the end of the day, the reference librarian is frustrated, the students are frustrated, and little has been learned from the exercise.

Frequently at night and on weekends, high school students outnumber the college students in the library of many metropolitan universities. These students can be expected to lack the kind of sophistication that comes with maturity, lack scholarly purpose, and lack respect for library materials. On those occasions when the mix includes younger students and students who are not college-bound, the problems can be magnified. In the same vein, Brenda Johnson (1984) found that the sheer numbers created when high school students or any other group were allowed to use the library increased the need for seating, required that more security precautions be in place, and required increased support for users simply as a function of increased numbers. Russell, Robison, and Prather conclude that "the external user may be the most omnivorous of the library users because he/she usually knows little or nothing about the particular library" (1989). While this conclusion may be an overstatement, it does provide a graphic description of the problem facing librarians with open use policies.

THE ACADEMIC LIBRARY RESPONDS

The response of academic libraries in urban settings to the demands placed upon them by high school students has varied from place to place. Many private universities have moved to exclude these students from the library, along with others who have no connection with the university. These universities feel that while they are located in the city, their primary obligation is to a student body that is national and international in character and to those who pay for the output of university research programs. Others provide limited services to special clienteles that are of particular interest to the university or to groups that have traditionally associated with the university.

Even some libraries that would describe themselves as urban libraries feel the need to curtail the provision of services to high school students as they try to accommodate this clientele within the context of their regular service program. Some of these provide limited services to nonuniversity students and frequently allow them to enter the library and use materials on the premises while limiting the students' borrowing privileges or their access to online searching, micro-computing facilities, or interlibrary lending services. Still others target specific groups of students for special services, typically advanced placement or college-bound students or students who have specific, well-defined needs that cannot be met in other ways. Other libraries provide a full array of services to this client group. Generally speaking, the level of service offered represents a compromise among philosophical commitments to free access to information, a commitment to service by the university, and contractual obligations to provide access to things like government documents collections and the resources that are available to serve all of the clients of the library (Miller and Russell 1987).

In recent years, a number of attempts have been made to find ways to accommodate high school students in the academic libraries. For some time there has been a realization that the library cannot simultaneously serve this clientele well and prevent it from interfering with its service to other client groups unless some system is developed to orient these users to the library more efficiently. As noted earlier, high school students are coming to the academic library no matter what the service policy is, and rather than banning them from the building, many libraries are coming to grips with the problems they present. As a result, a number of service delivery programs are being developed based on bibliographic instruction models that have been in use in libraries for some time. In general, these kinds of programs are based on traditional bibliographic instruction. They include library orientations for high school classes, tours, the provision of library materials designed to help introduce students to the library collections and services, and privileges for special groups like gifted classes or workshops.

One of the most sophisticated programs has been developed at the University of Vermont. This program began in 1977 and is based on an instruction program lasting one-half day that includes an orientation to the library, some instruction on how to use the facility, and exercises that encourage students to explore the resources of the library on their own. The university offers the program to teachers from any school in Vermont, and, in the main, they have found it to be successful on several levels. Classes come as a group with their teachers and are put through the program as a unit, an exercise that provides teachers with an opportunity to understand what their students know and how to use this knowledge in the classroom. As an instructional device, the program provides students from all over Vermont the opportunity to use and become accustomed to an academic library that is often the largest library to which those students have ever been exposed. From a public relations standpoint, it has been used to show that the university has an interest in the citizens of Vermont who live outside of the Burlington area. Its primary limitation has been that it accepts entire classes, which often include students who are not college-bound and who are not interested in the program (Jean 1981).

A more typical program has been developed by the University of Tennessee at Knoxville. A survey done by the staff of the university library determined that the available library resources were adequate for the majority of high school students in the Knoxville area. The researchers found, however, that 20 percent of the senior classes in the area high schools who were involved in advanced placement programs needed more library support than was currently available to them and that additional resources were needed to support the professional development of teachers in the high schools. As a result, a program was initiated whereby free library cards for the university library are given to every high school senior and every teacher involved in advanced placement classes. An orientation program featuring tours of the library was initiated to show them how to use the library. Letters sent to teachers at the beginning of the academic year announce the program, and groups of between 25 and 60 students are brought to the campus throughout the year. The expectation is that students will leave the library with a feeling that it is a friendly place and a resource for their education (LeClercq 1989).

At the University of Alabama in Huntsville, a program has been developed that is designed to tailor instruction to the needs and limitations of the local school systems. This program features an offer to any school system in the service area of the university to extend borrowing privileges to any high school student who participates in an orientation conducted by the library faculty or staff. Several options are offered for delivering this orientation to students. The teacher can choose a tour of the library or a visit to the high school classroom by a library staff member. In addition, one-day sessions are offered twice a year for those who would like to have more in-depth instruction. Library cards are also offered to teachers from secondary schools in the area to encourage them to find out what is available in the library for their students. The university draws 75 percent of its students from the local area, and while it boasts a strong student body, many of those who might be expected to enroll in the university are neither honor students nor students enrolled in the advanced placement program. As a result, the audience for the orientation program was designed to be as broad as possible to ensure that those students who were likely to attend the university were included. In a typical year more than 2,000 user cards are authorized, and roughly one-third of those are used by high school students in the area.

While the evidence is not entirely consistent, it appears that the most successful programs of this kind tend to take place in smaller cities. It appears that these cities provide enough high school users to test the system properly without overwhelming it. In addition, there are fewer communications problems between teachers and librarians when fewer high schools have to be served.

Even in this setting, there seem to be real problems in making this kind of program work. The first of these relates to the difficulty in communicating with everyone within the schools who needs to be aware that the program exists. For instance, the first year that the University of Alabama in Huntsville tested its program, an arrangement was made to have the school librarian in one of the high schools to be served coordinate the program through the English department. In the middle of the program, the advanced placement chemistry class was sent to the university library to do a project on a weekend. When the librarians inquired, they were told that the university's help might have been appreciated had it been offered earlier. The conclusion reached and reinforced in later conversations was that teachers within the schools do not communicate well among themselves and that contact with any one individual, be it the school librarian or the principal, is likely to be only partially effective. Each year the library has found that more people have heard of the program, but each year it has also found any number of people who do not know that the program exists. The only hope is that as more people are exposed to the effort, understanding will be more widespread.

The second problem relates to the seeming detachment of high school librarians from the teaching process. These librarians do not appear to have much impact on what is taught in the classroom, and efforts to use them as contacts for the program have had varied results. Most of the arrangements for helping students to use the university library are made directly between the classroom teacher and the university library, and efforts to include the school librarian in that process have been only partially successful. In addition, it has not always been possible to convince school librarians that there is a need for supplementary instruction and for the additional effort required to coordinate the programs.

The third problem comes from the cursory nature of the orientations that are given. Bringing students into a library orientation program is clearly more effective than sending librarians to the class but can be difficult to arrange if it requires the students to come to the university. Class hours are viewed as precious, and it is difficult to get students to come after school because of jobs, extracurricular activities, or other activities. In general, class tours conducted in the university library can be expected to reach only small groups of the most interested students at any session and do not meet the needs of others. Even when it is possible to get classes to come to the library, short tours can expect only to leave the impression that the library is not an unfriendly place to expose the student to the library's layout. On the other hand, lectures given in the classroom are more difficult to make relevant, even though they do reach a larger population. In either case, the techniques used have little hope of impressing on students the complexity of the library or of teaching them how to use the tools that are available to them.

A fourth problem relates to the resources that are available for the program. It is important to understand that most of the programs now in place for serving high school students have been developed on a shoestring and have used existing resources. Most of the rationales for these programs reflect the idea that students will use the library with or without instruction and that libraries can cope with this usage more effectively if instruction is provided. As these programs expand, however, it is unlikely that they will prosper unless universities or others in the community recognize the importance of alliances between educational institutions and find supplementary funding to support them.

It is also unlikely that programs designed to introduce students to the academic library can be successful unless they include a variety of libraries in the community in an integrated program. Multitype library cooperation has been fashionable for some time, but few efforts have been mounted to make high school students intelligent consumers of what various types of libraries have to offer and how to choose the ones that meet their specific needs. If libraries expect that students will be able to determine whether the school, public, or academic libraries in their areas can best serve them at a specific time, they should be exposing those students to all three in a common program so that comparisons can be made. With this kind of integrated instruction program, libraries might also come to the kind of mutual understanding that will allow them intelligently to refer patrons to other libraries that are better suited to meet a specific need and encourage cooperation among the libraries in a variety of areas.

In the final analysis, it is critical that students come to understand how to operate in an information-rich society. In *Alliance for Excellence: Librarians Respond to a Nation at Risk* (1984), it is recommended that academic and other libraries be open as many hours as possible to the general public so that students and others can have as much opportunity as possible to gain access to the information contained in those facilities. It is important that librarians do everything that they can to help students understand how much information is available to them and how to use that information well. As the impact of technology continues to manifest itself on the library and its program, this process will be increasingly important, and it is important that all kinds of libraries develop mechanisms to serve all of their clients at as early an age as possible. While the urban academic library is designed to serve students and faculty of the university, increased pressure will be felt to meet the demands of local high school students. Reaching into the high schools to serve these students well will put additional pressure on the library to develop innovative programs to meet the needs of these clients.

REFERENCES

Boyer, Ernest L. 1983. *High school: A report on secondary education in America.* New York: Harper and Row.

Breivik, Patricia Senn. 1977. *Open admissions and the academic library.* Chicago: American Library Association.

Craig, Hardin, and Perrine, Richard. 1962. Problems of Urban Universities: Library services for the high school student. *Library Trends* 10 (April): 469.

Craver, Kathleen W. 1987. Use of academic libraries by high school students: Implications for research. *RQ* 27 (Fall): 53–66.

Grobman, Andrew B. 1988. *Urban state universities: An unfinished national agenda.* New York: Praeger.

Jean, Lorraine A. 1981. Introducing the college-bound student to the academic library: A case study. Arlington, VA: ERIC Document Reproduction Service, ED 200236.

Johnson, Brenda L. 1984. A case study in closing the university library to the public. *C&RL News* 45 (September): 404–7.

LeClercq, Angie. 1989. High school library access to an academic library. In *Reaching and teaching diverse library user groups*, ed. Teresa B. Mensching, 11–17. Ann Arbor, Pierian Press.

Miller, Rosalind, and Russell, Ralph. 1987. High school students and the college library: Problems & possibilities. *Southeastern Librarian* 37 (Spring): 36–40.

Rudnick, Andrew J. 1983. *The American university in the urban context.* Washington, DC: National Association of State Universities and Land-Grant Colleges.

Russell, Ralph E.; Robison, Carolyn L.; and Prather, James E. 1989. External user access
    to academic libraries. *Southeastern Librarian* 39 (Winter): 135–38.
U.S. Department of Education. 1984. *Alliance for excellence.* Washington, DC: U.S.
    Government Printing Office.

7

Cooperation: Private Academic and High School Libraries

Kathleen Tiller

The age, the look of uncertainty, and the tentative, garbled request for information are the same. The research topic is as familiar as the obvious lack of knowledge about how to use reference sources and tools. The student standing before the reference desk, however, is not the college freshman who has participated in the required library orientation session or completed a carefully designed bibliographic instruction exercise. A few more questions usually identify the patron as a high school student.

This scenario is apt to occur during evening or weekend hours when perhaps a single librarian is available to answer questions and handle telephone requests. The academic reference librarians in such situations face a serious dilemma in terms of time, priorities, and loyalty, to say nothing of the genuine desire to help, which probably led them into the public services area in the first place. The American Library Association (ALA) Code of Ethics states: "Librarians must provide the highest level of service through appropriate and usefully organized collections, fair and equitable circulation and service policies, and skillful, accurate, unbiased and courteous responses to all requests for assistance" (American Library Association 1982, 585).

A nearby academic library can be attractive to high school students for a number of reasons. Sophisticated, electronic research tools that are within walking distance or a brief bus or car ride away are tempting to both the serious high school student and the teacher of an advanced placement or college-bound class. Teachers taking advanced degree courses are often impressed with the wealth of reference material, indexes, CD-ROM products, and periodical and book collections that they have used at the library for their own research. They are eager to expose their students to these resources. The late and weekend hours and the presence of a reference librarian during those times are also attractive features of the academic library. High school libraries generally remain open only 45 minutes, at most, after regular dismissal, with only an aide or secretary left in charge. With the trend toward fewer study halls, about the only opportunity for any kind of research is in either a public or an academic library.

PROBLEMS OF PUBLIC SERVICE TO THE HIGH SCHOOL STUDENT

How much service should be offered to library patrons not affiliated with the university is a real dilemma. In a state institution supported by tax dollars, the problem can be addressed with the rationale that all citizens have contributed to the library's existence and are therefore entitled to some level of service. On the private level, however, where high tuition rates help maintain the quality and state-of-the-art library technology, another issue surfaces. Does the tuition-paying freshman needing an explanation of the *MLA International Bibliography* have priority over the high school senior whose teacher has recommended that source? Is it fair to the high school students for their teacher to give an assignment that can be completed only in an academic library? Is it reasonable to expect the academic librarian to help with the assignment? The meaning of public service for an academic librarian in this situation needs some close examination.

Many private academic libraries have always opened their doors to any user, with restrictions limited to charging out materials. Use of the reference room and periodical collection is assumed, and requests for assistance or answers are routinely handled. Many Catholic institutions have a nearby high school staffed by the same religious order affiliated with the university. Students from the high school use the academic library regularly, and usually the only problems that arise are missing materials on popular term paper topics or a group's enthusiasm reaching an unacceptable noise level. Since the college and high school are, in a sense, "related," handling these problems is usually never considered to be a matter for policy. Use of even private college libraries by outsiders has increased to the point where the problem is not an occasional annoyance but a real concern in terms of time and materials.

Policy statements are time-consuming to formulate. They are essential, however, and they may be the only way to deal with increasing use of the academic library by high school students. The popularity of CD-ROM indexes and online computer catalogs and rising computer literacy levels of younger users have created serious competition for the use of these products and the materials that they access. High school students who have dial access from a school media center to a college online catalog find CD-ROM products equally tempting. They experience new information needs and know that the college library can satisfy those needs. They want to know how to find the material, but time used to instruct individual high school students in the use of electronic or print reference tools is taken away from university students needing similar help. A bibliographic instruction session and library tour for a high school class can tie up two librarians for several hours, put a strain on the use of terminals, indexes, and periodicals, and try the patience of university students and faculty needing to use the same resources. A mission statement promoting the strong service orientation and quality public relations in contacts with the general public may sound inspirational, but it is no substitute for clear guidelines about who may use the library and under what circumstances. Private institutions, especially those with religious foundations, pride themselves on service to more than the university community; however, the desire for, and the reality of, providing services that are expensive to install and maintain are frequently at odds.

ENCOURAGING OR RESTRICTING ACCESS FOR HIGH SCHOOL STUDENTS

In an effort to establish specific policy guidelines defining who has the right to use which services and materials, it is essential to examine the reasons for encouraging or discouraging high school student use of the academic library. The most common reason for allowing a high school student to use the university library is recruitment possibilities. Highlighting the library's friendly and competent assistance, the latest computerized research tools, and vast collection is supposed to convince prospective students to choose the university. A trip to a college library to complete a homework assignment is not, however, a likely factor in college selection. The rationale of community service or public relations is more realistic. The accessibility and friendliness of a university library can go a long way toward dispelling notions of an elitist intellectual community in an urban setting. The poor image of librarianship that many worry plagues the profession can receive a boost, as can the value of a college education. Exposing high school students to an academic library can reduce the intimidation and lack of adequate preparation experienced by first-year college students.

Perhaps the most important reason for encouraging high school students to use the academic library is the concept of lifelong learning. *A Nation at Risk* called for the creation of a ''Learning Society'' committed to a ''system of education that affords all members the opportunity to stretch their minds to full capacity, from early childhood through adulthood, learning more as the world itself changes'' (U.S. National Commission on Excellence in Education 1983, 13). A specific recommendation from *Alliance for Excellence* states clearly that ''school media centers and public and academic libraries be open, to the fullest extent possible, to elementary and secondary school students and area residents'' (1984, 18). These recommendations have serious implications for cooperation with high school libraries and service to high school students.

RECOMMENDATIONS

Several things need to be addressed if the private academic library is to survive increasing use by high school students and still offer quality service to its immediate and most important users. The value of a clear policy defining users and the extent of use by each category has already been mentioned.

In practical terms, policy is valuable when explaining to a high school English teacher that bringing a class of 50 students to the library is not possible during the term paper rush. Extent of service and borrowing privileges for nonuniversity users can be clearly spelled out. If direct borrowing by high school students is acceptable, the number of books can be limited; this policy is particularly useful if an entire class is doing similar research. Books can be checked out, through prior arrangements, to the teacher or school librarian if concern for return of materials is an issue. More difficult to control, but still necessary, is exactly when students may use the library. Some libraries have declared Sunday afternoons and evenings, certain weekday evenings, or specific periods of the university's academic calendar off-limits to high school patrons.

A second consideration is the impact of high school student use on noncirculating materials and library personnel time and attention. While not much can be done to lessen the use of the periodical collection, prior arrangements with high school teachers and library media specialists can make the visit to an academic library less troublesome. The visit should never be considered a field trip, but rather a working session resulting in a specific and clearly demonstrated amount of research accomplished. Adequate supervision of the students as defined by the academic library is paramount, no matter what assurances of behavior are promised by the classroom teacher. If possible, chaperones should be the school librarian and other teachers, not parents. Ideally, the chaperones should be familiar with the library and the kind of tools the students will be expected to use. Early contacts between high school teachers and librarians and the academic librarian should establish what background and skills the visiting students should have before using the college library and what the specific assignment will be. Having a detailed assignment sufficiently in advance of the class visit will enable library personnel to prepare any special material. It is essential that high school students have an understanding of the nature of an academic library and an introduction to the one they will visit before they attempt any research.

This type of introduction can be handled in several ways. The academic librarian can visit the high school and introduce Library of Congress call numbers and subject headings, general and subject specific encyclopedias, and indexes. How to narrow a topic and follow a search strategy can be covered by the classroom teacher, and the interpretation of bibliographic citations and appropriate practice drill can be part of the high school librarian's presentation in this team-taught approach. Appropriate exercises to measure library skills can also be developed by the school librarian. If such a trip is not possible, an introductory tour, brief bibliographic instruction session, and explanation of the catalog, especially if it is online, should be given when the students arrive at the library. Such a session will necessarily be brief so that students have most of the time to spend completing the assignments. Still another possibility is a set of worksheets designed to teach students the skills they will need to use a university library. The worksheets should be completed and evaluated by the teacher or school librarian prior to the class visit or as a prerequisite for using the library on an individual basis. Samples of such exercises and projects are available as ERIC documents.

A third consideration is that increasing numbers of high school students using academic libraries may indicate a real or perceived inadequacy of high school library collections. A needs assessment was conducted by the library at the University of Tennessee, Knoxville, in preparation for the development of a model for providing access to the university library resources for area gifted high school students. Only 41.8 percent of teachers surveyed reported that the school library adequately met the research paper and project needs about 50 percent of the time. Fifty-six percent of the teachers said that students needed greater access to periodical indexes and abstracts and more than 50 percent indicated that they would assign more research and short papers if their students had better access to an actual research collection (LeClercq 1986, 14–15).

If these figures are indicative of how other teachers feel, there is definitely a need for closer cooperation between high school and college libraries. Rosalind Miller and Ralph Russell cite the need for proactive, rather than reactive, measures (1985, 10). Time-consuming, one-on-one bibliographic instruction of high school students can be replaced with an academic librarian–initiated cooperative workshop for area teachers and school media specialists. Such a workshop could alert potential and previous users to the possibilities, limitations, and preparation necessary for a successful experience in the academic library. Arrangements can easily be made with individual teachers and school librarians. If a larger session is desired, a workshop as part of a scheduled faculty development day might be investigated, inviting representatives from all the high schools that used the library in the past. Arrangements can be handled through the library director and school principal. Here the library director's role can extend beyond helping determine policy. If there are several academic libraries in a city, the directors could coordinate efforts to make alternate libraries available when one college cannot accommodate a high school class.

In her review of the literature, Kathleen Craver emphasized two objectives concerning the use of academic libraries by high school students and the need for well-articulated bibliographic instruction: "to ease the transition of the student from one educational unit to another" and "to link the education process into a lifelong learning condition" (1987, 63). These goals are not specific to the classroom teacher or one particular area of librarianship. They are the desires of any librarian, high school or academic, sincerely interested in helping individuals succeed. A few observations are inescapable. The information needs of high school students are becoming increasingly sophisticated. They are eager to use academic collections and the latest computer and CD-ROM technology. Academic libraries have demonstrated a general reluctance to limit service to only the university community. Academic and school librarians will need to formulate strategies directed at making academic, public, school, and special libraries "full partners in a dynamic Learning Society" (*Alliance for Excellence* 1984, 47).

REFERENCES

Alliance for excellence: Librarians respond to A Nation at Risk: Recommendations and strategies from libraries and the learning society. 1984. Washington, DC: U.S. Department of Education, Office of Educational Research and Improvement, Center for Libraries and Education Improvement.

American Library Association. 1982. Librarians' code of ethics. *American Libraries* 13:595.

Craver, Kathleen W. 1987. Use of academic libraries by high school students: Implications for research. *RQ* 27: 53–66.

LeClercq, Angie. 1986. The Academic Library/High School Library connection: Needs assessment and proposed model. *Journal of Academic Librarianship* 12: 12–18.

Lorraine, Jean. 1981. *Introducing the college-bound student to the academic library: A case study.* ERIC. ED 200 236.

McClure, Charles. 1981. *Chickasha cooperative bibliographic instruction project: Final evaluation.* ERIC. ED 269 024.

Miller, Rosalind, and Russell, Ralph. 1985. *Implications of high school use of academic libraries.* ERIC. ED 269 024.

Ratzer, Mary V. 1986. *Information retrieval and university level research.* ERIC. ED 266 782.

U.S. National Commission on Excellence in Education. *A Nation at risk: The imperative for educational reform: A report to the nation and the secretary of education.* 1983. Washington, DC: National Commission on Excellence in Education.

PART III

Services to Internal Population Groups

8

Reference and Information Service

Carolyn A. Sheehy

Providing reference and information service in an academic library in an urban or metropolitan setting offers the reference librarian particular challenges and opportunities. The librarian must not only be effective but also be efficient in meeting users' information needs. While the demands on an urban academic reference librarian can be intense, the richness of the urban setting offers the librarian a unique and stimulating experience.

PATRONS

Every library has a variety of users; however, in an academic urban library that mix of patrons can be even greater. In addition to the usual academic classifications (from undergraduates to graduate students and faculty), the urban academic library can have a wealth of community users. Though public and private libraries differ in their abilities to screen users, all are affected by the urban population's accessibility to them.

Public institutions attract a particularly diverse group of community users. Elementary and high school students preparing papers ask questions at the reference desk. Students from other area colleges and universities—both private and public—search for another institution's materials at the reference desk. Business executives use the reference department's *Value Line* and other financial services. Police personnel look for materials on criminal justice to study for upcoming examinations. Editors from local publishing companies seek citation verification. Recently arrived immigrants look for copies of their hometown newspapers. The nontraditional user sometimes appears to be the norm rather than the exception in an urban academic library's reference department.

A reference librarian in an academic urban library needs good language skills, an openness to people from all countries, and a willingness to try to communicate to patrons lacking adequate English language abilities. The urban student population contains many students from foreign countries, many students who are the sons and daughters of recent immigrants, and many minority students. The community user group also consists of numerous people recently arrived from other countries. Both foreign- and native-born population groups contain individuals with poor English language skills. Patience is a necessary virtue for an urban academic reference librarian. A librarian trained in English as a second language is a particular boon to such a reference department.

In addition to encountering language problems at the reference desk, the urban academic librarian also faces communication difficulties due to educational deficiencies. Many students are returning to college or university life after their studies were interrupted. Some are working their way through school. Many are the products of inferior secondary schools. Whatever their background, the number of what I term "bibliographically needy" patrons is especially high for the urban academic reference librarian. Students coming to the reference desk lack basic library skills, such as knowing what a call number is or having any experience using an online public catalog. They have difficulty knowing how to ask for what they want or need.

On the other side of the educational spectrum are graduate students and faculty who expect the urban academic reference librarian to be well versed in the research materials of their discipline, particularly those that are online. Many urban academic institutions are noted research facilities; their reference librarians must be able to provide in-depth reference service to those individuals conducting scholarly research. This duality of needs means, for example, that the librarian must be able to switch quickly from looking for obscure conference proceedings for a faculty member to explaining to a young student what the numbers on the spine of a book mean.

Though many individuals use the urban academic library's reference department, repeat patrons can sometimes be rare. In a residential urban academic institution the reference librarians may get to know their clientele better than in an institution where both the student and faculty populations are commuters. In the latter, it is sometimes difficult to establish a sense of community. Moreover, the times when a reference librarian is on desk usually fluctuate from week to week, so one can never even be sure of seeing the same patrons frequently during an academic term. The satisfaction that can be gained by assisting one patron a number of times can often be missing for the urban academic reference librarian.

SERVICE HOURS

Hours of reference service in an urban academic library are directly affected by the extent to which the institution is a residential community or a commuter school. If the institution is a residential community, service on the reference desk will be heavier on nights and weekends than in a commuter environment.

Commuter students usually travel to school early in the morning, so until 8:30 or 9:00 A.M. the reference desk is quiet. The activity level at the reference desk is highest during the lunch hours (noon–2:00 P.M.), when students are usually free from class and come by the library before, during, or after their lunch break (food in an academic urban library where students are commuters is a serious problem). The other busy hour during the day is from 5:00 to 6:00 P.M. Day students are making their final trip to the library before they travel home, and evening students are making a quick trip to the library before their classes begin. Few evening students come to the library after their classes end. After a day of work and an evening class, these students are usually tired and want to go home, or for safety reasons they want to travel earlier, rather than later, in the evening. Therefore, reference desk activity can usually be curtailed by 8:00 P.M. or 9:00 P.M.

Reference desk activity at a commuter school is very low on weekends, since most commuter students do not come to campus on Saturdays and Sundays. (For example, at the Main Library of the University of Illinois at Chicago, during the academic year 1989–1990, 65,797 questions were asked at the reference desk; of these, only 5,060 occurred on weekends.) Rather than double or triple staffing at the reference desk, as is customary during the week on commuter campuses, the reference desk can usually be single-staffed from 10:00 A.M. to 5:00 P.M. on Saturdays and on Sunday afternoons. Sunday afternoon activity is so low that it can be debated whether or not any reference assistance is needed at all. Saturday activity includes students from other institutions who seek books and journals that their home library does not possess, elementary and high school students, and community users. The one exception to this activity level is during the few fairly predictable weekends in the middle of a term when students are busy completing papers.

In a residential urban library, students may not feel the pressure to utilize reference service during their lunch hour, but they do use it in the early afternoon and evening. Also, individuals not affiliated with a residential institution may be allowed to use the library during the day without showing identification, but they may not be allowed to use it on nights and weekends. Although evenings during the week are often devoted to study, residential students do not have far to travel at night, and reference service can be needed until 10:00 P.M. or 11:00

P.M. on weeknights. Weekend reference service activity, particularly on Sundays, in a residential urban academic library can be high. The only similarity between commuter and residential environments appears to be Friday and Saturday nights, when many students seem to avoid the library.

Another difference between residential and commuter campuses is reflected by holiday hours. Though most private institutions with residential facilities close on major holidays, many public institutions with commuter populations remain open on these holidays, if they fall within the academic term. As a result, many reference departments in public institutions find themselves serving students from private institutions on those days.

Even when the library is not open to users, many urban campuses provide reference services for their patrons electronically. Instead of coming to the library, students can have dial-up access to the library's online catalogs from their homes or dormitories. They can ask reference questions or request computer searches electronically. Reference librarians usually answer electronic reference questions within 24 hours. This responsibility may be shared among all reference librarians (with each librarian handling "LIB-REF" questions for a week) or may be permanently assigned to one member of the reference staff. In either system, these questions should be read and answered daily. Computer search activity may be relegated to an electronic appointment book or the downloading of search results but must also be handled in a timely fashion.

INSTRUCTIONAL SERVICES

Because of the changing nature of the urban student population, the reference department's involvement in instructional services needs to occur on many different levels, in a variety of formats, and at different times. Unlike a rural or suburban institution, where the student population tends to be more homogeneous and remain intact for four years, the urban student population ebbs and flows. Students may work full-time for a few years and then go to school for a year or two. They may be part-time students one semester and full-time students the next term. They may transfer between two different institutions once or twice during the course of their degree program. The first time students even set foot in the library may be as seniors, when they finally take the required composition course that most rural and suburban students take as freshmen. Therefore, it is imperative that the reference department offer a variety of instructional services at different times.

Tours, bibliographic instruction sessions, information management workshops, research consultations, and other formal instructional programs must accommodate the needs of faculty and students alike. Scheduling hours must be flexible. Nontraditional evening and weekend students should not be left out of the instructional program. Bibliographic instruction sessions are best held during normal class periods, since so many students work. It is extremely different to find alternate times for a class to meet.

It is important to note that a considerable amount of teaching will also occur informally at the reference desk. Since so many urban patrons are unfamiliar with libraries, it is important to document the high rate of instructional services given by librarians at this service point. In addition to the more traditional statistics kept at the reference desk for known item, directional, and reference questions, statistics on instructional service activities at the reference desk should be kept. Particularly in public institutions where community usage is high, reference librarians can spend a great deal of desk time showing patrons how to use online public catalogs, periodical indexes, CD-ROMs, and other informational tools.

Instructional services are not confined to formal and informal sessions with the reference staff. Reference department publications also serve to instruct the user when a librarian is not present or is engaged with another patron. For this reason, these handouts need to be exceptionally well written, brief, and preferably clearly illustrated. The harried urban student does not have time to pour over pages of documentation. Whether it is learning how to do keyword searching on the online public catalog or locating sources for literary criticism, these publications need to be clear, concise, easy to read, and not difficult to understand. Given the variety of language and comprehension abilities within the urban population, the skill with which these documents are written is critical.

In addition to print materials, nonprint instructional sources offered by the reference department can serve as independent study aids for individual learners. For example, a Hypercard tour of the Main Library at the University of Illinois at Chicago can be operated by patrons on a personal computer to help orient them to the library. This tour is available at all times the library is open, even during those hours when a reference librarian is not on duty, and has proved to be a very successful teaching tool.

Given the library's urban setting, the reference department may be called upon to give library tours to city high school students, bibliographic instruction sessions for local teachers' institutes, and instructional sessions to other community groups. The decision on whether the reference department will participate in such community activities will be dependent on staffing levels and the nature of the institution's commitment to the community. These calls may be frequent, so the reference department's policy needs to be clear. For the sake of community relations, all reference librarians must be conveying the same set of guidelines.

REFERENCE DESK SERVICES

Except for private institutions that sometimes control entry to their library, most urban academic reference librarians do not ask callers or in-house patrons their institutional affiliation before they attempt to answer questions presented to them at the reference desk or by telephone. As a result, the range of subject inquiries at an urban academic library's reference desk can be enormous and can challenge the mental abilities and stamina of any reference librarian. Because of the commercial and cultural activity of any metropolitan area, the reference librarian has to be well versed in a number of fields, including business, technology, the arts, and sports. Whether the question is on real estate, chemical formulas, or a local architect, and encyclopedic mind is an asset to any urban reference librarian.

The number of undergraduates and community users seeking help at the reference desk usually exceeds the number of graduate students and faculty members. (Instructional services provided at the reference desk are given primarily to undergraduates and community users.) Although attempts can be made to reach the graduate and faculty populations through the reference department's computer search services and research consultations, reference desk activity appears highest for the undergraduate and community populations.

Most urban library reference departments offer computer search services. These services may be free or fee-based. Cost for a search is usually related to whether the patron is affiliated to the institution. These services are used heavily by graduate students and faculty members but may also serve the needs of alumni or community users. If sufficient staffing allows, they can also be publicized to the business community as a revenue-generating operation.

Phone questions can account for almost one-fifth to one-quarter of an institution's reference desk activity. (Unlike a suburban or rural area, this may also include a higher number of incorrect referrals from directory assistance and crank, obscene, or "phone pal" calls.) The greatest number of questions asked at the reference desk—either in person or by telephone—is usually known item questions; that is, a specific item that is known to exist as opposed to a question for information that is not known. Most patrons want to know if the institution has an item for which they are looking. Because of the amount of staff time known item questions may take, most reference librarians responding to a telephone inquiry will search only their own institution's holdings. They will check other institutions only if they do not have other patrons waiting.

One characteristic that distinguishes reference desk activity in the urban academic library from that in a rural or suburban setting is that the urban academic reference librarian on duty needs to know the holdings of other repositories in the city. Not only will reference librarians need to check the usual state and national online catalogs (for example, corporate, government, and special libraries). Urban students have a wider range of institutions available to them to find materials than a rural or suburban student. It is the urban academic reference librarian's responsibility to be knowledgeable about these sources.

In addition to being aware of the city's bibliographic richness, urban academic reference librarians should also know their colleagues in other local libraries. One phone call to the appropriate librarian can save a patron much time and effort, and is particularly helpful when a patron is searching for manuscript or nonprint material that may not be online but may be held locally. For example, in studying genealogical resources in a city, the reference librarian should know which repositories collect in this area and should have contacts at those institutions, for much of this material cannot be located in print or online sources. A reference librarian's professional contacts can be invaluable.

Because the library world in a large city is really a small town, it is especially important to observe professional courtesies and protocol. If a private institution has an item that a patron needs, the librarian should make sure to check all public institutions before sending the patron to the private one, as the colleague at that institution will not appreciate being sent a patron unnecessarily. It is also important to speak only positively of other institutions and point out their strengths and not their weaknesses. Whatever is said to a patron may be said to a colleague. Contrary to popular thought, there really is no anonymity in being an urban librarian. (For this reason, some urban academic reference librarians prefer not to give their full names to a patron when they are returning a telephone inquiry or when there is a complaint.)

SPECIAL SERVICES

Reference service to patrons with special needs—learning disabled, visually impaired, or physically handicapped students—varies among urban academic libraries. Some institutions provide no special equipment to assist such students, have no specially trained staff to work with them, and comply only with the barest interpretations of state and federal regulations. Some institutions refer students with special needs to other campus offices that deal with the disabled to arrange for hiring a reader or an assistant to help them with their library research. Other institutions may offer appropriate equipment, have librarians whose primary function is to work with students with special problems, and offer informal and formal instructional sessions to disabled users and their readers and interpreters. These sessions may include large print, brailled, or audio-taped library guides.

For deaf and hearing-impaired students, it is important to have a reference staff member who knows American Sign Language or finger spelling. For these students and visually impaired, blind, or dyslexic students, it is important to have a reference librarian who is knowledgeable about a variety of aids, such as scanners, speech synthesizers, large print systems, typing aid systems, special magnifiers, talking calculators, closed circuit television, telecommunication devices, and TDDs. CD-ROM stations can now be equipped for disabled users and offer an opportunity for independent research. Training students in the use of these machines or workstations can take enormous amounts of time (up to 12 hours of instruction for a device such as the Kurzweil Reading Machine), but it is critical that access to online public catalogs, computer databases, and print sources be available to all patrons.

Although it is important to have reference librarians on staff with specific talents and training to serve disabled users, it is equally crucial that all members of the reference staff be sensitized to work with disabled patrons. Those users who approach the reference desk with poor speech or communication abilities need the assurance that the reference librarian will deal with their questions patiently and considerately. Although no reference librarian should be expected to do students' research for them (whether able or disabled), in a very busy urban academic library it is important that the reference staff be aware of the difficulties disabled students face in using the library and approaching the reference desk. In some instances, setting up an appointment with disabled students or their assistant will help get them started on their research. It may mean referring them to another campus agency. Since reference librarians are in a position to witness the needs such students face, if the institution is not providing adequate library access, they are also in a position to lobby for increasing that access.

SECURITY

Urban and metropolitan libraries are at times used by patrons not affiliated with the institution. Sometimes these patrons are interested not in the library's book and periodical collections but in users' personal possessions. Theft can be prevalent in urban life, and librarians need to be streetwise. In a rural or pastoral setting, a reference librarian might step out of the office without locking it. In an urban area, if one leaves one's office for even a minute, care is immediately taken to lock it. Likewise, the reference center, reference office, computer search service office, library instruction room, and any other physical space controlled by the reference department must be locked whenever no staff member is present.

Signs must be clearly displayed warning patrons to be careful with their personal belongings. Instructional sessions and tours should include information on thefts and caution patrons to take appropriate care of their possessions. At times, a friendly bit of advice to a patron is also warranted. For example, reminding patrons to take their purse with them when they leave a study table to check the online public catalog can save the patrons from a possible theft.

Because of the pressure with which many urban students, particularly commuter students, live and their need for immediate information resources, more noncirculating reference collection books may "walk" from an urban library than from a library in a rural setting. Though security devices can stop some of these items from disappearing, some extremely popular reference books may need to be removed from the ready reference collection if the reference desk is not staffed at all times. These works could be placed on a truck and removed to a secure area if a staff member is away from the reference desk and then returned to the collection when a staff member is present.

It may be necessary to hold patrons' identification card or driver's license at the reference desk when they borrow a book from the ready reference collection. If a patron fails to return a book to the ready reference collection, it is important to charge that patron not only a fee for the replacement of that item but also a fine similar to that charged for not returning an item to the reserve collection. The inconvenience caused to librarians and patrons when a ready reference collection item is stolen should not be underestimated. A penalty needs to be imposed.

Some individual reference items may be popular because they are being used for specific classes. In these instances, it is appropriate to find out the classes for which these reference items are being used in order to purchase additional copies and place those copies on reserve. Some categories of reference materials may be popular because the topic or subject they cover is extremely timely. For instance, college guides, career materials, or résumé writing books may need to be placed in the reserve collection. In these cases, the head of the reference department needs to work with the head of the reserve room in establishing separate reserve collections of reference materials. These collections would be the responsibility of the reference department. Weeding old titles or adding new ones to these reserve collections would be a reference department function.

A final area of security concern may be with automated equipment. Patrons can become very creative when faced with the prospect of using library computers for nonlibrary use. It is particularly important that such equipment be kept in view of the reference staff in secured areas or one may discover a CD-ROM being used for word processing.

RECRUITMENT AND RETENTION OF
REFERENCE LIBRARIANS

Working in the reference department of an academic library in an urban or metropolitan area can be exciting and rewarding. It can also be exhausting and frustrating. Recruitment and retention of professional staff can sometimes be more difficult than in suburban or rural settings.

Applicants hear of greater crime statistics and have questions regarding personal safety. These questions cannot be ignored, yet there are very real answers to them. Most urban academic libraries provided some kind of escort system (student patrols or fraternity members) to assist staff working evenings. Experienced urban librarians can provide new librarians with information on safe travel routes. With proper precautions, working in an urban library can be as safe as working in a nonmetropolitan setting. Librarians, however, must take greater responsibility for acquiring information on necessary security measures and faithfully follow those guidelines.

Since city life in general is hectic and fast-paced, the activity level in most academic urban reference departments is also high. If one yearns for a quiet day on the reference desk, work in an urban academic library is not the solution. A hearty constitution is necessary for the survival of the urban reference librarian. One may answer in one hour on the urban academic library's reference desk the same number of questions one's suburban or rural counterpart might answer in one day! Phones ring constantly, and patrons line up to ask their reference questions. Fatigue at the end of the day is not uncommon. Yet, for librarians who like to be challenged and who like to think of themselves as a ''walking encyclopedia," there is much satisfaction to be gained by helping a tremendous number of patrons who might otherwise remain confused or perplexed.

For many new librarians this rate of activity is frightening. Yet, with proper on-site training, an urban reference librarian learns the skills of reference survival or what I term "fast-food reference." One learns when facing a queue of patrons how within the space of a few minutes to get one person started on the online catalog, answer a short known item question, inform a telephone caller that one will be available momentarily, and direct a user to the government documents collection. The necessity of keeping the line moving, getting as many people as possible started on their research as quickly as possible, and retaining a positive welcoming attitude is a skill and a challenge to learn, but with its mastery comes a sense of professional satisfaction.

Recruitment and retention of professional staff can be affected not only by safety and activity concerns but also by institutional requirements for continued employment. In some academic urban libraries, reference librarians are administrative staff and are reviewed only in terms of their librarianship. At others, they are members of the faculty and are judged not only on their librarianship but also on their service and research and publication records. Some departments have very steady levels of employment, while others have great turnover. Whatever the institution's requirements for continued employment, the challenges of academic urban reference librarianship and those institutional requirements must be taken into consideration when analyzing staffing patterns.

CONCLUSION

Urban academic reference librarianship reflects the excitement of living in a metropolitan area—the variety of patrons, the wealth of local bibliographic resources, and the opportunity to experiment with creative approaches to providing information service to users with an array of special needs. The very vigor of urban life makes reference work in this setting constantly challenging.

REFERENCES

DeDonato, Ree. 1988/1989. Commitment beyond location. *Urban Academic Librarian* 6, no. 7:50–57.

Dunlap, Barbara. 1988/1989. The essence of urban academic librarianship. *Urban Academic Librarian* 6, no. 7:25–29.

Holley, Edward G. 1972. Organization and administration of urban university libraries. *College and Research Library News* 33, no. 3:175–89.

Huang, Samuel T. 1989. Reference services for disabled individuals in academic libraries. *Reference Librarian* 25–26:527–39.

Padnos, Mark, and Roff, Sandra Sholock. 1988/1989. Urban academic libraries in the literature. *Urban Academic Librarian* 6, no. 7:74–76.

Rettig, James. 1988/1989. Cakes and ale in the city. *Urban Academic Librarian* 6, no. 7:14–19.

9

Local Information in Federal Sources

Catherine M. Dwyer

The U. S. Depository program has existed since 1813 to make government information available to the public (McClure and Hernon 1989, iii). Federal publications are distributed to over 1,300 depository libraries nationwide. All types of libraries are represented; 768 are academic. The federal government provides a classification system for its documents known as the Superintendent of Documents or SUDOC system. The publications are indexed by a variety of sources, one of which is the *Monthly Catalog of United States Government Publications*. Recently, privately produced indexes on CD-ROM have also become available. This well-developed and evolving system eases access to federal information, but this information continues to be underutilized by our teaching faculties. Emily Jean Fraser and William H. Fisher's study of science and engineering faculty reports that the faculty use the sources they are familiar with and refer their students to these same sources (1987, 33–44). In fact, "the most commonly cited reason for limited use of government documents is the belief that the government publishes little or nothing in a faculty member's field of interest" (Fraser and Fisher 1987, 33–44). The reality is that there are few fields in which the federal government does not take an interest, and that interest is frequently at a local level. The U. S. government compiles information on a county, city, and even a block level.

As faculty do research, they often begin in their own backyards and use urban and metropolitan areas as a microcosm of the nation. State and local documents are excellent sources for this type of material, but federal documents have a number of advantages. They are widely accessible through both distribution and the indexing available. Furthermore, federal documents are often the primary source material for information published at a state and local level. Faculty who do research, consult for business and government, or are active in social agencies need government documents. Librarians need to become aware of local information in federal sources and promote this material to their faculty patrons. This chapter will look at a number of these sources in four general areas: demographics, business statistics, government finance, and climate and environment.

Demographics impact on many areas of research. The Department of Commerce, Bureau of the Census is responsible for the decennial count of our nation's population and its characteristics. Census information is distributed in hard copy, microfiche, maps, and, beginning in 1989, CD-ROM. The Bureau of the Census has its own definitions of some geographic areas. Edward Herman warns not to "assume that your concept of a geographic area matches that used by the Census" (1987, 69–75). One of the most commonly used geographic areas in the 1990 census is the standard metropolitan statistical area or SMSA. SMSAs are urban areas with a centralized population of 50,000 or more. These areas may include more than one county if the counties have close economic or social ties. SMSAs are divided into smaller areas known as census tracts. Tract boundaries are fairly permanent from census to census, and each has 2,500 to 8,000 residents. Census tracts are further divided into blocks. Each block is fairly rectangular and bounded by streets or roads. Other geographic areas include consolidated metropolitan areas (CMAs), metropolitan statistical areas (MSAs), and primary metropolitan statistical areas (PMSAs). To avoid confusion when using a census volume, check the appendixes for definitions of geographic terms.

General Population Characteristics (SUDOC C3.223/6:) are issued for each state and supply data by state, county, American Indian reservation, and places of 1,000 to 10,000 residents. As the title states, the information provided is general. Population totals, age, sex, race, and household characteristics are some of the statistics listed. *Detailed Population Characteristics* (C3.223/8:) are also issued by state but cover SMSAs, central cities, and rural areas as well. Each volume is split into social characteristics and economic characteristics. Years of school completed, marital status, citizenship, and language spoken at home come under social characteristics. Economic characteristics include labor force, income of persons, families, and households, and poverty status. Not all data are provided for every geographic level, but a finding guide is included in the front of each volume.

Continuing to narrow geographically, the next publications are the *Census Tracts* (C3.223/11:). There is a tract for every SMSA, and in a few instances tracts exist outside of SMSAs. Each tract is assigned a four-digit code and frequently a two-digit prefix. Statistics are listed by these codes, and the user must consult the *Census Tract Maps* (C3.223/11: maps) to identify specific locations. For each tract there are both population and housing characteristics. Numbers are given for total population, household type and relationship, journey to work, enrollment in school, home heating fuel, number of rooms, and source of water.

Census information about individuals is kept confidential for 72 years. Names, addresses, and other information about individuals are not released until that time passes. Data that might reveal any of this information about individuals are also suppressed. Blocks are the smallest area for which the census publishes data, but some of them are suppressed to ensure privacy. Blocks, like tracts, are identified by numerical code. *Block Statistics Maps* (C3.224/5: maps) are necessary to identify the codes. *Block Statistics* (C3.224/5:) include population and housing characteristics, such as total population, age, and number of boarders. Block statistics and maps of 1990 were made available on CD-ROM.

There are two more census of population decennial reports that are especially useful for their local data. *Number of Inhabitants by State* (C3.223/5:) provides population totals from the current census and past censuses by state, county, and SMSA. Graphs and charts supplement the usual tables. *Summary Characteristics for Governmental Units & SMSAs* (C3.223/23:) is also published for each state. Counties, incorporated places, and minor civil divisions are some of the governmental units listed. Statistics cover a wide variety of topics, general population and housing, social and economic characteristics, employment, and detailed housing characteristics.

The decennial population and housing count is not the only census taken. The economic censuses are taken once every five years in years ending in "2" and "7". Since 1972 the economic censuses have been divided into three parts, retail trade, service industries, and wholesale trade.

The *Census of Retail Trade Geographic Area Series* (C3.255/5:) compiles data from businesses that sell goods for personal or household use. These establishments may also provide services related to those goods. A volume is published for every state and contains statistics on the number of businesses, payroll, sales, and number of employees. Within each state volume there are summary data for the state and then a breakdown by CMAs, PMSAs, counties, municipalities of 2,500 or more residents, and other geographic areas.

Service industries are defined as businesses that provide amusement, education, or repairs. The *Service Industries Geographic Area Series* (C3.257/2:) provides statistics for states, SMSAs, counties, and places of 2,500 or more residents. For each there is information on payroll, receipts, revenue per establishment and employee, number of businesses, and number of partnerships. Counties and places of 2,500 or more are ranked by the volume of their receipts.

The third piece of the economic censuses is wholesale trade, which is the sale of merchandise to retailers by businesses with at least one paid employee. The *Wholesale Trade Geographic Area Series* (C3.256/2:) data include payroll, sales, number of establishments, and number of paid employees. As with retail trade and service industries, the information is listed by state, county, SMSA, and place of 2,500 or more residents.

The Bureau of the Census also collects business statistics annually and publishes them in the *County Business Patterns* (C3.204/). There are reports for every state, the District of Columbia, and Puerto Rico and a U. S. summary. Data are compiled on mining, insurance, construction, agriculture, manufacturing, public utilities, and transportation. Information for each is similar to what appears in the economic censuses: number of businesses, payroll, and number of employees. The U. S. summary is published after the state reports and may reflect corrections made to state data.

Local Area Personal Income (C59.18:) is published by another agency within the Department of Commerce, the Bureau of Economic Analysis. This five-volume set is issued annually. Volume 1 is the national volume with data for regions, states, and metropolitan areas as well as the United States. Volume 2 covers New England, the Mideast, and Great Lakes, volume 3 the Plains, volume 4 the Southeast, and volume 5 the Southwest, Rocky Mountains, Far West, Alaska, and Hawaii. For each county per capita income is given with details on sources of personal income. Graphs depict the percent change in income over a period of time, and each volume contains maps.

The Department of Commerce is not the only agency of the U. S. government that compiles business statistics for localities. The Department of Labor produces *Area Wage Surveys* (L1.121/). This series is a basic reference source and should be available in every metropolitan area academic library. *Area Wage Surveys* has changed its frequency over the years. Starting in 1990, a survey is published for each of 32 selected areas on an annual basis. Other areas will be split into two groups of 29 and done in alternate years. Areas covered include SMSAs, PMSAs, and a summary of selected metropolitan areas. Users always have high hopes for the *Area Wage Surveys*. They expect that for a given occupation in a local area an average salary will be listed. In reality the surveys cover a small spectrum of occupations: secretarial, clerical, custodial, truck drivers, and a few others. Listed for each are median, mean, and middle-range salaries. There are also tables on employee benefits.

Employment and Earnings (L2.41/2:), issued monthly by the Department of Labor, is based on a survey of the labor force conducted at the same frequency. Coverage of local areas is selective and includes average weekly hours and earnings, number of employees on payrolls by industry, number of employed, and number of unemployed. The text gives summary information for the nation and some comparative data.

One of the biggest businesses in this country is the business of government. The Bureau of the Census conducts the Annual Survey of Government Finances. *County Government Finances in [year]* (C3.191/2–7:), *City Government Finances in [year]* (C3.191/2–5:), and *Local Government Finances in Major Areas* (C.191/2–9:) provide similar data for different levels of government. Each lists total revenue and then breaks it down by type of tax or income from other governmental units. Expenditures are also listed in totals and then broken down by function, such as education or social services. Expenditure and income data are also given per capita. The introduction will often give a national overview of governmental finance for a specific local level. Graphs supplement the usual tables. This information is useful to faculty teaching in a variety of disciplines, including political science, public administration, and social welfare. Faculty who do consulting for their local governments will use the data to draw comparisons with other local areas.

The *Consolidated Federal Funds Report* (C3.266/2:) is another publication of the Bureau of the Census. Data on federal expenditures to local governments are gathered from a variety of sources and reproduced in this document. This annual publication is comprised of two volumes, county areas and subcounty areas. Funds reported for each area are grants, procurement contracts, loans, and insurance.

Faculty are generally aware that the U.S. government is concerned about the characteristics of our nation's population and businesses. Less well known is the federal government's concern with climate and the environment. Climate has an impact on business location, insurance rates, and construction. Even lawyers research the weather as they try to ascertain conditions at the time of an accident. Weather data for the nation are compiled and published by the National Oceanic and Atmospheric Administration (NOAA). *Local Climatological Data Monthly Summaries* (C55.286/) is issued for selected cities around the United States. Readings are generally taken at airports, and figures are presented for every day of the month. Temperature, precipitation, wind, sunshine, and weather type are listed day by day. Similar information is observed and reported at three-hour intervals during the day. *Local Climatological Data Annual Summaries* (C55.286/) examines local weather over the course of a year, draws comparisons, and gives typical weather conditions for the area.

Climatological Data (C55.214/:) is published monthly for every state. Rather than a day-by-day look at conditions, this document gives a monthly summary for each weather station in the state. Graphs detail temperature and precipitation over a range of years. Maps for the state depict variations in average temperature and precipitation. Some issues contain text on weather patterns during the month. An annual summary for each state compiles weather data and presents them by month. This series is distributed to depositories in microfiche. *Hourly Precipitation Data* (C55.216:) is also a monthly, state-by-state document issued in microfiche. Daily and hourly precipitation is the only data in these brief reports. *Storm Data* (C55.212:) contains maps and satellite photographs of major storms. This monthly publication lists storms or other severe weather conditions for each county. Snowstorms, tornadoes, drought, and high winds are some of the conditions reported. This publication is distributed to depositories in microfiche.

Mother Nature is not the only one that affects our environment. The Environmental Protection Agency has created a *Toxic Release Inventory (TRI) Database*. TRI is a compilation of annual estimates of toxic chemicals released into the environment as a result of manufacturing. The database is currently accessible online through the National Library of Medicine. TRI is available from depository libraries in microfiche (EP5.22:) for 1990. Businesses submit their names, addresses, and estimates of the amount of toxic chemicals that they release into the air, water, or land or that they inject underground. One purpose of the TRI is to make the public aware of toxic releases in local areas so people can work together to reduce risk. Science faculty need this information to research the effects that toxins will have on the environment, as they assist their local areas in reducing risk. Business faculty should also use this information when they advise their communities or chambers of commerce on the type of industries to recruit. Statistics are provided in a variety of ways, and local information should be easy to identify.

When Peter Hernon investigated the use of government documents by social scientists, he found that "interview subjects also emphasized the value of statistical data, both current and retrospective" (1979, 10). All of the sources discussed in this chapter are statistical in nature and have been issued in some form over a course of years. Statistical data are not the only type of information available. Maps of local areas and monographs on local concerns are published by the Interior Department. Hearings and reports on local concerns or national issues that have a local impact are distributed by Congress. In addition to local information the federal government produces thousands of subject-specific documents. These should be included in any metropolitan area academic library to support the curriculum. Much of this information can be obtained through depository libraries and interlibrary loan. Libraries can purchase copies of individual documents or subscriptions to titles through the Government Printing Office. For prices and other ordering information, contact the nearest depository.

As this chapter demonstrates, a wide variety of local topics is examined in federal sources. The smallest local area is studied in detail, and the results are available in different formats. These are basic local information sources that should be available in every urban and metropolitan area academic library. Faculty should be encouraged to use these sources for research and to prepare to do consulting, as well as teaching. Federal documents must be heavily promoted through bibliographic instruction, pathfinders, and bibliographies. Librarians may also want to provide a current awareness service to faculty by providing lists of new publications about a local area or on a specific topic. As Fraser and Fisher (1987, 33–44) discovered, faculty are aware of government document resources. As librarians we need to ensure that documents are made available to our faculty users through selection, promotion, and reference services.

REFERENCES

Fraser, Emily Jean, and Fisher, William H. 1987. Use of federal government documents by science and engineering faculty. *Government Publications Review* 14, no. 1:33–44.

Herman, Edward. 1987. Developing community profiles. *Documents to the People* 15 (June):69–75.

Hernon, Peter. 1979. *Use of government publications by social scientists.* Norwood, NJ: Ablex.

McClure, Charles R., and Hernon, Peter. 1989. *Users of academic and public GPO depository libraries.* Washington, DC: U.S. Government Printing Office.

10

Audiovisual Services: Strategic Planning

Donna R. Leone

AUDIOVISUAL SERVICES IN THE ACADEMIC LIBRARY

In *The Fourth Revolution*, the Carnegie Commission on Higher Education (1972) took an in-depth look at "instructional technology" in higher education. In the "fourth revolution" (development in electronics), behavioral scientists have been active in accenting the importance of learning objectives and understanding the learning process in order to implement media in higher education in the best way. On April 26, 1983, the findings of the National Commission on Excellence in Education, an extensive report on the quality of education in America, were presented to Terrel H. Bell. The 36-page report, entitled *A Nation at Risk: The Imperative for Educational Reform*, has received wide attention among educators, lay citizens, politicians, and the media (Mann 1984). One of the report's major implementation recommendations in the area of "standards and expectations" was that "new instructional materials should reflect the most current applications of technology in appropriate curriculum areas, the best scholarship in each discipline, and research in learning and teaching" (Mann 1984, 49).

The library professional literature regularly addresses this issue with words of support. Professional librarians realize that they cannot deny the growing need for various formats of information being utilized and demanded by faculty researchers in their institutions. Faculty who must examine, evaluate, and integrate technological advances in their teaching and research are concerned with the availability of resources on their campuses. There are a growing number of faculty who recognize their students' sophistication with the use and experience of media audiovisuals (AV) in their learning development. These students arrive at colleges and universities with the expectation that media resources will be readily available for their study and research. Both faculty and students are looking to the library to provide a centralized, accessible collection of learning resources to fully meet their teaching and research needs.

One of the most respected professional librarian journals, *Library Trends*, devoted an entire publication (Summer 1985) to "media collections and services in academic libraries." In the introduction Phyllis Geraldine Ahlsted and Paul Graham began by quoting Franklin Patterson: " 'The college library must not only reflect our culture, it must also be this culture. A library is not shelves of books; it is a process; it is communication in print, and today we must add, in sound and in image. For we are no longer print-bound, and the library neglects these new media at its peril' " (Patterson 1970, 255). This quote is an excellent example of librarians' recognizing the logical and necessary inclusion of media in their collection. *Library Trends* has supported the idea that media collections are fundamental to library services. Both in 1967 and in 1971, an entire issue was dedicated to a discussion of media relevance in library collections. The 1967 issue outlined the need to redefine the library function to include the newer media (Ahlsted and Graham 1985).

In their introduction, Ahlsted and Graham further demonstrated the support for audiovisual integration in university libraries when they outlined their goals of the journal issue with the purpose that it "illustrates how media constitutes an integral component of any balanced repository of educational resources. At the same time, it seeks to encourage among administrators, librarians, and other personnel a more sophisticated appreciation of the wealth of information—both in substance and style of audiovisual formats" (1985, 6). They also pointed out in their introduction that a major roadblock to this integration is funding, a problem of growing concern for academic libraries. The explosion of information and access success through print and database technology causes a strong focus of funds in academic library reference departments. A relatively new technology is the compact disc format for storage and retrieval of indexes, abstracts, and reference books. This format allows microspeed availability of resources and access to them, providing library users with ready references they need. Computer data banks and online catalogs of library collections are proliferating and being used widely in research libraries. These technologies are providing a wealth of print information to the library researcher, and involvement of libraries in this new technology requires additional staff, equipment, and format subscription costs. Added to these increasing budgetary needs for research libraries are journal subscriptions, which have increased in cost to a staggering degree. The question of how to continue subscriptions or whether to seek database resource sharing is under serious discussion in research libraries. This area of technological focus with such budget costs has great impact on the audiovisual integration in libraries.

If libraries are to develop and expand their information offering and integration of its formats, they must outline and follow specific goals within their mission and thereby substantiate their needs for sufficient funding.

Library administrators, once they recognize the relevance of audiovisuals within library collections, must set about a plan of action and objectives to integrate them. Thus, the already established standards and guidelines for research libraries would integrate audiovisuals into their coverage.

DEVELOPING A PLAN OF ACTION FOR AV SERVICES

There are numerous questions that need to be addressed in developing a plan for AV services in the library. The following questions involve integral steps necessary in the planning process:

1. What kinds of media will the library purchase?
2. Will the media circulate?
3. Will the library have equipment to use with the media collection? How much is needed to handle use?
4. What are the staff requirements in number and training?
5. What kind of budget is necessary, and how will it be allocated?

Many of these questions can be addressed in a strategic plan with understood proposed stages of development. The plan requires integration in established budgetary areas such as collection development/technology support for teaching and research.

One of the most efficient and accessible approaches to AV services is a multifunction AV laboratory. An AV lab can be designed with carrels/booths and/or countertops/tables where equipment is located for use along with the library AV collection. The lab can be operated similarly to a reserve collection in a library in that students check out media to use with the lab equipment for in-house use only. The lab can be expanded by increasing the number of carrels/ booths and/or the physical space to incorporate AV systems for cable satellite reception, control rooms for directing audio and video services, and interactive video/computer setup. The expansion and development of a lab are limited only by budget and space. Thus, in preparing the proposals for various stages and potentials of this technology, one plans and justifies according to curriculum, faculty, student, and administrative needs. As increased understanding and awareness of technology-based instruction/research media occur, the needed expansion of collection, equipment, systems, and trained staff will be apparent.

The initial setup of an AV lab and collection is totally dependent on budget. If you are proposing an initial system setup with a control room, you will need to contact AV companies for comparative costs and capabilities. There are numerous national companies as well as local AV companies that can install a lab with equipment and wiring to your specifications and within your budgetary requirements. Many of these systems are analyzed and discussed in the literature. If you attend the annual conference of the Association for Educational Communications and Technology (AECT), you will be able to see the systems in the exhibits and discuss with vendors the capabilities and specifications. The American Library Association (ALA) annual conference also includes media systems and collections in its exhibits. Two vendors that offer audio expansive systems as well as video/computer interfacing capabilities are Tandberg and Sony.

ADDRESSING THE QUESTIONS WITH AN AV LAB

What Kinds of Media Will the Library Purchase?

The most frequently collected media formats in libraries are records, audiocassettes, slides, and videocassettes (videos). Records have been the historical format for music and the spoken arts. Both music and spoken arts curriculum support are requiring integration of the audiocassette format and/or compact disc in accordance with user preference, sole source, quality production, and long-term use/preservation.

Traditionally, films have been a preference for large screen projection and subject matter unique to this format. This situation has changed with the explosion of videocassette use and subject coverage. Videos are less expensive than film and can be easily used in an AV lab setting. The subject research coverage of excellently produced videos continues to increase demand by professors for use in their teaching. The televised showings on the Public Broadcasting Stations (PBS) and other television networks of individual videos and series increase awareness and use in universities. Faculty who view a video from a video rental store, on television, or at a meeting/conference may request the video for purchase to use in their classes and research. Many universities are involved in instructional video creation and course offerings. These kinds of videos can be readily acquisitioned, housed, and scheduled for use in AV labs.

Thus the kinds of media the library purchases depend on the collection development policy. The collection development policy will need a section for the media collection that outlines curriculum/research support and the types of media the library collects. The policy can be a development in stages that indicates that due to budgetary and equipment limitations, certain media are currently being purchased.

Will the Media Circulate?

Setting up an AV lab with fixed function equipment and systems allows and supports a noncirculating media collection. This operates similarly to a book reserve collection in which class assignments are more readily available for use within a limited time. An AV classroom provides access to class use and large group viewing/listening outside of class time. Professors often do not like to use class time to view a video and may want to assign the class to view it outside of class time much as they assign reserve readings. The library can schedule the time and room location for this type of AV use.

The library may want to circulate media as it does books. Media can be cataloged and processed for checkout use. The unique variations of size and packaging of media determine decisions on storage and access. There is a vulnerability in security and damage to media that requires due consideration for handling circulation, return of items reviewed for damage, shelving/storage of items, and procedures for locating items and use by the patrons. In general, media best serve on a limited loan basis. This means that circulating media for long periods of loan or the same as books creates problems in multiple use needs/ requests within a limited subject collection.

An initial library setup of a circulating media collection works best when there is an AV lab/classroom support area to handle limited loan/use reserve needs by faculty and students.

In summary, the decision to circulate media depends on understanding the needs of the public served and long-term preservation/use of the collection. Other questions addressed in this chapter concerning staff, budget, and equipment support available for media use are involved in setting a circulation policy.

Will the Library have Equipment to Use with the Media Collection? How Much is Needed to Handle Use?

Librarians understand the logic and obvious support that equipment provides to use media. Basically two factors affect the decision to purchase equipment; one is the budget limitations in libraries to purchase and maintain equipment/ systems, and the other is whether equipment is available on campus elsewhere to schedule for classroom use. These factors require careful review by a library concerning its decided and understood support of media use. Even though there may be equipment elsewhere on campus, it does not eliminate the question of what is necessary to set up the best access, support, and use of a library media collection.

As already discussed, an AV lab provides efficient use of media for classroom/ teaching assignments as well as immediate research access. An AV lab can be initially set up with one piece of equipment to service each kind of media format in a collection and expand as use increases and budget is available. An academic administration responds to faculty/department needs for technology required in their teaching and research. Statistics on use and increased need for expanding an AV lab can be addressed in budget requests.

What are the Staff Requirements in Number and Training?

The staff number needed to operate an AV lab is dependent on the size of the collection and the equipment/system operation. Initially, a staff member assigned to develop or supervise an AV operation needs clear direction from the library director concerning the purpose, goals, and budget allocation. If a staff member is assigned to investigate these areas and outline a proposal, then the stage development approach is recommended. This involves meeting with campus administrators, faculty, students, and AV-related personnel on campus and off to learn needs, ideas, comparative AV operations, and costs involved. It is advisable initially to establish an AV committee or task force with varied campus representatives to study and outline a development plan and proposal. Whether the AV lab and media collection will initially be integrated into an existing department or service in the library or whether they will be created separately will affect assignment of existing staff or hiring new staff.

It is advisable that any needed staff to be hired should have AV experience and/or education. As the collection and service grow in use and equipment support, it is crucial to have staff familiar with equipment and media system capabilities. Cataloging and processing media as well as equipment installation, directions for use, and patron access also require skilled and trained staff.

Librarians have excellent professional skills in investigating what is necessary to initiate a new service or collection in a library. They are actively involved in this process with the computer catalog and CD-ROM/database searching records and equipment. Since the main purpose of a library is to provide information and access to that information regardless of format, an AV collection and service parallel this technological development in libraries. The challenge of these new developments and their successful integration in libraries are dependent on learning and acquiring the necessary skills as well as hiring future personnel prepared to develop and support the technology.

What kind of Budget is Necessary, and How Will it be Allocated?

Budget is always crucial to the development of a new service in the library. One of the problems in the technological development in libraries is a misconception concerning budgetary need. Administrators often expect the development of technologies in libraries to lessen the budgetary needs. This simplistic presumption requires libraries carefully to outline and distinguish the unique requirements of the various technological developments that justify the additional budgetary requests. Combining the various technological developments into an existing traditional budget allocation area often severely stresses the continuing budget and is not understood by the administration as a new service or expanded capability.

In terms of media collection development, combining media with books in a budgetary allocation can present several problems. When a faculty or department is allocated one budget figure from which it can choose to purchase books, periodicals, or media, an unbalanced, potentially biased collection development program can result. It is advisable to separate the allocations so that regular funding is provided for books/periodicals and media. The steady, stable growth of any collection requires regular funding dedicated to that purpose. It also provides balance in the library collection and any limitations within specific budget allocations, and also applies to the equipment budget. Libraries need to continue clear communication of equipment budget requirements for each of the technological developments to assure yearly growth and development.

An AV lab operation offers a clear distinction of service and budgetary needs. It is important in the planning and proposal stage to outline the budget needed initially for implementation and the ongoing regular budget necessary to maintain and develop its growth and use. The budget amount should be specified as a percentage of the book and equipment budgets. Thus, an initial beginning allocation might be 3 percent of the book budget and 3 percent from the equipment budget to be allocated yearly from these existing budgets. Therefore, if these budgets vary in their yearly allocation amount, then all library collections and services will be affected. This system avoids erratic budget allocation in which media receive an allocation one year, and do not the next year. The success of this policy is dependent on whether a library integrates technology/media into its required collection development or instead perceives it as superfluous and not required in a viable research/teaching support academic library. The percentage a library decides to allocate should be consistent on a yearly basis and increased as use of the service and collection justifies and as they meet the research and teaching need.

There is an inherent problem facing academic libraries and their technological collection development. Recognized organizations and standards do not include media in their statistics and formulas. This lack creates ongoing problems in understood budgetary allocation and support as well as recognition in statistical reports. As academic libraries increase their understanding and support of collecting media in order to continue their mission of providing information access regardless of format, they will need collectively to communicate to national organizations the need to recognize these formats in standards, statistics, and formulas for budgetary allocation.

REFERENCES

Ahlsted, P. G., and Graham, P. 1985. Introduction. *Library Trends* 34, no. 1 (Summer): 3–7.

Carnegie Commission on Higher Education. 1972. *The fourth revolution: Instructional technology in higher education.* New York: McGraw Hill.

Mann, E. B. 1984. Federal government, 1983. In *School library media annual,* ed. S. L. Aaron and P. R. Scales, vol. 2, 45–68. Littleton, CO: Libraries Unlimited.

Patterson, F. 1970. The library as arbiter. *American Libraries* 1: 255.

11

Library Services
for Faculty in the
Urban University

Floyd C. Hardy

The university faculty and the university library both claim to be the "heart of the university." In reality, all units of the university must work cooperatively and constructively for the institution's success. Part of an institution's success is measured by the impact it has on the students who elect to enroll in its programs. Because of their respective roles, faculty members are generally in direct contact with students to a greater extent than are librarians. Librarians, however, have opportunities to participate in the teaching process by providing resources and services that stimulate inquiring minds. Decisions on providing appropriate resources and services are made easier by close cooperation between the teaching faculty and the librarians and by a clear understanding by each group of the other's role in the university.

FACULTY IN THE URBAN SETTING

Information sources abound in the urban environment. Faculty members who do not find the academic library useful will seek alternative sources of information and will fail to encourage their students to become avid and resourceful library users.

The task of the academic librarian is to determine the information needs of the faculty and to design a system within which those needs can be supplied. In the urban university, librarians must recognize and make allowances for characteristics of city living that have an impact on information-seeking behavior.

Although our society frequently bemoans the ills of urban living, metropolitan areas frequently have tremendous resources suitable for strengthening the urban academic library. The existence of educational, cultural, and religious institutions representative of, and in close proximity to, an ethnically diverse population can enrich immensely the intellectual life of the entire university community.

A typical American university, as projected by the media and by their promotional literature, consists of majestic buildings on a campus with well-defined borders. This image is accurate for many universities and colleges in small town and rural settings but is not a true picture of the typical urban university. Physical boundaries of the urban university are often nonexistent, and its buildings often blend into the city environment. Although the physical characteristics of the urban university campus are frequently indistinguishable from its immediate surroundings, there are often striking social and psychological divisions. Urban university faculty who live a considerable distance from campus may inadvertently contribute to the alienation that sometimes exists between the university and its environment. Local residents may view some of the faculty as outsiders, who do not come into the area unless they have a class to teach.

A concerted effort is required by all units of the university to reduce or eliminate the hostility that often mars relationships between the university and its local community. Fortunately, many faculty members are sensitive to the needs of the local community and take pride in external university service. Librarians can contribute to the process of building ties to the community by supporting the faculty's external activities. Librarians need to identify those faculty members who have a strong interest in local and state affairs. In some cases, faculty members consider their involvement in state and municipal affairs as an extension of their teaching and research activities. The information needs of these faculty can often be met by maintaining substantial databases about state and local government affairs, public and private schools, and civic, social, and cultural organizations. Faculty members are delighted when librarians demonstrate resourcefulness by scanning data sources and bringing these items to their attention. This service is an excellent way to cultivate faculty supporters who will emphasize library usage in their lectures and who will give library-centered assignments.

IMPACT OF URBAN SETTING ON
LIBRARY SERVICES

In the process of gathering information about the local community for faculty, librarians may have opportunities to gain knowledge and skills required for effectively interacting with the university's neighbors. Contacts established in the community can be used for future projects, such as submitting joint grant applications with public libraries and identifying prospective members for a Friends group for the library.

Traditionally, the academic library has been satisfied to leave responsibility for aggressively collecting local materials to the public library. Public libraries have built a well-deserved reputation in collecting local materials. Although needless duplication should be avoided, extensive background information on the local community is necessary for some urban universities to accomplish their goals.

LIBRARY SERVICES AND FACILITIES
FOR FACULTY

Space conducive to study is not always readily available on the urban university campus. Lounges and study rooms for faculty and students that are located in the library can provide attractive meeting places for continuing dialogues that start in the classroom. Comfortable faculty study carrels can enhance the image of the library as a desirable place to spend time and will provide opportunities to build professional relationships between faculty and librarians. If the library succeeds in providing for students and faculty a convenient setting in which to interact in a productive manner, it will have accomplished a major part of its mission.

If space is available, the library can derive benefits from having professors arrange to meet and teach their classes in the library. Faculty members can use this approach to break down the artificial barriers that sometimes separate the library from the classroom. Class meetings in the library may reduce the monotony that inevitably creeps in when all sessions are held in the same classroom. It is also a subtle strategy for introducing to the library building some students who are strangers to the facility.

A high percentage of faculty and students in the average urban university are commuters. Working students with family obligations try to make the most of the time they spend on campus. Faculty members are under similar time constraints and try to accommodate their students. In this environment, unencumbered, efficient access to information is essential. Faculty members expect appropriate responses from the library and are highly pleased when accorded special privileges and arrangements that facilitate access to information. Professors often experience stress and fatigue from working in the urban university and thoroughly appreciate any resources and services that reduce the pressure they encounter on the job. Private study rooms, personal computers, and special privileges in the use of periodicals, reference materials, and other restricted items are among the perquisites that can assist faculty members.

PART-TIME FACULTY

There has been an increase in the number of part-time faculty, mainly because most of them are paid less than full-time faculty. Generous benefits enjoyed by full-time faculty are not often offered in part-time contracts (Abel 1984, 70–83).

Some of the characteristics that describe full-time urban university faculty are even more pronounced among part-time faculty. Because part-time faculty members tend to live a considerable distance from campus, they are likely to spend fewer hours on campus than full-time faculty. Some of them have full-time, demanding jobs that consume most of their time and energy. Because of their relationship to the university, the library must decide if any or all of the special privileges designed for full-time faculty will be extended to part-time faculty. Decisions must also be reached with respect to incorporating the information needs of part-time faculty into the overall plans of the library. Part-time faculty have a relatively high turnover rate (Abel 1984, 82–83), a fact that could conceivably make it more difficult to retrieve library items they have borrowed.

The library staff must work particularly hard to establish communication links with the part-time faculty, because there are fewer opportunities to contact this faculty component. Unless the library keeps in touch with the academic departments, it is difficult to determine departmental plans and to make decisions that support the faculty's objectives. Where part-time faculty are involved, it is useful to know if a faculty member will be teaching for a single semester or whether an extended commitment has been made by the university. Long-range planning is easier when information needs can be predicted based on established patterns of use. Part-time faculty in the urban environment can be an asset to universities that are seeking to build partnerships with local businesses and industries. They can sometimes provide valuable linkages to external resources beneficial to the university. Cooperative arrangements between academic libraries and special business libraries can develop from the involvement and participation of faculty members who use both facilities.

Because they are ineligible for some of the benefits of their full-time colleagues, the university may have a different set of expectations for part-time faculty. Their emotional ties to the campus may not be especially strong. In some cases, they may work at more than one university and have divided institutional loyalties as a result (Abel 1984, 83–85). Part-time faculty may feel that they do not spend enough time on campus to justify establishing strong ties with the library or to warrant giving their students extensive library assignments.

CORPORATE AFFILIATIONS

Partnerships are often arranged between universities and corporations for the purpose of research and special projects. Some universities and corporations are attracted to these arrangements because of the potential prestige and financial rewards. Faculty members who are also corporate employees may gravitate to the corporate library if it is convenient and less crowded than the university library. Even the most helpful, accessible professors need time and space for research without being bombarded with questions from their students whom they happen to meet in the library. Faculty members may continue to use the university library if it has a strong collection in their area of interest. If the university administration places a high value on successful joint ventures with corporations and perceives an efficient, high-quality library as necessary to achieve this goal, additional funds may be assigned to the library. Library funds earmarked to support research projects conducted jointly with companies provide opportunities for strengthening library resources and services. Since universities need to guard against external funds that detract from their central missions (Fairweather 1989, 393–95), it seems reasonable to advise libraries to take similar precautions when external funds are received.

Partnerships with industry may tend to increase the percentage of faculty who opt to work full-time in industry and part-time in the university. For some faculty, this arrangement may be temporary, while others may establish permanent patterns of full-time employment in industry and part-time work in the university. Part-time faculty who do not spend a great deal of time on campus may not have the time and energy necessary to become involved in library affairs and may fail to make a meaningful contribution to improving library services. Assignments made by these faculty members may tend to require the use of routine materials without creative dimensions or innovative content. In these situations, the professional staff can use its resourcefulness to identify materials that will enrich the assignments given by these professors.

On the other hand, part-time faculty members who are engaged in research in industry may bring dynamism and energy to their teaching responsibilities. Because they may be well informed about the knowledge and skills required on the job, they may be equipped to offer valuable suggestions for library resources in their disciplines.

Partnerships with industry are not new for universities, but pressure to form these arrangements has increased as funds available to universities have decreased. Industry sees the university as fresh repositories of highly trained talent. The university sees industry as a potential job market for its students and as an opportunity for the university to engage in high-profile, external ventures. Partnerships that have been formed between universities and industry have again sparked debate about whether faculty members can be productive researchers and effective teachers at the same time. Historically, libraries have purchased materials that support both teaching and research. Universities tend to regard research and teaching as compatible activities that complement each other. During periods of scarce resources, however, universities may be tempted to emphasize research, if this activity yields financial benefits (Fairweather 1989, 393).

Private industry has encouraged collaboration and formal ties with academe, because it sees resources in the university that can be used in a highly competitive economy. Although the most visible links with industry have occurred at large research universities, there is a possibility that these activities will trickle down to smaller urban universities and other institutions.

Universities that are accustomed to using partnerships with industry to acquire new laboratory equipment may tend to overlook opportunities to obtain additional library resources. Faculty members who are involved in partnerships between the university and industry and who have not been particularly active in library affairs may have to be reminded to be alert to possible spin-offs that could benefit the library. The librarian's responsibility is to initiate contacts with faculty members and aggressively explore whether the library could use to its advantage some of the resources resulting from joint ventures between the university and corporations.

Partnerships between industry and universities often involve research in the natural and exact sciences. Trends showing disproportionate growth of these collections when compared to the social sciences and the humanities must be corrected by vigorous oversight by the professional library staff.

COMMUNICATING WITH FACULTY

Communications links with faculty can be used by librarians to determine which library resources are suitable for the institution's academic programs. Librarians in the urban environment should evaluate their resources and services to determine how they can cooperate with faculty in preserving a climate conducive to exciting teaching and intellectual growth. Traditional approaches for faculty-librarian cooperation should be considered as well as new directions presented by the dynamics of the urban environment.

The library committee is a standard vehicle for bringing faculty and librarians together. One of the drawbacks of the library committee is the difficulty of providing adequate representation for all departments of the university. Unless guidelines are carefully established for departmental representation, the same faculty members will return year after year. This arrangement has the advantage of providing continuity, but it restricts opportunities to bring fresh ideas. Stagnation sets in unless the chairperson of the committee has a deep commitment to the library and has the required time and talent for motivating the committee. Participation in the library committee will gradually decline unless there are clear objectives, relevant projects, and ideas to which members of the committee can ardently subscribe. It is hard to change the course of a library committee after it has gained a reputation for sluggishness, complacency, and inactivity. If members of the committee attend meetings at which nothing significant takes place, an ineffective group will be the inevitable result. Attendance will decline if meetings follow a predictable course of voluminous discussions and meager outcomes. Concerns of faculty and students must be foremost in the deliberations of the library committee. If the library committee establishes a record of giving priority to and taking action on faculty and student concerns and of delivering services that effectively articulate the mission of the university, able and eager participants will be attracted to it from faculty and student ranks.

In the urban university, a satisfactory level of committee participation may be even more difficult to achieve than in other situations. Involvement in any campus activity must compete with the time constraints characteristic of the urban environment. An extra effort will be necessary to provide representation from part-time faculty, who often comprise an important segment of the urban university faculty. Participation is likely to suffer unless the library committee successfully develops a stimulating agenda and compelling focus. Although the chairperson of the library committee is usually a faculty member, its members usually expect a librarian to provide guidance, agenda items, and a large part of the energy required to propel the committee.

Accreditation visits provide good opportunities for generating enthusiasm about library issues. When an institution is being prepared psychologically for an accreditation visit, a high level of anxiety is created on campus. This time is appropriate for the librarians and the faculty jointly to articulate their visions for the library within the framework of the self-study effort and to present a blueprint for how these visions can be realized. Ideas for ambitious projects that may not be seriously entertained under normal circumstances may receive a fair hearing in the tension-filled atmosphere of preparing for an accreditation visit. Even if these ideas are not immediately implemented, the library will have received the high visibility necessary for faculty and students to reflect on the importance of the library to the academic enterprise. Faculty members and students will see library services as a vital component of the accreditation effort and will work energetically to support the library's programs. If sufficient momentum is generated during the accreditation visit, it should continue after the visiting team leaves campus. Ideally, the heightened sense of purpose and collegiality established during the accreditation visit will survive as useful instruments for future joint activities and endeavors by faculty and librarians.

Each campus presents unique opportunities for librarians to create and cultivate effective communication channels with faculty. Librarians can participate in and contribute to formal and informal discussion groups in which faculty members present the results of study and research to their colleagues. Librarians can submit grant proposals jointly with faculty members. Faculty members can be invited to library staff meetings to discuss research they are engaged in or talk about books and articles they have written. Faculty members are usually delighted to have the library display their articles and books. Exhibits are excellent vehicles for showcasing faculty research activities and for identifying long-term, productive supporters of the library.

Faculty members, like students, appreciate individual attention, and librarians should devote a reasonable amount of time giving them appropriate treatment. Faculty members tend to view favorable courtesies afforded by the library befitting their academic status. If faculty members suggest the purchase of certain books and subscriptions, they are usually delighted when the library orders these items and exhilarated when they are promptly and consistently notified about their arrival. When seeking ways to communicate with faculty, librarians can also consider the following approaches: (1) interviewing faculty to construct profiles of their writing, teaching, and research activities, (2) contributing to faculty newsletters, (3) holding workshops for faculty to inform them about new materials and technological advances, (4) distributing library newsletters, acquisitions lists, and bibliographies, and (5) becoming active in campus committees and attending faculty receptions and social functions (Sluss 1988, 71–73).

Friends groups are good points of contact between faculty and librarians. These organizations provide informal settings, sometimes away from the campus, in which faculty and librarians can exchange ideas. Friends groups also provide important units for nurturing the traditions of the university, particularly when faculty retirees are active members.

LIBRARY RESOURCES AND
TEACHING STRATEGIES

Librarians are part of the teaching team, and their work should be designed to reinforce and strengthen concepts and skills introduced in the classroom. Although there are many aspects about the teaching and learning process that are not understood, there are some concepts that librarians may find useful in making decisions about which resources to make available for supporting classroom instruction. One of these concepts is that students should be active seekers rather than passive recipients of learning. This concept is compatible with the thinking of librarians who advocate teaching students how to find information, rather than actually finding answers to questions that students ask. Another teaching concept is that it is difficult to learn ideas that are very similar unless the differences between them are emphasized. Conversely, it is easier to learn disparate ideas if their similarities are emphasized. This concept suggests a need for variety in learning resources. A third concept of learning is that images are more easily remembered than words (Lowman 1984, 101–2). Clearly, this concept underscores the importance of providing audiovisual resources in the university environment. A fourth learning concept deals with the effectiveness of developing thinking skills by assigning original documents as reading materials instead of textbooks. Librarians have been longtime advocates of building collections that supplement and enrich the material found in textbooks, rather than duplicating these sources. Original documents have the capacity to present stimulating and provocative ideas and concepts in a robust, unadulterated form before they have been homogenized, packaged, and dispensed in textbook form (Lowman 1984, 167).

All of these concepts can be used by the librarian to help the faculty break the monotony created by one-track teaching routines and offer students several approaches to learning. In an article on college teaching, Thomas Guskey writes that the exceptionally effective teacher ''recommends specific alternative learning resources, such as learning laboratories, computer-assisted instruction facilities, tutoring services or the library'' (1988, 23). Librarians will be in a position to support teaching efforts if they are familiar with the approaches professors are using in the classroom. Sometimes teaching strategies can be determined by reading course syllabi. Clearly, where a strong partnership between librarians and professors exists, the task of introducing to professors library resources that support teaching is facilitated.

Although faculty members constantly seek new ways of teaching, the lecture method remains the dominant mode of instruction. Case studies, field experiences, self-paced modular methods, personalized systems of instruction, peer teaching, and the use of media and computers are among the new instructional methods that have been tried. Some of these approaches have been used extensively in community colleges and have been tried in attempts to reach highly diverse student populations (Gross and Gross 1980, 1–68).

Universities have been criticized for failing to experiment with innovative teaching techniques. Libraries have also moved cautiously in using their scarce resources to promote innovative teaching, because they seldom have the luxury of experimenting in areas that do not have full faculty support. At universities where innovative teaching is emphasized, the library can serve as a center for the exchange of ideas. Information and materials about innovative instructional approaches can be collected and brought to the attention of the faculty. Librarians can contact faculty members who have a special interest in new ways of teaching and offer library support in implementing their ideas. Librarians could also use forums or workshops to introduce faculty to library resources selected for their potential to inspire new teaching approaches. Faculty members from other universities who have used innovative teaching techniques successfully, as well as librarians at those institutions who have supported their initiatives, could be invited to discuss their experiences.

IMPLICATIONS OF EMERGING COMMUNICATIONS TECHNOLOGY

Faculty members use the library to do research in connection with publishing papers, reading for self-improvement, and finding materials required for a course. When seeking information, faculty members are inclined to take steps in the following order: (1) scan their own collection, (2) consult with a colleague, (3) try the university library, and (4) do without the item. Not only is the library perceived as one of the last sources from which to seek information, but faculty members who come to the library are unlikely to consult a librarian for assistance (Pinzelik 1984, 333–34).

Some research suggests that faculty members perceive the librarian as a limiting factor who actually sets up barriers to using the library. Some faculty members see the arrangement as confusing and illogical (Pinzelik 1984, 333–36). If faculty members have these attitudes and perceptions, similar attitudes and perceptions will rapidly spread among their students.

If students and faculty are reluctant to use the library because they find it confusing, the growing popularity of using remote computers to access library collections is understandable. Faculty members and students have a tool at last with which to search the contents of the library without visiting the facility.

Computers permit them to use some of the search strategies and techniques with which they are familiar. With the computer, faculty members and librarians have a common tool that both can use to access the library with equal levels of expertise. Perhaps this circumstance will mark the beginning of a productive collaboration between faculty and librarians for the purpose of improving library computer technology.

Library services have been decentralized to a certain extent by terminals in remote locations. Faculty members who tend to use the library as the last resort will be less inclined than ever to come to the library. Accessing the library from the privacy of their office or home is especially appealing to those faculty members who have always preferred to use their personal collection or perhaps their departmental library. Decentralization trends will probably move rapidly in the urban university environment and may contribute to a decline in the number of patrons using the library as a place to conduct research (Lewis 1988, 291–96).

If the university adjusts appropriately to this new environment, it has the potential of increasing its impact on the university community. Faculty members, like other professionals, tend to place a high value on autonomy and flexibility in their work. If the library promotes and supports their autonomy and flexibility, the faculty will perceive the library as a resource capable of making immense contributions to their work. If the library chooses to place needless restrictions on access, it will continue to be regarded as an obstacle to be avoided.

Networks exist for the benefit of their participants. Recently, the Coalition for Networked Information was formed as an affiliate of the National Research and Education Network (NREN) for the purpose of playing a "major role in the reform and enrichment of learning, teaching, and research in the 21st century by reshaping the informational infrastructures of a significant group of higher education institutions while working in close cooperation with a wide array of scholarly, scientific, commercial, and governmental constituencies" (1990, 1–3). Through this network, scholars will have access to comprehensive collections by using the combined library resources of participating universities.

At the local level, networks provide the technological enhancements necessary to connect terminals, printers, fax units, microcomputers, modems, e-mail, licensed software, and voice and video functions. If the library is integrated with the resources on campus that have the technical skills and the financial resources necessary to build networks, it will still have a chance to remain in the forefront as the premier provider of information on campus. For this integration to occur, viable communication channels must be maintained by the library with campus network participants. Communication with the faculty and computing personnel is an essential part of this process.

Local area networks (LAN) are used for the efficient transmission of data. Faculty are using them to connect a variety of devices because they are cheap, easy to install, and expandable. The primary advantage of a local area network is that it helps to share resources. Libraries have a long and distinguished record of sharing information and will enthusiastically embrace LAN technology for this reason. Libraries have usually concentrated on sharing information among themselves, but local area networks promise to create an open environment in which information is exchanged and data manipulated from a variety of sources. As scholars seek to set up workstations, the library will represent just one alternative on an impressive menu of information possibilities.

Technological innovation often enables us to perform old tasks better, but it also helps us to do things that could not have been done at all without the new technology. While local area networks are currently helping to perform old tasks well, the future promises exciting new communication concepts made possible by this technology (Byers 1984, 10). One development that is expected to produce unpredictable consequences for the academic library is network access to the full text of documents traditionally stored in libraries. This and similar developments may have an impact on how frequently faculty visit the library and will ultimately influence student library use. Local area networks also raise questions about the level at which libraries will be supported and how their budgets will be used. The increasing compatibility among computers portends mergers of campus computer centers with academic libraries.

Faculty productivity (with respect to publication output), allocation of library resources, decentralization of information services, and decisions about access authority are among the issues that must be examined within the context of the new information environment.

SUMMARY AND CONCLUSIONS

During the early years of the history of some of America's oldest universities, professors frequently served as part-time librarians. Although academic librarianship eventually emerged as a separate profession, some aspects of the roles of professors and librarians have remained inextricably intertwined. A strong library can contribute to the vitality of the academic program. Within this context, professors and librarians remain partners in the teaching process.

Faculty members and administrators in urban universities are often commuters, and as a result, sometimes there is a need to build sustaining relationships with the surrounding community. Librarians can contribute to building these relationships by gathering information related to the local area that is tailored to the needs of the university as a whole and to individuals.

Librarians need to know which resources are appropriate for supporting specific teaching techniques. Intelligent responses to teaching needs can be made by communicating directly with the faculty. Library committees, faculty workshops, displays of faculty publications, newsletters, and bibliographies are among the ways to communicate with faculty.

Future technological developments, particularly networks, will probably provide some faculty members with greater flexibility in seeking information. Although the importance of the library as a place to visit will probably decline for some faculty members, it is expected to retain its standing as a significant resource for study and research.

REFERENCES

Abel, Emily K. 1984. *Terminal degrees: The job crisis in higher education.* New York: Praeger.
Byers, T. J. 1984. *Guide to local area networks.* Englewood Cliffs, NJ: Prentice-Hall.
Coalition for Networked Information, Washington, DC. 1990. *News Release.*
Fairweather, James S. 1989. Academic research and instruction: The industrial connection. *Journal of Higher Education* 60 (July/August):338–407.
Gross, Beatrice, and Gross, Ronald. 1980. *A review of innovative approaches to college teaching.* Sarasota, FL: American Accounting Association.
Guskey, Thomas R. 1988. *Improving student learning in college classrooms.* Springfield, IL: Charles Thomas.
Lewis, David W. 1988. Inventing the Electronic University. *College and Research Libraries* 49 (July):291–303.
Lowman, J. 1984. *Mastering the techniques of teaching.* San Francisco: Jossey-Bass.
Pinzelik, Barbara P. 1984. Conflicting perceptions of the academic library. *Proceedings of the ACRL Third National Conference, Seattle,* 333–36.
Sluss, Sara B. 1988. Bailiwick bibs: Improving communication between classroom faculty and librarians. *Urban Academic Librarian* 6 (Spring):70–73.

12

Bibliographic Instruction for Students

E. Ray Hall

Knowledge is expanding exponentially, resulting in access to specific information that is becoming increasingly complex. This complexity of access is often coupled with the need for timely information. Persons who do not possess the essential library use skills to acquire the needed information quickly are at a decided disadvantage, because the ability to find information is as important as, if not more important than, the information itself. Students who lack these library use skills will not fare as well as those who have them, both in the classroom and in the competition for quality employment after graduation. They may consider their college/university to have inadequately prepared them to meet the rigors of life, both on campus and in the "real world."

Bibliographic instruction is an effort by teachers and librarians to improve the library use skills of their students. One main focus of attention is to educate individuals in the process of information gathering—not just providing answers to specific problems. While all instruction tends to be specific for one library and its holdings, the most effective instruction is general enough so the principles taught can apply to any library. Bibliographic instruction should impart basic transferable skills.

Library instruction programs vary from college to college, university to university, and library to library. All instruction programs, however, can be grouped into three broad categories—orientation, basic instruction, and detailed instruction.

ORIENTATION

Orientation is a one-shot effort to present a class with "everything we want you to know about XYZ Library." It is often synonymous with a tour of the physical features of the library. In addition to the information about the library building itself (where "things" are located), the orientation session usually gives a "once over lightly" presentation concerning departments, service desks, and staff; specific services such as computer searches and interlibrary loan; policies and procedures; collection organization; and staff helpfulness.

Most academic libraries have some type of orientation program. How effective they are at meeting the information needs of their students is not easily generalized.

While the already mentioned tour is one technique utilized for orientation, there are several other methods available.

Self-Guided Tours

Audiotape Tour

In this method the users go to a predetermined location to pick up a cassette player with headphones. They then listen to a cassette tape, which can be stopped and replayed as desired. The users may take the tour at their own pace, at their own convenience, and without disrupting library services (the way a large guided tour might). One consideration, however, is "that a poorly produced audiotape would be worse than no tape at all. Have several people try it out, preferably people not familiar with your library. It must be easy to understand. . . . If at all possible, get the help of professionals in planning such a show. If you choose to adopt this medium, do a good job with it" (Rice 1981, 54).

Print-Supported Tour

In this method print materials, rudimentary or detailed, are used instead of cassette tapes. Usually the print materials include a floor plan and other general information for the user. It might also include several questions designed to test the effectiveness of the tour.

Audiovisual Presentations

Videotape

Videotape presentations can be used successfully. The most effective method is to prepare a video presenting the information desired. A number of libraries have prepared successful videotapes. While some are more serious than others, most try to inject humor into the script. Jean Smith makes the following observation:

Many overlook the usefulness of humor as an attention grabber and a gimmick that goes far in helping to realize affective objectives. Even bibliographic instruction librarians must admit that sometimes what we are trying to teach is not the most fascinating information to a typical undergraduate. Humor in the form of an occasional sight gag is a successful technique used in several videos. A quick shot of a dog sitting at a table reading a book or surfboards parked in a bike rack makes students wonder what will happen next. Also, in an environment where many of our students come from high schools where libraries are primarily detention centers, humor can help to correct negative attitudes students may have about the library and its staff (1988, 111).

One example of videos using humor in bibliographic instruction is *Battle of the Library Superstars*, produced by the Ohio State University Library System, which is a parody of television sports competition. Student reaction to the videotape has been very positive, although some students found the humor rather broad (Segal and McNally 1983, 797). Another example of video humor is *The Malti's Chicken*, produced at the University of Minnesota, which uses a detective in the Sam Spade/Humphrey Bogart tradition. Student response to this video was also positive, although some criticized it and called it "corny" or "overplayed" (Chiang and Kautz 1985, 145–46).

Expense is a major consideration in video production. While production costs can skyrocket, it is possible, with assistance, to produce a videotape on a low budget. (For two different views of the production process see Nancy French and H. Julene Butler's "Quiet on the Set! Library Instruction Goes Video" and Smith's "Teaching Research Skills Using Video: An Undergraduate Library Approach"). One main ingredient, however, is creativity and enthusiasm for the project.

Slide Tape Orientation

This is one of the most widespread methods of orientation. It consists of a set of slides accompanied by an audio narration. It has the advantage of being quite flexible—slides can be added or deleted easily. Moreover, it is also relatively inexpensive to produce. Slides tapes are also portable and can be presented in many locations. One factor to remember, however, is that a slide tape presentation can take 300 hours or more to produce (Palmer 1972, 8). Mistakes can also occur; for example, slides can be upside down or out of sequence.

James Rice notes:

One mistake that is commonly made in library orientation is to try to introduce a group away from the library. A classroom presentation, for example, should never be used as the single mode of introduction. Furthermore, effective library orientation cannot be accomplished *solely* by videotape, slide-tape, or any device which is presented away from the actual library areas and materials. . . . Another common mistake is the practice of overwhelming students with the complexity and sophistication of our business. . . . Another mistake that is made far too frequently is attempting orientation with groups that are too large" (1981, 47–48).

Orientation is often the only method of bibliographic instruction a user encounters. For this reason, it is imperative that whatever method is utilized, the tone of the presentation should emphasize the friendliness of the staff and their willingness to assist the user in his or her information needs (Rice 1981, 59).

BASIC INSTRUCTION

This involves a series of sessions (usually fewer than 10) on specific library tools or materials. Typical components in this type of library instruction might include use of the online catalog, CD-ROMs, or the card catalog; use of the periodical indexes; use and access of the microformat collections; use and access of reference materials; use and access of government publications; and use and access of the audiovisual collections.

There are several methods of teaching for basic library instruction. The traditional method is the *lecture*, in which the librarian presents the body of knowledge to the students. It should be noted, however, that student retention of information is maximized when there are learning activities that reinforce the information presented in the lecture. Some type of exercises that the student will complete and then have critiqued will greatly improve the retention of desired information.

In addition to the lecture method of basic library instruction, there are other approaches that may be utilized. *Point of use instruction* is usually a one-on-one presentation at the exact time the student needs to know how to utilize a specific library tool. Point of use instruction focuses on immediate information needs. A variety of audio and/or visual support materials can often be developed to support this type of instruction. *Learning programs* are usually a combination of media and materials, for example, workbooks and workbooks with supporting media. This type of instruction can be infinitely tailored to meet varied needs but at the same time is possibly the most difficult to develop for that same reason. *Computer-assisted instruction* is a method that has particular appeal. Utilizing the computer offers several educational advantages, such as students' ability to receive immediate feedback, to work at their own pace, and to work individually with no loss of self-esteem if they do not readily understand a body of knowledge. A disadvantage to computer-assisted instruction is the cost of equipment and software if a large number of students is involved. (For a more detailed discussion of these approaches, see Rice 1981, 70–80).

DETAILED INSTRUCTION

This type of instruction goes beyond the basics and delves into advanced topics. It is often associated with a "Use of the Library" credit course. This type of instruction introduces students to research methods as well as materials. One of the goals of detailed library instruction is to make the student a self-sufficient user of the library and its resources. This goal can be critical for a strong undergraduate program from which a significant percentage of students may be expected to go on to graduate programs.

FACULTY PARTICIPATION

While most faculty members would agree that a basic knowledge of the library, its collection, and its services is desirable for their students, this agreement does not mean that all faculty will eagerly sign up for bibliographic instruction sessions. It is also a given that there will never be 100 percent participation in a bibliographic instruction program. What methods, therefore, can one use to increase faculty participation in bibliographic instruction?

One possibility is to utilize the faculty orientation sessions that are typically held for new faculty at most institutions. Work with the administrators coordinating these sessions to have yourself included on these programs to promote the availability of general and course-specific bibliographic instruction sessions. Definitely get on the agenda and get enough time really to make your case. If a campus tour of facilities and services is part of the orientation, attempt to schedule a brief demonstration of what bibliographic instruction can do for faculty teaching.

Another idea is to utilize faculty who have scheduled bibliographic instruction to promote your program to their new colleagues. In addition to promoting bibliographic instruction sessions to new faculty, your existing network of supporters can often sell a colleague in their department/school on the advantages of your instruction program. Do not overlook departmental or administrative secretaries. They can often provide insights about departmental or college/school policies and priorities. They may also suggest faculty members who would be most interested in your instructional program.

A possible method of increasing instruction is to target those courses that have a library research component in the curriculum. One approach is to examine the college catalog and read course descriptions to discover which ones indicate a research project as a part of the course requirements. Another is to talk with students who are using the library for term/research papers to determine the courses in which they are enrolled (Beaubien, Hogan, and George 1982, 239). Ask the school deans or the vice president of Academic Affairs for their assistance in getting into the program. You may need to be aggressive here.

Another facet to consider is that there may already be some type of bibliographic instruction program in an academic department. It may be a separate course or a component of a course. In this case the librarian might cooperate with the instructor by helping design instruction or exercises and by offering to work together as colleagues. An important consideration is not to alienate the teaching faculty. Sincerity really is vital here.

INSTRUCTION FOR CREDIT

All of the above scenarios presuppose bibliographic instruction sessions that do not carry academic credit for course completion. If, however, your college/ university offers or is anticipating offering a bibliographic instruction course for academic credit, the problems of support are somewhat different (see Jacquelyn Morris's "Gaining Faculty Acceptance and Support of Library Instruction: A Case Study"). In this case, gaining support from faculty may be compounded by the fact that academic departments look askance on a course that competes with departmental offerings for credit hours generated. A strong faculty supporter of the bibliographic instruction program can often do much to counter this type of thinking.

The success of bibliographic instruction credit courses often depends on how well you, the librarian, promote your program in a strong public relations campaign. There are several aspects to this; one is faculty contacts. If your school uses faculty advisement, the faculty are a key to whether the courses are full or not. Promote the course with these faculty and inform them about it; make sure, for example, they understand course content and which students will be best served by the course. If your campus has a salaried group of academic advisers, the same promotional program used for faculty advisers applies.

Other successful methods of promoting the course include fliers posted around the campus; announcements in library, departmental, or campus newsletters; a news article in the campus or local newspaper; or other creative ways to catch the students' attention. "One enterprising librarian took advantage of his paper's personal column to insert messages (Lori: Remember the rough time you had finding info for your paper last semester? Don't forget to sign up for LIB200 and learn how to do it the right way.)" (Adams and Morris 1985, 21).

ADULT STUDENTS

Much has been written in recent years about the increasing number of adult students. Adults enrolled in college or university programs have always been a part of urban/metropolitan institutions; however, they are receiving a higher profile in today's educational environment, which features declining numbers of traditional students. In fact, today's student enrollment is less homogeneous than in the past. The majority of all college students are women, the adults 25 years of age or older comprise over 40 percent of all college enrollment. (Epstein 1987, 2). Another study found that of those students 25 years of age or older, about three-fourths were 25–34 years of age. After age 35, women were more likely than men to enroll in a college degree program. Most adult students attended school part-time; had attended a 2-year, 4-year, or technical school previously; had delayed the academic program for family or job responsibilities; and had returned for job or career reasons (Sewall 1986, 8). A survey by the College Board reported in the *Chronicle of Higher Education* predicted that nontraditional students could rise to 50 percent by the year 2000 (Hirschorn 1988, A35). Brian Nordstrom has noted that adults who return to college tend to be in transition and are experiencing crises in their lives (e.g., divorce, unemployment, or geographic relocation). They tend to be sacrificing more than traditional students to attend college and to be more highly motivated, although they are often lacking in self-confidence (1989, 17).

In past years little was done to accommodate adult students and assist them with their educational needs. That situation is no longer true, as many urban/ metropolitan universities are devoting considerable resources to assist these students. For the bibliographic instruction program, these nontraditional students pose special problems: time limitations because of family and/or job commitments; distance to library facilities; and "library anxiety" as these students are often faced with a bewildering array of electronic tools that contemporary university libraries utilize. Bibliographic instruction programs need to reflect the differences between traditional and nontraditional students and move to meet the needs of both.

Because there are significant differences between traditional and adult students, the successful bibliographic instruction program should recognize that adult students often have more clearly defined goals than do traditional students. Bibliographic instruction should address this situation and prepare sessions that address the specific informational needs. The bibliographic instruction program should also recognize that adult students bring a tremendous variety and wealth of experience to the bibliographic instruction session, that adult students are often more interested in the process of information gathering and not solely in the information itself, and that adult students may require some modification in time and/or location for bibliographic instruction presentations. Because many adult students are enrolled in evening or weekend courses, often in an off-campus location, bibliographic instruction presentations should be scheduled at times and locations convenient for their schedules. The bibliographic instruction librarian should be prepared to travel to these sites.

Nicholas Tomaiuolo has noted that "bibliographic instruction must be tailored to its audience. Presentation and content must reflect the patron's priorities, proclivities and preparation" (1990, 51). How, then, should the bibliographic instruction librarian proceed? By recognizing that the adult student is significantly different from the traditional college student, the bibliographic instruction librarian should not attempt to duplicate instruction for both groups. One recommendation is that "large doses of library instruction for adult students is not recommended. Their time constraints, focused objectives, and autonomous personalities, combined with the immediate nature of their research questions, make the case for more practical library instruction" (Tomaiuolo 1990, 51), with one-on-one assistance.

Sheila Howard has noted: "The fact that adults are often short of time means they may want to progress from little or no knowledge to conducting a meaningful information search in one visit" (1983, 153). The same author suggests that librarians might adopt a more passive approach, utilizing written instructions and handouts as well as informative signs and graphics that "can orient, direct, inform and remind the adult without inducing the feelings of dependency and inadequacy which can be by-products of having to constantly ask for help" (152).

Providing support and assistance for nontraditional students is a dynamic part of bibliographic instruction. They bring an enthusiasm for learning that is often lacking in traditional students, and the rewards for working with them are many and varied. These can take the form of cookies and candy, describing you as a "life-saver," thank-you notes or letters, and word-of-mouth promotion of your program. While working with nontraditional students may involve more time than with traditional students, it is certainly time well invested.

Taking extra effort to provide services for nontraditional students in the academic library may help students become reacquainted with library research skills, will introduce them to the new technologies of online catalogs and databases, and may foster library independence. Furthermore, working with these students will become more than a pleasurable part of the academic librarian's job—it will also prepare librarians for the large numbers of future nontraditional students that are predicted to turn up on college campuses and in academic libraries (Wyman 1988, 33).

CONCLUSION

An effective bibliographic instruction program produces a win-win situation; that is, no one loses. For the user, timely and appropriate instruction can provide self-confidence in doing research, streamlining that research, and making it more thorough. For the librarian, it enhances skill and subject area expertise. Positive public relations can be gained by the library's having an effective bibliographic instruction program. The college/university benefits in that its students are wiser consumers of information and are able to utilize resources more effectively and make wise decisions based on the information they have located. Academic disciplines and faculty find students who are more knowledgeable about their discipline and critical in their thinking processes. Finally, society benefits from a more self-sufficient citizen who can make rational decisions based on sound research (Beaubien, Hogan, and George 1982, 251–52).

A final thought is that for effective bibliographic instruction to develop, one needs to have commitment and dedication—a commitment by all involved (i.e., librarians, faculty, and administrators) to provide students with quality instruction and the dedication to bring this commitment to fruition.

REFERENCES

Adams, Mignon S., and Morris, Jacquelyn M., 1985. Teaching library skills for academic credit. Phoenix, AZ: Oryz Press.

Allen, David Y. 1982. Students need help in learning how to use the library. *Chronicle of Higher Education* 24, no. 15 (June 9): 6.

Beaubien, Anne K.; Hogan, Sharon A.; and George, Mary W. 1982. *Learning the library: Concepts and methods for effective bibliographic instruction.* New York: R. R. Bowker.

Chiang, Katherine S., and Kautz, Barbara. 1985. *The Malti's Chicken*: A different kind of video. *Research Strategies: A Journal of Library Concepts and Instruction* 3, no. 3 (Summer): 143–46.

Clark, Alice S. 1974. Computer-assisted library instruction. In *Educating the library user*, ed. John Lubans, Jr., 336–49. New York: R. R. Bowker.

Culkin, Patricia B. 1972. Computer-assisted instruction in library use. *Drexel Library Quarterly* 8 (July): 301–11.

Engeldinger, Eugene A. 1988. Teaching only the essentials - the thirty-minute stand. *Reference Services Review* 16, no. 4: 47–50, 96.

Epstein, Howard V. 1987. *College students come of age.* Arlington, VA: ERIC Document Reproduction Service, ED 278 904.

Fisher, Raymond K. 1979. Academic libraries and part-time adult students. In *New horizons for academic libraries*, ed. Robert D. Stueart and Richard D. Johnson, 529–33. New York: K. G. Saur.

French, Nancy, and Butler, H. Julene. 1988. Quiet on the set! Library instruction goes video. *Wilson Library Bulletin* 63 (December): 42–44.

Griffin, Mary L. 1988. Bibliographic instruction, reference, and the teaching/learning process. *Reference Services Review* 16, nos. 1/2: 93–94.

Hirschorn, Michael W. 1988. Students over 25 found to make up 45 pct. of campus enrollments. *Chronicle of Higher Education* 34, no. 29 (March 30): A35.

Howard, Sheila. 1983. Library use education for adult university students. *Canadian Library Journal* 40 (June): 149–55.

Iovacchini, Eric V.; Hall, Linda M.; and Hengstler, Dennis D. 1985. Going back to college: Some differences between adult students and traditional students. *College and University* 61 (Fall): 43–54.

Lansing, John A. 1988. The library-faculty partnership in curriculum development. *College and Research Libraries News* 49 (January): 7–10.

Lutzher, Marilyn. 1982. Full-time thinking about part-time students. In *Options for the 80s: Proceedings of the Second National Conference of the Association of College and Research Libraries*, ed. Michael D. Kathman and Virgil F. Massman, 247–54. Greenwich, CT: JAI Press.

McCarthy, Constance. 1985. The faculty problem. *Journal of Academic Librarianship* 11 (July): 142–45.

Morris, Jacquelyn M. 1976. Gaining faculty acceptance and support of library instruction: A case study. In *Faculty involvement in library instruction*, ed. Hannelore B. Rader, 57–73. Ann Arbor, MI: Pierian Press.

Nordstrom, Brian H. 1989. *Non-traditional students: Adults in transition.* Arlington, VA: ERIC Document Reproduction Service, ED 310 686.

Palmer, Millicent C. 1972. Creating slide/tape library instruction: The librarian's role. *Drexel Library Quarterly* 8 (July): 251–67.

Rader, Hannelore B. 1984. Bibliographic instruction programs in academic libraries. *New directions for teaching and learning* (Increasing the teaching role of academic libraries) 18 (June): 63–78.

Rice, James, Jr. 1981. *Teaching library use: A guide for library instruction*. Westport, CT: Greenwood Press.

Segal, Jane D., and McNally, Tom. 1983. Battle of the library superstars. *Library Journal* 108 (April): 795–97.

Sewall, Timothy J. 1986. *Nontraditionals in traditional setting: Why older adults return to college*. Arlington, VA: ERIC Document Reproduction Service, ED 267 257.

Simon, Rose Ann. 1984. The faculty/librarian partnership. *New directions for teaching and learning* (Increasing the teaching role of academic libraries) 18 (June): 55–61.

Smith, Jean. 1988. Teaching research skills using video: An undergraduate library approach. *Reference Services Review* 16 nos. 1/2: 109–14.

Solomon, Lewis C., and Gordon, Joanne J. 1980. *The characteristics and needs of adults in postsecondary education*. Arlington, VA: ERIC Document Reproduction Service, ED 198 750.

Steffen, Susan Swords. 1988. Designing bibliographic instruction programs for adult students: The Schaffner Library experience. *Illinois Librarian* 70 (December): 644–49.

Tomaiuolo, Nicholas G. 1990. Reconsidering bibliographic instruction for adult reentry students: Emphasizing the practical. *Reference Services Review* 18: 49–54.

Wood, Richard J. 1984. The impact of a library research course on students at Slippery Rock University. *Journal of Academic Librarianship* 10 (November): 278–84.

Wyman, Andrea. 1988. Working with nontraditional students in the academic library. *Journal of Academic Librarianship* 14 no. 1: 32–33.

PART IV

Extended Campus Considerations

13

Extended Campus Library Services

Mary Joyce Pickett

The subject of this chapter is the provision of library services for extended campus programs.

In recent years the profile of the student body at most academic institutions has changed significantly. At more and more institutions the 18- to 24-year-old full-time undergraduate is being outnumbered by older adults who are often fully employed and taking courses part-time. These older adults are enrolling for many reasons: to complete a bachelor's degree started many years before, to prepare for a career change and/or reentry into the job market, to advance in their present position, and to obtain a graduate degree. To serve this new pool of students better, colleges and universities of all types and sizes are offering courses at sites removed from their main campuses.

These extended campus programs come in literally all shapes and sizes. Some-times satellite campuses are developed that come close to replicating the services and facilities of the main campus, only on a smaller scale. More typically, even where there are satellite campuses, their services and facilities differ in nature as well as in scale. Many programs offer courses at other institutions (e.g., libraries, high schools, community colleges, corporations, military bases). Tele-vision, videotapes, and computer networks enable some students to take their classes at home or at other sites, where they may be the only student.

Concern with the provision of extended campus library services has increased in recent years. Four national conferences on off-campus library services (St. Louis, October 1982; Knoxville, April 1985; Reno, October 1986; and Charleston, October 1988) sponsored by Central Michigan University have been well attended, and the proceedings of these conferences make a significant contribution to the literature of the field (Lessin 1983, 1985, 1987, 1988). The Extended Campus Library Services Discussion Group within the Association of College and Research Libraries (ACRL) has been revitalized within recent years, and in January 1990, the ACRL Board of Directors approved the creation of the Extended Campus Library Services Section of ACRL.

ACRL GUIDELINES FOR EXTENDED CAMPUS LIBRARY SERVICES

Increased concern was also evident in the 1988–1990 work of the Task Force to Review the ACRL Guidelines for Extended Campus Library Services. Many members of ACRL participated in the hearings held by the task force, and contacts with accrediting agencies indicated that many of them are more closely examining library services when reviewing off-campus programs. The latest revision of ''The ACRL Guidelines for Extended Campus Library Services'' was approved January 1990 by the ACRL Board of Directors. These guidelines provide a framework for establishing, implementing, and evaluating library and information services to the extended campus community.

At the hearings many persons who worked with off-campus programs testified. Their testimony confirmed the diversity of programs and the need for flexibility in planning and implementing off-campus services to take into account local programs. At the same time the testimony clearly called for a statement in the guidelines emphasizing the importance of providing the extended campus community with library services equitable to those provided to the on-campus community. Among other changes requested were clarification of the parent institution's responsibility for providing financial support and clearer definition of the library's management role in providing services.

The guidelines are directed to ''library staff planning for and managing these extended campus services, other library staff working with extended campus library staff, faculty, administrators at all levels within the educational institution, and sponsors of academic programs, as well as accrediting and licensure agencies'' (Association of College and Research Libraries 1990, 354). They are a very good starting point for anyone establishing a new program or evaluating an existing program. (The guidelines as printed in the April 1990 *College and Research Libraries News* contain a minor error in the introduction; however, the major portions of the guidelines are printed accurately. If desired, corrected reprints may be requested from the Association of College and Research Libraries).

The major topics covered in the guidelines include management, finances, personnel, facilities, resources, and services. The rest of this chapter will draw heavily upon those sections of the guidelines. An attempt has been made, where appropriate, to draw attention to issues unique to (or of particular importance to) urban and metropolitan academic libraries.

Management

This section of the guidelines spells out the responsibility of the library administration in planning and overseeing library support for extended campus programs. The specific steps outlined stress the leadership role the library must take in assessing needs and developing goals and objectives for extended campus library services. At the same time, the importance of working closely with academic administrators and faculty is emphasized. This is important for at least two reasons. First, only by communicating and working with the rest of the academic community can librarians understand the needs of that community. Second, those extended campus library services programs that have been most effective have had the support of the administrators and faculty of the programs. That support is most often present when librarians have worked with administrators and faculty in developing programs and services.

One management step recommended is to "assess existing library support, its availability and appropriateness." When extended campus programs serve widespread and rural areas, there is often little library support available other than that provided by the parent institution. The proliferation of libraries in urban areas sometimes leads to an attitude on the part of the parent institution that students can get sufficient library service from other libraries located near their course site or home. This assumption can do a grave disservice to students. For example, the materials in a nearby public or community college library will probably not be advanced enough for students in many upper division or graduate-level courses. In cases where classes are offered in corporations either live or via interactive TV networks, some of the corporation libraries may have holdings appropriate for course work, but many will not.

Availability of other libraries does not absolve the parent institution from responsibility in providing resources for its students. Educational institutions develop a negative image when they refer masses of their students to academic, special, and public libraries that happen to be located near their extended campus sites. To avoid that image and to allow the free referral of students, written agreements should be made with local libraries where appropriate.

Finances

The ACRL guidelines spell out that continuing financial support for extended campus library services should be provided by the parent institution. This financing should be included as part of the normal budgeting process and identified in the budget and expenditure-reporting statements. This financing should cover all funds directly expended by the library and any expenditures required to cover agreements with external agencies such as local libraries.

Personnel

Since the programs and needs vary so greatly from institution to institution, there is not one single most effective personnel structure for providing extended campus library services. There are certain factors relating to personnel, however, that are common to most programs.

First, the provision of library services to the extended campus community is a labor-intensive process. It requires qualified professional and support personnel serving in many different capacities. There obviously must be "a librarian to plan, implement, coordinate, and evaluate library resources and services addressing the information needs of the extended campus community" (Association of College and Research Libraries 1990, 355). In addition, there is usually a need for other professional and support personnel designated to serve the extended campus programs. These people may work in branch libraries or from an office in the main library or travel from site to site. Less obvious are the other personnel required to carry out a program. When an extended campus library services program is established, there is increased demand on existing personnel in all departments of the library. For example, the administration is involved with management of the program, the reference department is expected to provide backup services of various kinds, interlibrary loan or some other department must retrieve and photocopy to fill requests for document delivery, and the technical services units will have additional materials to order and process.

Second, personnel working in these programs must be flexible and creative. For example, the most appropriate method for delivering library service to students taking classes via interactive TV at 30 different sites may be quite different from the service methods used to serve the extended campus community when all courses are taught live at one or two sites removed from the main campus. Personnel must be familiar with resources available and be willing to try new ways of delivering those resources.

Facilities

The facilities for offering library services vary depending on the location and nature of the course offerings. The ACRL guidelines give three examples of suitable arrangements. One possibility, as noted earlier, is to arrange to use the facilities of a nonaffiliated library. This arrangement works well when there is a library on or near the course site. Appropriate compensation for this use can be monetary, but in many cases it involves other compensation, such as provision of personnel at the site, the addition of certain items to the site library's collection, provision of terminals to access the online catalog of the contracting library, or special privileges for the site library's clientele at the contracting library.

A second possibility is to have designated space for certain functions at the course site or in the main library. In most cases provision of a branch library at all sites is not practical. An alternative is to provide at the site more limited facilities providing at least some of the following: a ready reference collection, course reserves, an online catalog terminal, provision for computerized database searching (via CD-ROM, files loaded on a campus mainframe, Dialog, and so on), telefacsimile equipment to transmit requests to the main campus, and document delivery from the main campus and other libraries.

If a large number of students are enrolled at a given site, it may be feasible and necessary to provide a branch or satellite library. This type of facility would come closer to duplicating the services of the main campus library; however, there must still be a very close working relationship with the main campus library. No institution can afford to duplicate all the services and materials that might be required by extended campus programs.

Urban universities and colleges offering courses at extended campus sites within the same metropolitan area may be tempted to say that their students can come to the main campus for library materials and services. This attitude, however, defeats one purpose of offering extended campus programs, which is to offer courses at sites close to where people work and live so that people who do not have time to come to the main campus will enroll. It may be appropriate that they occasionally have to make a trip to campus for library or other reasons; however, facilities should be provided to keep this need to a minimum.

Resources

Access to library materials required by students in completing their academic work is essential. In addition, faculty and administrators located at extended campus sites need resources to support their teaching, research, and administrative functions. The resource needs of the extended campus community may require the purchase of duplicate materials and/or additional materials unique to the needs of these programs.

Services

The ACRL guidelines give nine examples of library services that can be used to help meet informational and bibliographic needs of the extended campus community. A great deal of creativity and flexibility is required in the development of these services. There are undoubtedly other services that can be provided, but these nine listed below with comments are a good starting point.

1. Reference assistance. Reference personnel and resources should be available to all extended campus students. They might be provided by contracting with an existing library near the course site or by employing a librarian to work at the course site. With many scattered sites in a metropolitan area, it will not be feasible to have reference assistance at each site, but one possibility would be to select one or two strategically located sites. The telephone and electronic mail are also useful in providing reference assistance. For instance, students working on a business project may not know that

the public library two suburbs north of them has one of the best business reference collections in the metropolitan area. The extended campus services librarian does know about them and can refer the students there. They have 10 minutes to drive rather than the hour to the main campus.

2. Computer-based bibliographic and informational services. Terminals to access the main library's online catalog and state/regional/national library databases can be provided at course sites. Similarly, databases can be accessed on CD-ROM or via a commercial online vendor such as Dialog (online access might be either intermediary searching done by the librarian's or end user's searching, particularly in the evening hours with the lower rates on Knowledge Index, BRS Afterdark, and so on).

   The potential for these services is growing by leaps and bounds, particularly as more and more students have access to computers both at home and at work. From their personal computer at home they can access the library's online catalog (in some states such as Illinois they can access a statewide catalog), indexes and other databases that have been loaded on their campus mainframe, commercial end user services such as Knowledge Index, and so on.

3. Consultation services. Consultation with a librarian can be either in person at the course site or by phone.

4. A program of library user instruction designed specifically to meet the needs of the extended campus community. Many of the students in extended campus programs are older adults who are fully employed and taking courses part-time. In many cases they have not taken classes for a number of years. Because of their busy schedules and the many new developments (e.g., online catalogs and other computer-based services) since they were in school, it is especially important that these students have library user instruction.

5. Assistance with nonprint media and equipment. Library personnel may need to assist with the use of various kinds of nonprint media.

6. Reciprocal borrowing, contractual borrowing, and interlibrary loan service. Resource sharing is increasingly important in providing materials even to faculty and students on the main campus. The extended campus community should have access to the same reciprocal borrowing and interlibrary loan services as those on the main campus. Whether interlibrary loan services should be handled through the main library interlibrary loan department or by library personnel at the site depends on local circumstances. In some cases additional reciprocal borrowing and/or contractual borrowing agreements should be established to improve the extended campus students' access to libraries near their course site.

7. Prompt document delivery, such as a courier system or electronic transmission. Document delivery is one of the most basic services typically provided to the extended campus community. Many decisions have to be made as to how best to provide this service. Following are some questions that might be helpful to ask in planning such a service: How do we accept requests for documents to be delivered? U.S. mail? Phone? Fax? Electronic mail? Who in the library processes them? Is there already a courier system that goes to the sites and into which the library might tie? (Sometimes there is a system to deliver assignment sheets, exams, and so on between faculty and students.) If not, should we set up a system? Is the U.S. mail or UPS a possibility? Should materials be sent only to course sites or directly to students' homes? Should

we utilize telefacsimile to transmit photocopies and with what guidelines? Are the costs of photocopies passed on to the client or absorbed in the library budget?

8. Access to reserve materials. Materials can be placed on reserve at the course site or a nearby library. Taking into account local circumstances, the library and faculty member should work together to determine the most reasonable loan periods. Certain types of extended campus programs are particularly problematic for the provision of reserve materials. For example, courses offered by interactive TV or by videotapes will have students in the same course at many different sites. These situations may require the purchase of multiple copies or students' coming to a central site to use reserves.

9. Promotion of library services to the extended campus community. Library services will be utilized only if students and faculty are aware of their availability.

EXTENDED CAMPUS ISSUES UNIQUE TO ACADEMIC LIBRARIES IN URBAN AND METROPOLITAN AREAS

Many of the issues relating to establishing library service to students in extended campus programs are the same whether the setting is in an urban setting or not; however, some unique factors arise in the metropolitan setting.

If a student is taking courses at a rural site 200 miles from campus, it is obvious that coming to campus is a considerable inconvenience. If a student is 35 miles from campus with a one-hour drive to campus when traffic is pretty clear, the inconvenience of coming to campus is not quite as obvious. In this situation are occasional trips to campus justified? If so, how does this kind of proximity affect planning for library service to these students?

Related to the closer geographic proximity is another problem faced by providers of urban extended campus library services. What about those students who are enrolled both on the main campus and at the extended campus site(s)? Occasionally a student enrolled on the main campus will take a course at the extended campus site because that is where the needed course is offered. What about document delivery to these students?

Many urban libraries feel a considerable impact from the demands of students from other institutions. In many cases these students are in extended campus programs where the parent institution is not even in the same metropolitan area and has made no arrangements for library services for its students. These nonlocal institutions assume that since there are many libraries in the area, their students can depend on those libraries for their information needs. As mentioned under "Management" above, there is sometimes the temptation when setting up extended campus programs, even within one's own metropolitan area, to assume that students can get the materials they need in libraries near where they live. Both to be certain that students are getting the support they need and to maintain positive relations with other libraries in the metropolitan area, it is important carefully to assess what is available and develop agreements with other libraries where appropriate.

CONCLUSIONS

Institutions offering courses at extended campus sites have an obligation to provide library resources and services in support of their extended campus programs. The library administration must take responsibility for planning and implementing the services necessary to meet the information needs of the extended campus community. To be effective, they must do so in cooperation with the college/university administration and faculty. If the academic administration does not provide appropriate financial support, programs cannot be implemented. Faculty must be consulted concerning the needs of their students and must also be informed of the resources and services available.

The level of success achieved in providing quality library and information services to the extended campus community is heavily dependent on the personnel running the program. Creative personnel can make a big difference in whether a program meets the needs of the extended campus community. The personnel are, however, still dependent on having adequate support from the library and the college/university administration. If there has not been solid planning and there is not financial support, no program can flourish as it should. Institutions that refer to the "ACRL Guidelines for Extended Campus Library Services" will find considerable guidance as they undertake the planning process.

REFERENCES

Association of College and Research Libraries, Task Force to Review the Guidelines for Extended Campus Library Services. 1990. ACRL guidelines for extended campus library services. *College and Research Libraries News* 51 (April): 353–55.

Lessin, Barton M., ed. 1983. *The Off-campus Library Services Conference Proceedings, St. Louis, MO, 1982*. Mount Pleasant, MI: Central Michigan University Press.

———. 1985. *The Off-campus Library Services Conference Proceedings, Knoxville, TN, 1985*. Mount Pleasant, MI: Central Michigan University Press.

———. 1987. *The Off-campus Library Services Conference Proceedings, Reno, NV, 1986*. Mount Pleasant, MI: Central Michigan University Press.

———. 1988. *The Off-campus Library Services Conference Proceedings, Charleston, SC, 1988*. Mount Pleasant, MI: Central Michigan University Press.

14

The Perception of Distance: Networking Among Libraries

Susan Anderson

In 1990 the Smithsonian Institution's National Museum of American History opened a new exhibit: "Information Age: People, Information and Technology" (Linden 1990, 59). The exhibit makes very clear that what is certain about the future is that it is uncertain.

Even the most futuristic librarian of the 1950s, 1960s, 1970s, or early 1980s could not have predicted the impact on resource sharing that has resulted from optical scanning, telefacsimile, and laser discs since 1985. As if overnight, telefacsimile machines have arrived in libraries and provided a simple method to transmit printed documents over common telephone lines. Compact disc technology has made possible the storage of very large amounts of bibliographic information. One compact disc can store 550,000 typewritten pages, or enough paper to make a stack nearly 200 feet tall. Encyclopedias, periodical indexes, and library collections are now stored and accessed inexpensively in this format. These and other developments of the information age and those we have yet to imagine change not only the ways we store and retrieve information but also our opportunities for developing library collections and sharing resources. Where information is stored or how it is stored becomes much less relevant if the information can be accessed and made usable.

SHARING ACADEMIC RESOURCES

Academic libraries are change agents in the concept of sharing services and information between different institutional libraries. Academic consortia, cooperatives, and networks developed because of the need for cooperative collection development, the costs associated with archival collections, and the need for scholars to access information. In urban locations, academic libraries created avenues to share materials and information out of economic necessity and because scholarship, by its nature, requires that information be available regardless of institutional affiliation.

"The campus library often is described as the university's heart, but those in charge of the university budget might be more likely to describe it as a 'black hole' in the university's midst" (Arms 1990, 5). Those first networks of urban libraries sought to overcome this reality by sharing resources through collaboration.

It is true that the cost of academic monographs, serials, and periodicals has far outpaced any expectations based on inflation rates (*Bowker Annual* 1988, 362). In geographic locations with several academic libraries, it was natural for concerned librarians to investigate effective management of financial resources by sharing information resources. Union lists of periodicals, microform projects, and interinstitutional faculty borrowing privileges resulted from these efforts.

At the same time, computers became practical for storing and accessing bibliographic information. Far-sighted librarians, such as those who formed OCLC, BALLOTS, ILLINET, and other automated networks, were addressing both resource sharing and conservation of financial resources. Early electronic systems soon crossed the boundaries of geographic constraints. Almost by the time The Online Computer Library Center (OCLC) was formed, it ceased being restricted to Ohio college libraries. The Research Library Group (RLG) was created in 1974 to share the resources of major academic institutions in the northeast. Four years later, in 1978, it had expanded to a national network and adopted Stanford University's automation system as a framework to support storage of bibliographic information. Today nearly 100 major voting members are associated with the network.

Where does this leave such networks as the Council of Research and Academic Libraries (CORAL) of San Antonio, Texas; the Chicago Academic Library Council; the Richmond, Virginia, Academic Libraries Cooperative; and a myriad of other academic library networks? (Wareham 1986). For the most part, library automation has supplanted the need for these local academic library networks and cooperatives to exist. The Chicago Academic Library Council disbanded, according to Bernard Sloan, executive director of ILLINET Online (Sloan 1986). The Library Council of the Consortium of Universities in the Washington, DC, area, founded in 1964, transferred its responsibilities in 1990 to the new online system in that area, the Washington Research Library Consortium (WRLC) (*WRLC Newsletter* 1990).

Although the CORAL group continues to serve libraries in southeastern Texas, its focus has changed. According to Virginia Bowden, librarian at the Health Science Library of the University of Texas, San Antonio, CORAL is still alive, but it is no longer solely an academic library network (Bowden 1990).

There are 29 to 30 members, which are very diverse, ranging from small to large, from special to academic to public to military. The military component comes from the large installation of bases near San Antonio, but, according to Bowden, this component is probably not a strength, since there is heavy demand from the military bases for materials from the university.

The network received state funding to develop a union list of serials, which was loaded into OCLC. Some of the problems encountered by CORAL resulted from just such grants; that is, someone had to account for the funding, do the reporting, and oversee the project. Additionally, not all libraries contributed to the union listing of serials and not all libraries participate in the delivery system. A part-time executive director served for a time, and now the elected president has a paid assistant.

As the cooperative has evolved, a fee schedule has developed. This schedule is based on the size of the acquisitions budget of the library and ranges from $200 to $1,500. This disparity in dues in some ways penalizes the larger library.

Another library consortium that exists in Texas is the Herrington Consortium, which began in 1984 in Amarillo, Texas, with four members, three of which were academic. The consortium now serves 24 different libraries of all types. Governance is controlled by the four original libraries, which are referred to as the Council. The remaining libraries are formed into a users group referred to as Herrington Users Group (HUG).

The conclusion that can be loosely drawn from the development of these cooperative networks is that libraries and librarians are committed to resource sharing and will innovate in finding ways to share resources.

It is more productive for many academic libraries to cooperate in regional, multitype library consortia that provide access to the resources of many types of libraries, in OCLC for cataloging and interlibrary loan and in RLG, when possible, for collection development, than it is to network academic libraries by locality. Yet, there remain viable urban academic library networks because of idiosyncrasies of location and special resources that can be shared most effectively through this mechanism.

PATTERNS OF COOPERATION

Interinstitutional Faculty/Student Circulation Privileges

A very common practice of urban academic libraries is to provide borrowing rights to all academic faculty without regard to institutional affiliation. A less common practice is to allow materials to circulate to all college/university students within the locality.

There are obvious problems inherent in these practices that need to be carefully addressed by the institutions involved. The benefits to the individual scholars involved are the reasons that institutions seek to provide these services, but the process is not always easy. Some institutions are willing to loan materials to students from another college but balk if these students are in some way atypical, such as enrolled in both high school and college at the same time, or they are willing to loan to full-time faculty, but not to adjunct faculty.

In Austin, Texas, for example, the University of Texas provides circulation privileges for a fee for anyone not associated with the university. To provide services to Austin Community College students, it serves up to 200 community college students without charge upon recommendation from the community college library staff. The community college accepts responsibility for payment of fines or lost book fees. Austin Community College also contracts with St. Edwards College to provide services to students. The effort is to make locating materials and information convenient for students, and it extends beyond the concept of cooperation between academic institutions. One of the most valuable service agreements, in terms of students needs, is that the Austin Community College underwrites the borrower's fees for its students who are not residents of the city of Austin and who want to borrow materials from the public library. The students have proven more interested in the convenience of using the local public library than in using the resources of the university (Hisle 1990).

In San Diego, California, cooperation between academic libraries has resulted in faculty guest borrowing cards, but students at the colleges and universities must use the ILL (Interlibrary Loan) system to borrow materials. ILL, for all its success, is little comfort to students who have located a book and must wait for it to be mailed to their own college. A cooperative activity that is very successful is a film consortium of the educational institutions in the area, including the public school system (Stevens 1990).

In the real world legal and administrative constraints often restrict the hopeful endeavors of librarians to share resources. Two important restrictions are institutional reluctance to assume financial obligations of individuals and legally defined service groups.

For example, three hypothetical academic institutions in an urban area want to provide reciprocal faculty borrowing privileges. The first institution is a private university with a small, full-time faculty. The second is a private college with a small, full-time faculty. But the third is a public community college with a large number of faculty equally divided between full- and part-time. The college and university arrive at an agreement for cooperative faculty use of library collections and agree to assess each other for any financial obligations incurred by their faculties, such as fines or lost materials. The community college is prohibited from assuming the financial responsibilities of individuals and because of the large number of faculty involved is reluctant to be a collection agency so cannot participate in the agreement. Additionally, the small college was founded by a religious group, and its charter restricts it to serving only those adhering to that religious affiliation.

Shared Libraries

In states with rapidly growing populations, such as Florida, Texas, and California, universities and colleges have opted to share buildings and collections in developing new campuses and enlarging existing ones. Once this takes place, differentiating between two institutions' collections, faculty, or student body becomes impractical.

In Florida, for example, there are nine publicly supported universities; of these, six are sharing libraries on at least one campus site with a community college. Three of the universities, University of South Florida, University of Central Florida, and Florida Atlantic University, are sharing library facilities on various campuses with more than one community college.

The usual case has been that the university has sought to expand services by offering courses on or adjacent to an established community college campus. The benefit to the institutions is that the "newcomer" can use the established library as a base to build and enlarge collections and both institutions can realize financial savings in providing library services in terms of both materials and personnel.

Shared Databases

The next step in resource sharing is interinstitutional shared databases. There are many examples of local, state, regional, and national databases that are shared by several institutions. Many of these are shared databases of multi-type libraries such as the Tampa Bay Library Consortium (TBLC), the Illinois Library and Information Network (ILLINET), Southeastern Library Network (SOLINET), and OCLC.

In Indiana, the eight campus libraries of Indiana University are open to all users. A combination of public and private funding has resulted in a computerized network linking the university to other academic libraries in Indiana (Gray 1990, 8). Beginning in 1985, Kentucky has developed, first, an automated system for the University of Kentucky and, second, an interconnected system for the state's 14 community colleges (Willis 1988, 10). In Florida, the state universities share an automated system, and the community colleges in 1990 were in the process of implementing a statewide system that would interact with the university system.

M.E.L. Jacob has written about the changing environment of electronic networks and what that means for libraries. In early 1990, the U.S. government began studying the need for a national telecommunications policy, under the auspices of the National Telecommunication and Information Administration,

U.S. Department of Commerce (Jacob 1990, 8). Already, certain states, such as North Carolina and Florida, are including libraries in their plans for state telecommunications networks.

Jacob thinks that today's libraries are dependent on telecommunications whether they are small libraries using telefacsimile machines or large libraries using the Research Libraries Information Network (RLIN). Whatever the final configurations of local library systems, "there will be increased emphasis on local communication systems within an institution and within a community. These linkages will provide essential channels for communicating with patrons and for delivering services" (Jacob 1990, 10).

Elaine Lemmond has defined library networks by differentiating them into Types A, B, C, and na (1990, 139). Lemmond identified 34 different networks, with 2 not yet operating. One of these 2, the College Center for Library Automation (CCLA), which is the state system for community college libraries in Florida, has an administrative unit formed and a vendor selected. The other, the Ohio Library Information System (OLIS), is still in the planning stage.

Type A networks have a central node and a union catalog. They share systems and use one type of software. Of the 10 networks classified at Type A, 6 are academic. These are such state systems as ILLINET and regional systems such as TBLC.

Type B networks are formed from independently automated libraries that communicate primarily through dedicated telephone lines. Each library maintains its own catalog, circulation files, and so on. They are centralized but do not have a union catalog. Examples cited by Lemmond are the Richmond Area Network (RAN) in Richmond, Virginia, and the Kanawha County Public Library Network in Charleston, West Virginia (141).

Type C networks link all types of libraries through a distributed network with a union catalog. Four networks were identified, and two are state library systems. Circulation and other services are locally controlled.

Type D networks do not have union catalogs. Six were identified; they are networks, such as the Colorado Alliance of Research Libraries (CARL) and the Southeast Florida Library Network (SEFLIN), that use telecommunication interfaces to link dissimilar systems. Circulation and cataloging are locally controlled, and connections are through dial access and dedicated lines.

NA or not applicable networks are the large bibliographic utilities, such as OCLC and RLIN, that did not fit the model of Lemmond's study. This study predicts the continued growth of large, centralized systems with union catalogs and an interconnection of these systems with others through open systems architecture.

As electronic bridges are designed to make communications between dissimilar automated systems transparent to the user, more scholars will access these bibliographic networks from their own workstations. It is becoming a common practice for faculty, researchers, and students to use a phone modem to call into their own institution's database. The next step is to extend the search for information to the databases of other institutions and to private sources of bibliographic data. The full text of a document may be available, as well as citations and abstracts. The information can be downloaded from the network, saved to a file, or printed. Some systems, such as the Educational Resources Information Center (ERIC), allow for courier or mail delivery of the document in print or in microformat. Scholars are no longer dependent on or even interested in where the information is physically located when they have the tools to locate it instantly and have it delivered at their convenience.

Informal Networks

Many localities have informal networks without charters, dues, or officers to facilitate interinstitutional access to collections. These networks often develop as a result of the personal and professional associations of library administrators, librarians, and faculty and their willingness to cross institutional lines of service. As one library administrator has said, "It is only those who don't have anything [in terms of library resources] who want to keep the doors locked" (Johnson 1990).

In Jacksonville, Florida, a state-funded grant to foster interinstitutional cooperation between the colleges and universities in that area included the establishment of a committee to develop interinstitutional library cooperation. When the grant ended, the committee continued as an informal interest group of representatives from the academic libraries. The informal network later invited school and public libraries to send representatives to the meetings of the interest group. All full-time faculty and administration have reciprocal borrowing privileges between academic institutions. Students must use ILL; however, the practice is to allow "walk-in" ILL to facilitate student access. A likely outcome of this informal activity is that a regional consortium of multitype libraries will result (Johnson 1990).

Creative Networks

Libraries have been described as everything from repositories of knowledge to dusty warehouses, but a description that is seldom applied to libraries is "creative." Yet many of the currently existing networks of academic libraries can be best described in that way.

WRLC

In the Washington, DC, area, a new network of academic libraries was established in 1987. This network was an outgrowth of the Washington Research Libraries Consortium, which had existed for 20 years as a cooperative effort between the eight major universities in the Washington area: American University, Catholic University of America, Gallaudet University, George Mason University, George Washington University, Georgetown University, Marymount

University, and the University of the District of Columbia. The mission statement of WRLC is "to enhance and expand the existing library and information resources and services of its member universities" (*WRLC Newsletter* 1990). Its rationale is as follows:

Because of the "information explosion," university students and faculty members are faced with increasing problems in identifying, locating and acquiring the pertinent information they need for their research or study tasks. Further, the expense involved in acquiring, cataloging, housing, preserving, retrieving and disseminating books and journals continues to grow. No university can, within its own library, provide the total support required for its instructional and research programs.

Howard University has become a full member of the consortium, and Trinity and Mount Vernon colleges have joined as associate members.

The plans for the consortium called for the implementation of an automated library system that would serve the needs of all of the institutions. The database uses the NOTIS library automation system and is now online. The database began with 1 million records, which will expand as collections grow.

The outcome of this collaboration between libraries is planned to be, in addition to a common database, cooperative collection development, cooperative delivery and telecommunications services, a plan for preservation and conservation of informational materials, a joint depository program for seldom used but important materials, and the construction of a facility that will accommodate these and other networking needs. Funds for this project have been provided by the institutions and by special federal appropriations from the U.S. Department of Education, the National Endowment for the Humanities, and the U.S. Congress.

It is apparent that the commitment is being made on the national level to support networking activities with the expectation that information resources will be more efficiently and more cost-effectively provided. The value of information is in its accessibility, and this network will provide that accessibility in an urban area that is both information-rich and information-hungry.

UIUC and ILLINET

ILLINET had its beginnings in 1980 in the development of the Illinois Statewide Library Computer System (LCS), which was an extension of the installation of the automated system developed for the University of Ohio at the University of Illinois at Urbana-Champaign (UIUC) library in 1978. UIUC library is the largest publicly supported academic library in the country, the third largest collection after Yale and Harvard, and a significant contributor to the holdings of OCLC (Sloan 1986, 27).

Although ILLINET is a statewide, multitype library network, the establishment of the system has "given the state of Illinois, and the nation, increased and enhanced access to the bibliographic resources of 27 academic libraries" (Sloan 1986, 28). The system also has designated research and reference centers to assist in fulfilling ILL requests.

What ILLINET has achieved with a statewide, automated library system is a model for other networks. The success of this project results from the conviction of librarians that cooperative activities were beneficial to institutions and library users, the support of the Illinois State Library, the University of Illinois, and the Illinois Board of Higher Education, the cost-effective aspects of statewide automation, and the implementation and support of delivery systems funded by the Illinois State Library. The development of ILLINET negated in many ways the need for local academic library networks. The result has been the disbanding of groups such as the Chicago Library Council because the need for the groups had been superseded.

SEFLIN

The Southeast Florida Library Network was incorporated in 1988 to "provide timely information access for library users through resource sharing and cooperation among member libraries (SEFLIN 1990, 1). The project was funded through the Library Services and Construction Act (LSCA) and the State Library of Florida as a demonstration project for three years prior to incorporation.

From its inception, the network served more than academic libraries; however, 5 of the 7 original members are academic institutions. The other 2 members are major urban public libraries. Membership has increased to 11, with 3 of the new members being academic libraries, so that currently 8 of the members are academic libraries. Academic members of the network are Broward Community College, Florida Atlantic University, Florida International University, Miami-Dade Community College, the University of Miami, Nova University Law Library, St. Thomas University, and Barry University. Public library members are Broward County Library System, Miami-Dade Public Library System, and Palm Beach County Public Library System.

SEFLIN was a pioneering network in using telefacsimile for document delivery. As in the ILLINET system, SEFLIN leadership determined that the delivery of documents was an essential component of resource sharing. Two systems are in place, a courier system for physical delivery and a fax network for electronic delivery. The development of a microfiche and a CD-ROM publication of a Union List of Serials for the network provided increased access to resources and demands on the delivery system.

The next phase in resource sharing for this network is the SEFLINK project. This is an electronic bridge system that links dissimilar library computer systems. Part of the project required the development of extended LANs (Local Area Networks) on existing telecommunications lines (SEFLIN 1990, 2). Software to run the system was developed and installed. The result is another pioneering advance in resource sharing that allows for communications between various different automated systems.

TBLC

The Tampa Bay Library Consortium began as a loosely organized interest group of librarians in seven counties on the central west coast of Florida in 1979.

The consortium was based on the success of the Greater Cincinnati Library Consortium. The original membership consisted of 12 academic institutions and four large public library systems. The consortium now has over 60 member libraries in nine counties and includes academic, public, special, and school libraries. Like SEFLIN, TBLC incorporated (1980) and has received LSCA funding and support through the Florida State Library.

The consortium provides document delivery service through telefacsimile and a commercial courier system, consultation services, and workshops and training and developed the SUNLINE database.

TBLC provides, operates, and maintains the central site computer system that runs SUNLINE, essentially a regional online system that provides automated services to member libraries. The SUNLINE database requires that the libraries purchase terminals and pay online costs, port charges, and other charges, so although any TBLC member can join SUNLINE, participation is an institutional decision dependent on each library's need for automation.

In the case of TBLC a local affiliation of primarily academic libraries has matured into a multitype library consortium and has made available an automated online database. A concentrated effort was made by this consortium to recruit membership from special libraries and county public library and school library systems. Although the consortium directors, officers, and staff have been committed to the idea that each library has unique records to offer, conditions of membership based on holdings, staff, and budget have been developed to ensure that all member libraries contribute in some way to the network and that the network is not used to substitute for institutional responsibilities. The success of this regional consortium has encouraged the development of similar regional networks in Florida such as the Central Florida Library Consortium (CFLC).

CARL

The Colorado Alliance of Research Libraries began in 1974 as an effort to increase resource sharing between the academic libraries in the Denver, Colorado, area and the Denver Public Library. Seven institutions—the University of Colorado at Denver, Metropolitan State College, the Community College of Denver, the University of Colorado at Boulder, the Colorado School of Mines, the University of Northern Colorado, and Denver Public Library—are the basis of the network. The first three of these institutions, all in Denver, are served by the Auraria Library which is administered by the University of Colorado at Denver. Recently, the community colleges of Colorado have joined as associate members. The CARL system software is in use in several other regions in Colorado so that what began as a local network has expanded to provide resource sharing capabilities throughout the state.

The success of CARL is related to one of the first projects undertaken by the network, the development of an online catalog of the holdings of the member libraries. The CARL system now offers access to the member databases through terminal and dial-access, access to an online encyclopedia, local statistical information, local business news from the area daily papers, and the tables of contents from member library journal subscriptions. The system also takes advantage of the capabilities of optical scanning and telefacsimile and is developing full-text delivery through this technology.

CONTINUING THE EFFORT

"Whenever the subject of inter-institutional cooperation is raised, academic administrators, almost without exception, assume library cooperation is a given. It appears so eminently logical to officials that libraries should cooperate" (Dougherty 1988, 287). Sharing resources through automated databases, improved document delivery, and other innovative ideas have demonstrated that libraries can cooperate; however, the issue of local access to materials and local development of collections remains a consideration (288). It is necessary to build on the success of such networks as OCLC and RLG and the regional and local networks that have developed and to continue the concept that access and availability of materials are crucial and that all libraries need to manage both information and financial resources to their best interest.

When we begin to evaluate where we have been with academic library networks and where we might be going, it is very clear that what is certain is that it is uncertain. The edges that delineated the differences between types of libraries were thought to be firmly etched. We find these edges blurred and softened. The role of the academic library cannot be determined by the institution it serves; it must find its place in the larger arena of libraries and in its community. The challenge will be to ensure that future networking and cooperation will enhance, but not replace, institutional libraries and that networking will benefit all participants.

REFERENCES

Arms, Caroline, ed. 1990. *Campus strategies for libraries and electronic information.* Rockport, ME: Digital Press.

Bedient, Douglas. 1990. Letter to Roland Person, Special Projects Librarian. Morris Library, Southern Illinois University at Carbondale, Carbondale, IL. April 20.

Bowden, Virginia. 1990, Health Center Library, University of Texas at San Antonio, June. Telephone interview with author.

Bowker annual of library and book trade information. 1988. New York: Bowker.

Breivik, Patricia Senn, and Shaw, Ward. 1989. Libraries prepare for an information age. *Educational Record* 20 (Winter): 13–19.

Cain, Mark E. 1978. The council of research and academic libraries: An example of interlibrary cooperation. Master's thesis, University of Chicago, 122.

Dalehite, Michele. 1990. Letter to author. Florida Center for Library Automation, Gainesville, FL, April 10.

Dougherty, Richard M. 1988. A conceptual framework for organizing resource sharing and shared collection development programs. 1988. *Journal of Academic Librarianship* 14 (November): 287–91.

Gray, Julie. 1990. Public-private partnership builds state-of-the-art library at IUPUI. In *Our Indiana*, Indianapolis: Indiana University Office of University Relations, June.

Hisle, W. Lee. 1990. Interview with author, Austin Community College, June.

Jacob, M.E.L. 1990. Libraries and national library networks. *Bulletin of the American Society for Information Science* 16 (June/July): 8–9.

Johnson, Judith. 1990. Interview with author, Florida Community College at Jacksonville, July.

Kinney, Thomas. 1988. *Toward telecommunications strategies in academic and research libraries. Ten case studies of decision-making and implementation.* Washington, DC: OMS Occasional Paper OP14. Association of Research Libraries. Office of Management Studies, October, 33.

Kroah, Larry A. 1983. *Resource sharing of printed materials among Dayton-Miami Valley Consortium Libraries in 1982: A descriptive study.* Dayton, OH: Eric Clearinghouse, 81.

Lemmond, Elaine Harman. 1990. A study of library networks by type. *Proceedings of the 5th Integrated Online Library Systems Meeting, May 2–3,* 137–49.

LIBRAS, Inc. 1983. *LIBRAS bylaws and articles of incorporation,* July 18.

Linden, Eugene. 1990. Dashed hopes and bogus fears. *Time* (June 11): 58.

Luce, Richard E. 1987. The open library system and networking: Current developments and future trends. *Proceedings: Conference on integrated online library systems 1987.* Canfield, OH: Genaway Assoc., 59–70.

McCabe, Gerard B. 1979. *The Library Committee of the Capital Consortium for Continuing Higher Education.* Paper Presented at the Biennial Institute Collection Development Update, Richmond, VA, May 3, 10.

Medina, Sue O., et al. 1987. *Network of Alabama Academic Libraries collection assessment manual. Alabama Commission on Higher Education.* Montgomery: Network of Alabama Academic Libraries.

Networking on campus. 1988. *OCLC Newsletter* 175 (September/October): 10–18.

Person, Roland. 1990. Letter to author. Southern Illinois University at Carbondale, Carbondale, IL, April 27.

Rutstein, Joel S. 1985. National and local resource sharing: Issues in cooperative collection development. *Collection Management* 7 (Summer): 1–14.

Schwarz, Philip. 1987. Selection of an automated library system for the University of Wisconsin. *Information Technology and Libraries* 1 (March): 40–56.

SEFLIN. 1990. *Board of Directors Meeting Minutes.* March.

SEFLIN INC. 1, no. 1 (Spring 1990).

Sloan, Bernard G. 1986. Resource sharing among academic libraries: The LCS experience. *Journal of Academic Librarianship* 12 (March): 26–9.

Stevens, Curtis L. 1990. Interview with author, Grossmont College, Grossmont-Cuyamaco Community College District, CA, April.

Trickett, David. 1990. Letter to author, Washington Theological Consortium, Washington, DC, April 11.

Wareham, Nancy L. 1986. *The report on library cooperation 1986.* Chicago: American Library Association, Association of Specialized and Cooperative Library Agencies.

Washington Research Library Consortium. 1989. (Brochure.)

Willis, Paul. 1988. Networking on campus. *OCLC Newsletter* no. 175 (Sept./Oct.): 10–18.

WRLC Newsletter. no. 3 (January 1990).

15

Joint-Use Library Services at Distant Campuses: Building Cooperation Between a Community College and a University

Yvonne L. Ralston and Adele Oldenburg

As is so often the situation in many states, legislative mandates for public education cannot be easily transmitted into efficient and effective operations. The framework for this chapter is based upon several issues for administrators who are charged with beginning library services at a new branch campus that is located some distance from the main campuses of a community college and a university serving a large metropolitan area and several counties.

During the past decade, a number of studies have investigated the growth of college branch campuses in the United States. A.G. Konrad defined branch campuses as "extension centers of universities or colleges, i.e. semi-autonomous residential institutions, two-year public colleges, or parts of multi-campus institutions . . . each an integral part of a parent institution or larger system" (1982, 1). R. Huitt attributes the growth in the number of branch campuses nationwide to cost and size: "Branch campuses make a college education more accessible to many students who can live at home, maintain a part-time job, and pay lower tuition than at a main campus. In addition, branch campuses solve a problem for community colleges and universities who are trying to limit enrollment at the main campus in the face of increased demand" (1972, 41).

Konrad maintains that branch campuses became increasingly important in higher education in the 1980s, and he suggests that failure to define an institution's role and goals as to building more branch campuses can create an inner-institutional conflict over students and resources. In the struggle for "parody of esteem," governing boards frequently neglect branch campuses, which are viewed as ancillary to the total institution. Role clarification is seen as essential to increasing the effectiveness of branch campuses. Rather than emulating the main institution, branch campuses are advised by Konrad to develop identities and activities reflecting a local community orientation.

J. Wynn (1972, 44) discussed the need for multicampus institutions to direct attention to basic questions of organization and control. In the state of Florida, *The Master Plan for Florida Post-Secondary Education* established principles for the creation of branch campuses to meet the emerging needs for undergraduate education in the growing areas of Florida. The master plan recommended that these criteria include needs assessments, examinations of institutional capacity, and "educationally and economically significant tests." The master plan directed public community colleges and universities to determine a compelling need for a new campus and develop a 2 + 2 (2 years of community college + 2 years at university) curriculum approach that would fully utilize joint programs and joint facilities for enhancing student transfer and decreasing capital expenditures.

The Florida legislature created the Post-Secondary Education Planning Commission and charged that commission with the duty to "advise the State Board of Education regarding the need for and location of new institutions and campuses of public post-secondary education." In 1983, the commission was required to recommend to the State Board of Education and the legislature the establishment of additional branch campuses of postsecondary educational institutions. No branch campus in the state of Florida may be established without a review by the commission and formal authorization of the legislature. In the state of Florida, there are six joint-use branch campuses that fit the definition of an instructional and administrative unit of a university and a community college with limited support services. These branch campuses do not necessarily offer a full range of instructional programs or courses. In joint-use branch campuses within the state, the community college is responsible for the first two years of higher education and the university is responsible for upper division and graduate programs in high demand disciplines. Support services are shared to the maximum extent possible, and one of those support units is the joint-use library.

For the purposes of this discussion, the distinction is made that joint-use campuses for a community college and a university are limited centers of instructional opportunities for geographically bound residents within one hour or more driving distance of a joint-use campus, but several driving hours from a main campus.

STRATEGIES FOR COLLECTION BUILDING AT A DISTANT CAMPUS

Documents such as standards and formulas for minimum library adequacy for collections, master plans, needs studies, demographic profiles of populations to be served, analyses of student demand for programs, and the requirements of the labor market all can provide insights into defining the library collection for a distant campus. (New libraries need to be planned at least two years in advance of the completion of construction of a new campus.)

The problem with building a collection for a joint-use library, whether it is new or established, is that there are two sets of philosophies and administration that must be melded into a useful system of library services for two distinctively different student populations. Also, decisions must be made as to other populations to be served in the geographic area.

An organizing framework for examining how the collection is developed is essential for two discrete institutions that embark on a joint-use venture. The following strategies provide insights into the complicated dimensions of two autonomous institutions living in one house.

STRATEGIES FOR BUILDING THE
BASIC COLLECTION

Identify as early as possible the planning team, a group of senior librarians from each institution charged with the responsibility of studying all documents such as those mentioned above and proposing a basic collection for the campus. Considerations in this phase of planning are given solely to the basic collection but predicated on the amount of space available for all aspects of the library. Dimensions of that collection should be taken first from nationally recognized formulas for small college libraries. No consideration during this planning phase should include the degree programs to be offered at the campus nor other community groups to be served by the campus nor where or how the collection will be purchased or acquisitioned. Sources from which the collection will be taken should be defined at later junctions in the planning process. The final basic collection report from the planning team should include extensive references to the nationally recognized formulas used for the analysis. Some assumptions here are essential.

In the 1990s colleges will find themselves in an explosive new trend, begun in the late 1980s. The "Information Society," the term commonly used to illustrate the characteristics of the next decade, has begun now. Information publications have proliferated at an astounding pace, and no more is it national or continental; it is global. Reference materials should illustrate the needs and preferences of both institutions. Close cooperation should exist between the faculty of both institutions and the director/coordinator of the shared-faculty distant campus library to eliminate duplication of expensive works and to ensure that the need of each institution is being met. A community college or university cannot, nor should be expected to, meet the information explosion problem in its entirety. It must select what is needed at its particular site but have access to other materials at other sites. This access requirement brings to the planners an entirely new thinking regarding facilities and library collections. Realizing that neither the community college nor the university will ever be able to have a complete library collection at each site, the strategies for building the basic collection should include extensive use of microforms for journals and periodicals and computerized sources for any reference tools available in these formats. In joint-use libraries, however, a shared facility must continually take into consideration that a community college and a university are not the same.

Additions to the Basic Collection–
Content/Subject Development

Plans for building additional resources at a joint-use library after the basic collection has been established should incorporate procedures for extensive borrowing from the home campus of the two institutions. The solution to the two institutions' being at one site has been utilization of resource sharing, or, as stated by Charles Lowry, "Interlibrary loan should be characterized as interlibrary sacrifice" (1990, 13). The large university institution generally is the major lender, and the community college is the larger borrower. This arrangement has been a viable solution to building a collection for two institutions. With new technology, however, librarians will be provided with more use of distant databases for delivery of library materials to patrons, and the charges may be taken out of the realm of lending goodwill into the harsh world of financial reality. The planning team must consider the costs of acquiring materials from other libraries and the extent to which such borrowing meets the demands of the patrons of the distant campus. This issue should be a separate planning strategy distinct from building the collection. The questions to be answered are, How much of the collection will be taken from the existing libraries of the two institutions, and what must be borrowed from other libraries or databases?

The building of the extended collection for two institutions then must deal with the content/subject development for support of the educational philosophies of the two institutions and their different missions as well as service to the community and to students. There is a need for analysis of the library organization, that is, decisions/control, fiscal limitations, expansion, and growth. These strategies must now be considered as separate steps in the planning process. While there are many other factors, not the least of which are library financial allocations, which will be presented as a later strategy, the additional collection building at a distant campus must consider the content/subject development in three areas: community college, university, and community.

Historically, the collections of community or junior colleges were based on what the returning World War II veteran needed to get for his education, degree, and place in the work world. Much of this collection was based on titles we have since designated "vocational" subjects. The trend since then and through the 1980s appears to have been toward developing collections commensurate with a course taught and/or by faculty request. This procedure is logical unless you have a faculty member who is outstandingly active in requests for book titles for a course of questionable duration.

If each community college branch campus cannot hope to have a complete collection, a shared library with a university certainly could not attain an adequate collection for a university branch campus. But the university can be a major lender to a branch campus. The university programs offered at a distant campus must be supported by an adequate collection; however, that collection does not need to be permanently housed at that campus.

Although it would be ideal to include materials for the community needs in the joint-use library collection, the foregoing comments illustrate how difficult such a service would be to implement. Accessing these materials would be possible, however, through interlibrary loan, and perhaps that is all that should be attempted at a distant site. Formulating an electronic union catalog of the holdings of each business and industry would be a step in providing easy, local access to wanted materials. Concomitant policies, procedures, and contracts would have to be formulated for the copying and for lending of these materials. Written cooperative agreements among lending and receiving institutions are essential as they provide road maps of how these actions will be performed, how much they will cost, and which institutions have responsibility for initiating and receiving requests for materials. The planning team should be responsible for identifying the potential lending institutions and initiating agreements for exchange of library holdings.

SOURCES OF HOLDINGS TO MEET DEMANDS

The previous strategies regarding relationships and cooperative agreements also apply to resource sharing. But there is another aspect of resource sharing: borrowing from the collections of nonacademic institutions. Community libraries in the surrounding environs of most distant campus libraries are poor in scholarly information, book titles, journals, and so on that are indigenous to the institutions they serve, such as hospitals, industries, businesses, foundations, city and county government, and chambers of commerce. Each of these entities has some kind of a collection, whether or not it thinks of it as such. A joint-use urban campus library could create a wealth of accessible, current, and otherwise difficult to obtain subject information by being the catalyst in creating an ongoing database of these community resources.

The planning team should investigate whether to spend a higher percentage of what is generally considered books and periodicals budgets in order to focus on a general access collection, which would entail a whole new milieu of standards, databases, data deliveries, vendors, equipment, and so on.

ESTABLISHING RELATIONSHIPS: A WRITTEN COOPERATIVE AGREEMENT

The patrons of community college/university libraries are sophisticated in demanding library service as well as diversity. To meet the needs of these patrons, there must be viable, mutually conducive relationships established between the campus institutions. These relationships are not only in the financial area but also between librarians and disparate faculty.

There should be formal agreements on collection development and on the operation of joint use of campus library—not a vague "We'll do this and maybe you can do that." Such agreements force joint-use library staff to look more closely at their collection and collection policies as well as operating hours, staffing, equipment purchases, operating costs, and ownership of all aspects of book, equipment, and furniture holdings.

Below are primary issues to be included in written agreements.

Mission and Goals

The joint-use library should set forth provisions for academic support for the university and community college students as well as services to the community within the geographic region. It should provide within the limits of available funding the statements about integrated library resources and the library service as to how it should be delivered. Economy, service, and cooperation, with the good of the student and the community patron in mind should be the primary concerns of developing the library support that the programs of each institution require. It should be recognized that the service needs of the student body of each institution would require different levels of intensity of service and a comprehensive staff as well as facilities to meet those needs.

Responsibility for Administration

Clearly identify the authority and responsibility for administration of the joint-use library and the obligation of each institution as to its continuity and upkeep. The staffing of the library, as well as its operating hours and appropriate administrative channels to solve problems and issues, should be identified.

Management Organization and Staffing

Identifying who is in charge is critical and should be included in the cooperative agreement. Which institution will be responsible for acquisition of materials as well as interlibrary loans and other resource-sharing devices and their limitations should be included in the agreement. Staffing should include a library coordinator or director and the duties of that administrator as well as the reporting relationship of that library administrator. There are several patterns of possibilities for employing and funding staff within the library. Each institution could provide positions to the library, or one institution could provide all staff to the library, and the cost could be divided between the two institutions, and the host institution could invoice the other; or a contract for payment for the salaries of those staff members could be devised. Whatever pattern is used, the cooperative agreement should be specific as to how the staffing should be funded.

Lending Policies

This process can be awkward and cumbersome unless a firm policy is stated that allows the distant campus to have complete authority over all procedures. Neglecting to give autonomy to the shared faculty in this particular service negates any other positive service accorded to its student clientele. Such individual points as the type of material loaned; service; the policy of notifying requests; loan period; obligations of borrower, fines, or other penalties; having cash available; and a policy of returning borrowed material must be spelled out clearly and agreed to by both institutions before service is enacted.

Reserve Policies

A firm policy should be enacted, after discussion of the director/coordinator of the distant campus with pertinent personnel of each institution, so that the same reserve time allowances are granted to all students. A computerized hookup to each institution should allow each institution to have immediate records of reserve transactions.

Resolutions of Conflict

Conflicts are normal when two different institutions live in the same house. Conflict resolution should be codified, so that each institution has a senior administrator named in a cooperative agreement for final resolutions of issues. The policies for interpretation of rules and regulations and the procedures for interpretation, amplification, and renegotiation or amendment of the agreement should be stated in writing.

Advisory Committee

An advisory committee of members of each institution should be defined in the cooperative agreement. It is recommended that the committee be composed of administrators and faculty from each institution, students from each institution, and senior librarians from each institution. The cooperative agreement should indicate how often the advisory committee should meet, and the parameters of recommendations from that committee should be identified clearly in the document.

Hours of Operation

Often one institution will require more or different operating hours than the other. Hours of operation should be clearly defined in the cooperative agreement and should be set only after consultation with the administrators of the two institutions as well as the library advisory committee mentioned above. Hours of operation should reflect the extent of services needed for all academic sessions of each institution as well as periods of term breaks, vacations, and those times when only one institution may be operating. Limiting library services during any time in which either of the two institutions has classes or examinations scheduled should be thoroughly analyzed before conclusions are made for appropriate, flexible hours of operation. These considerations should be set forth in the cooperative agreement.

Acquisitions

As previously discussed, there are a number of ways to acquire the library collection. Acquisitions for a joint-use library can be a function of technical services at each of the home campuses of the institution or can be part of the functions of the joint-use campus library staff. The purchases by each institution should be in accordance with the respective policies and procedures relating to the selection and acquisitions of books, nonprint materials, periodicals, serials, and subscriptions, as well as furniture and equipment at each institution. It is imperative that all users of a shared-faculty library at a distant campus be treated in an equal and equable manner, with no distinctions or privileges made for any.

Availability of Resources

If the two institutions have different catalog formats, circulation systems or other differences in resource availability these must be accommodated. Procedures should be set forth to meet the goal of economy, service, and cooperation for the good of the student and the community user. The goal of a joint-use library is that all resources should be open and available to all students, faculty, and staff of each institution, except reserve collections, which are identified at the beginning of each term. All materials that circulate should circulate to all students, faculty, and staff, and each institution should be responsible for making good any item not required by one of the students, faculty, or staff of that institution. A unified circulation system for users should be implemented as far as possible and its operation stated in the cooperative agreement.

Inventory, Replacement, and Disposal of Property

All books, periodicals, other print and nonprint materials, furniture, and equipment in the joint-use library belonging to each or other institutions should be consigned as far as it is practical, and a procedure for inventory should be set for the cooperative agreement. Procedures for replacing and disposing of property should be developed, approved, and implemented in the same manner as outlined for the acquisition of property. Such procedures should be in accordance with each institution's respective rules and procedures for replacement and disposal of property to minimize conflict between the two discretely different institutions.

Property, accountability should be defined as books, nonprint materials, periodicals, serials, subscriptions, furniture, and equipment. The property of the two institutions should be considered as being held by the joint-use library so long as a cooperative agreement is in force, and all property should be identified as joint-use library resources, with additional designations for the community college or university that funded the resources in order to maintain a clear inventory. The joint-use library director should be accountable to each institution for such property inventory on an annual basis.

Building the Collection

Building the collection should continue after the opening of the joint-use library. The cooperative agreement needs to set forth the procedures for adding to the opening day collection.

Equipment Needs

New equipment and furniture needs should be met as funds are available each year from each institution. The need for furniture and equipment items should be recommended by the library director and reviewed and endorsed by the library advisory committee before submission to appropriate administrative authorities in each institution for inclusion in the operating budget of each institution. The institution should cooperatively agree to the assignment of financial responsibility for the purchases of specific items of furniture and equipment to provide appropriately for each institutions' program and service needs.

Operating Expenses

Operating expenses should be defined in the cooperative agreement as cost ratios used to determine on an annual basis the community college's and university's share of operating the library, respectively. There are several means of creating these cost ratios. One would be to derive the number of students enrolled at each institution on the campus and assign the cost by a percent of head count of each institution. Another would be to count the number of students from each institution using the library.

The use of a written cooperative agreement between the two institutions can resolve many issues before they can become problems. The writing of the agreement should be assigned to the planning team.

PLANNING THE FACILITY

It is almost pointless to use the term *limited space* when speaking of a library, for as soon as it is constructed, the need for more space becomes apparent. This phenomenon is particularly obvious when the library is a joint-use facility.

Whereas a community college can, and often does, get its job done by providing
the basic monographs, periodicals, and indexes for the courses taught in the first
two years of college, the university curriculum must have a collection far more
diverse, sophisticated, and extensive. This entails many and large indexes, scholarly journals, voluminous abstracts. It takes very little time for a shared library
to find itself in a space bind. According to all of the research predictions, this
situation will worsen faster as our publications/information continues its global
intensity and new disciplines emerge.

Obviously we must rethink our ideas of the physical library. The book will
undoubtedly remain a necessary portable source of information, but we will have
to consider utilizing other technologies to access and dispense to our patrons
and making a library of physical walls less important than the information gathered. The use of technology will assist in the solution to this dilemma.

ONLINE COMPUTER SYSTEMS

There was a time when the computer was an alien force to library patrons.
Today, many of the students and faculty now using our libraries expect instant
and complete feedback to a subject search, and it is estimated that by 2010 "all
students will have been educated in the electronic age" (McNair 1989, 3). The
year 2010 is not that far off, and this thought can be frightening to a library
staff not educated for computer and information systems literacy. The planning
team should seek the advice of computer technologists and other systems experts
at this juncture of planning the joint-use library.

It is obvious that for an online system to be effective, particularly when it
serves a joint-use library at a distant campus from main libraries, several considerations must be met. Perhaps first of all, there must be a complete understanding and agreement between the two institutions' acquisition and cataloging
departments. Failure to reach a consensus on the fine points of cataloging,
classification, types of identification of materials for that shared-use facility,
responsibility of purchasing and types of purchases, bibliographic citations, and
so on can and will lead only to frustration not only for staff but most importantly
for the end users who have no interest in the intricacies of such matters but want
only the results—their requested information.

Second, the community college and the university should build their information infrastructure in such a manner that all types of information (print, video,
statistics, government publications) can be easily accessible online. The planning
team should outline each type of database it wants to access in the joint-use
library before meeting with the computer experts.

All computer systems should be compatible, even with the increasing number
of personal computers and private databases that many of our faculty and students
now use. Unfortunately at this time such is not the case. A major goal, therefore,
is to work toward such a harmonious integration. As stated by J. A. Turner,
"To avoid the demise of the library, librarians must take part in the planning

process as universities decide how to use computers and other technology as information tools'' (1985, 30).

In the planning of a joint-use library, criteria for selection of librarians who operate the library must include computer literacy. The planning team should study the current computing systems used by the institutions from which they will borrow and make recommendations for computing compatibilities in its strategic plan report.

AUTOMATED CIRCULATION SYSTEMS

In either a community college or a university main library, problems are seldom encountered in this area once the system has been selected and put in place. In a shared facility on a distant campus, however, the circulation system can be a major problem. At the distant campus, policies and procedures for automated circulation systems should be clearly delineated beforehand by both institutions if errors, snags, or frustrations are to be avoided. The cooperative agreement could set forth these conditions.

TELEFACSIMILE UTILIZATION

With many databases now available, with computers in libraries, and with many staff trained in researching, we can find the needed information in an incredibly short time span. Receiving that information, particularly if it is a monograph, is an entirely different situation. Some libraries still rely on the mail system to disseminate monographs. It is not unheard of for two to three weeks to pass from time of request to receipt of material. In a joint-use library at a distant campus, courier service must be utilized to move materials from a nearby parent institution but cannot be used to secure materials from a library hundreds of miles away. A quantum leap in solving this problem for document delivery is the telefacsimile machine now becoming apparent in many libraries. Telefacsimile (FAX) machines have been used since the 1940s but now they can be blended with computers to enable a library to send copies of documents in seconds via telephone lines. FAX machines should be purchased for the joint-use library.

JOURNALS AND PERIODICAL COLLECTION AND THE FICHE APPROACH

Historically, colleges and universities have subscribed to a hard copy issue for the current year of a journal, with back issues being bound and placed in the stacks. In recent years, with space decreasing, the viable alternative is to provide the back issues on microform. With some exceptions, such as large newspapers, where microfilm is less expensive and less space-demanding, microfiche has been the solution. Fiche has several advantages: it takes less space to maintain, the reader has random access to needed citations, and the equipment needed for fiche reading and printing is less expensive than that needed for film reading and printing.

A trend has been occurring in recent years that may have a profound effect upon creating even the current collection of journals and periodicals on fiche. At the 1989 American College and Research Libraries (ACRL) Conference, it was repeatedly stated that journal publishers, particularly some well-known ones in Europe, were pricing themselves out of the market. Libraries are traditionally on tight budgets, and they find themselves fighting not to cut titles from their journal collections. As a possible solution, it may become necessary for libraries to consider purchasing some of their current serial titles only on fiche, even though that step means that the patron will have to wait two to three months for the needed issue to arrive. This development would be unfortunate, and it is to be hoped that a more equitable solution will be forthcoming in the dilemma of the high cost of journals and periodicals. The planning team should identify fiche collections to be purchased very early in the planning of the basic collection and the additions to that collection for each institution.

SUMMARY

The combining of two different types of institutions can be simple to legislators, but the intricacies of the implementation of the endeavor can be very complicated. Identification of sound and efficient strategies early in the planning of these joint-use libraries can dilute the traumas and pitfalls that will occur, even with the best of staff resources and facilities.

REFERENCES

Adams, Herbert Baxter. 1887. *Seminary libraries and university extension*. Baltimore: Johns Hopkins University Press. (Reprinted 1973. New York: Johnson Reprint Corporation.) Original edition issued as number 112 of municipal government, history, and politics, which forms the fifth series of Johns Hopkins University studies in historical and political science.

Advances in the development of automated library systems in Florida. 1985. Tampa: ACRL Florida Chapter. Title from eye-readable header: Advances in the development of automated library systems in Florida.

Allen, Kenneth W. 1971. *Use of community college libraries*. Hamden, CT: Linnet Books.

Boss, Richard W. 1985. *Telecommunications for library management*. White Plains, NY: Knowledge Industry.

Breivik, Patricia S. 1987. Making the most of libraries: In the search for academic excellence. *Change* 19 (July/August): 44–52.

Cline, Hugh F., and Sinnott, Loraine T. 1983. *The electronic library: The impact of automation on academic libraries*. Lexington, MA: Lexington Books.

Dodson, Suzanne C., and Menges, Gary L., eds. 1984. *Academic libraries: Myths and realities*. Proceedings of the Third National Conference of the Association of College and Research Libraries, Seattle. Chicago: ACRL.

Duffett, Gorman Louis. 1976. A study of the goals and the goal formation process in the libraries of multi-unit district community colleges. Ph.D. diss., University of Pittsburgh.

Durrance, Joan C. 1984. *Armed for action: Library response to citizen information needs*. New York: Neal-Schuman.

Florida Postsecondary Education Planning Commission. 1988. *Automation and networking for Florida libraries*. Tallahassee: The Commission.

Florida Senate Committee on Governmental Operations. 1989. *A review of the benefits, costs, and feasibility of a statewide network linking the libraries of Florida*. Tallahassee: The Senate.

Flower, Kenneth E. 1986. *Academic libraries on the periphery: How telecommunications information policy is determined in universities*. Washington, DC: Office of Management Studies, Association of Research Libraries.

Fox, Beth Wheeler. 1988. *The dynamic library: Creative, practical, and inexpensive ideas for the director*. Chicago: American Library Association.

Gray, John. 1988. *National information policies: Problems and progress*. London: Mansell.

Griffiths, Jose-Marie, and Strain, Paula Meise. 1986. Final report of Phase III study of statewide automated library systems and networks for the state of Florida, *A statewide plan for library networking and automated library systems development in Florida*. Tallahassee: Florida Department of State, Division of Library Services.

Griffiths, Jose-Marie; Barlow, Diane L.; Strain, Paula Meise; and Allen, Jon M. 1986. *A three-year automation plan for the Charlotte-Glades Regional Library System*, Rockville, MD: King Research.

Harvey, John F. and Carroll, Frances LaVerne, eds. *Internationalizing library and information science education: A handbook of policies and procedures in administration and curriculum*. New York: Greenwood Press.

Harvey, John F., and Spyers-Duran, Peter. 1984, eds. *Austerity management in academic libraries*. Metuchen, NJ: Scarecrow Press.

Hastreiter, Jamie Webster; Hardesty, Larry; and Henderson, David. 1987. *Periodicals in college libraries*. Chicago: College Library Information Packet Committee, College Libraries Section, Association of College and Research Libraries.

Huitt, R. 1972. The 10,000 mile campus. *College and University Business* 53 (September): 41–45.

Josey, E. J. Ed. 1987. *Libraries, coalitions, and the public good*. New York: Neal-Schuman.

Kirk, Thomas G., ed. 1984. *Increasing the teaching role of academic libraries*. San Francisco: Jossey-Bass.

Konrad, A. G. 1982. Full partner or step-child: Extending functions of a university through a branch campus. Paper presented at the annual convention of the American Association of Community and Junior Colleges, April, St. Louis, MO. ERIC Document Reproduction Service No. ED 216751.

Leighton, Philip D., and Weber, David C. 1986. *Planning academic and research library buildings*, 2d ed. Chicago: American Library Association.

Library systems evaluation guide. 1983. Powell, OH: J. E. Rush Associates.

Lowry, Charles B. 1990. Resource sharing or cash shifting? The unequal burden of cooperative cataloging and ILL in network. *College and Research Libraries* 51 (January): 11–19.

McClure, Charles R. 1980. *Information for academic library decision making: The case for organizational information management.* Westport, CT: Greenwood Press.

McNair, Jeanne. 1989. Management issues in the nineties: Seminar I, Tampa (January): 27–28.

Martell, Charles R. 1983. *The client-centered academic library: An organizational model.* Westport, CT: Greenwood Press.

Martin, Rebecca R. 1990. The paradox of public service: Where do we draw the line? *College and Research Libraries* 5 (January): 20–26.

Monroe, Margaret E., and Heim, Kathleen M., eds. *Emerging patterns of community service.* 1979. Urbana: University of Illinois Graduate School of Library Science.

Moran, Barbara B. 1984. *Academic libraries: The changing knowledge centers of colleges and universities.* Washington, DC: Association for the Study of Higher Education.

Morein, Grady P., and Wells, Lea H. 1983. *Strategies and tactics for enhancing the role and position of the library within the college or university,* 2d ed. Chicago: Association of College and Research Libraries.

Morris, Leslie R., and Brautigam, Patsy. 1988. *Interlibrary loan policies directory,* 3d ed. New York: Neal-Schuman.

Newman, F. 1987. Adapting academic libraries to the future. *Change* 19 (July/August): 4–5.

Onsite access to library collections by visiting scholars. 1989. Washington, DC: Association of Research Libraries, Office of Management Studies.

Penland, Patrick R., and Mathai, Aleyamma. 1978. *The library as a learning service center.* New York: M. Dekker.

Ray, D. 1989. The meaningful and the procedural: Dilemmas of the community college library. *Journal of Academic Libraries* 15 (July): 147–50.

Rudolph, Janell, and Argall, Rebecca. 1985. *Academic libraries: Concepts and practice.* Dubuque, IA: Kendall/Hunt.

The report on library cooperation, 3d ed. Report on Library Cooperation Committee, Multitype Library Cooperation Section, comp. and ed. 1980. Chicago: Association of Specialized and Cooperative Library Agencies.

Schwartz, Ruth. 1988. *Multicampus libraries: Organization and administration case studies.* Metuchen, NJ: Scarecrow Press.

Simas, Robert J. 1983. *Assessment system for the evaluation of learning resources programs in community colleges.* Suisan City, CA: Learning Resources Association of California Community Colleges.

Spyers-Duran, Peter, and Mann, Thomas N., Jr., eds. 1985. *Issues in academic librarianship: Views and case studies for the 1980's and 1990's.* Westport, CT: Greenwood Press.

To Fiche or to reel: A seminar in microforms management. 1982. Florida Library Association, May.

Turner, J. A. 1985. Campus libraries seen threatened by other sources of information. *Chronicle of Higher Education* 31 (December 4): 30–31.

Veit, Fritz. 1975. *The community college library.* Westport, CT: Greenwood Press.

Wynn, J. 1972. Administering multi-campus junior colleges. *College and University Business* 53 (September): 44.

PART V

Security, Safety, and Preservation

16

Legal and Practical Aspects of Securing the General Collection in Academic Libraries

Carolyn L. Robison, John D. Marshall Jr., and Pamela J. Cravey

Research indicates that a library loses up to 6 percent of its collection per year to theft and mutilation (Hendrick and Murfin 1974, 402–11). Since medieval times, librarians have tried various approaches to securing their collections. Despite valiant, ordinary, and innovative approaches to securing the general collection, 73 percent of the chief librarians of 255 public libraries rated book theft as their number one problem (Burns Security Institute 1973, 10).

In his review of the literature, James H. Richards, Jr. (1979, 266–69) reported that the majority of articles relating to book theft and mutilation dealt with comparisons/evaluations of electronic book theft detection systems or with archival security. Most articles approached the topic of book theft by the case study method (Pegg 1981, 49–54) or by offering "shopping lists" of features to include in the acquisition of the ideal system (Bahr 1981, 31–37). By early 1983, the caliber of the published literature had improved only slightly. Such slight improvement supported the conclusion that security of the general collection was a myth (Cravey, Robison, and Russell 1984, 317). A more recent literature review indicated, however, that the situation may be changing. For example, *Library and Archival Security* has included articles relating to security of the general collection, patrons, and buildings, as well as legal issues, disaster preparedness, and current research. "The Protection of the Library and Archive: An International Bibliography" was published in the journal in 1983. Finally, monographs by Marvine Brand and Alan Jay Lincoln have helped focus attention on securing the general collection.

Philip Rappaport cautioned: "The most difficult part of the installation of an electronic security system is what to do with students or members of the public who are actually caught in the act of stealing a book. This problem *must be resolved* before the installation of a system takes place" (1977, 3–4).

A 1983 survey of 25 urban university libraries revealed that, although 94 percent of the respondents believed the need for an electronic security system was sufficient to justify the installation of one, only 22 percent had policies to support such a system in written form (Cravey, Robison, Russell 1984, 314).

Dana Weiss (1981, 314–47), Sarah B. Watstein (1983, 11–33), Carroll Varner (1983, 19–29), and Sharon Mast (1983, 31–51) discussed book and journal mutilation as a natural by-product of stringent security. John D. Edwards (1986, 447–64) indicated that the availability of parking, the presence of working photocopiers, and the nature of applicable state library theft laws may influence the security of the collection. Lincoln reported that vandalism to library materials is related to city size and volume of daily use of the facility (1989, 52). All indicated that something must be done to stop mutilation; Watstein indicated that something could be done (1983, 25). None of the libraries, however, suggested written collection security policies that include clear, concise definitions of mutilation and that spell out the apprehension and treatment of library users found with mutilated items in their possession. Lee B. Brawner and Norman Nelson suggested that each library should have a written "Security Plan of Action," which includes policy and procedures and which names designated library personnel responsible for implementation of each aspect of the plan (1984, 41–58). Alice Bahr argued that security training and information ought to be an important component of the preparation of librarians (1989, 42).

In 1980 the Pullen Library of Georgia State University wrote a detailed collection security policy and hired student assistant door checkers to monitor the exit gates of the electronic system that had been installed in 1976. Since then, the policy has undergone continuous administrative review, which has resulted in revisions—both minor and significant. In 1983, the library conducted a telephone interview with six urban libraries to support the thesis that a written policy among the urban libraries was the norm. None of the libraries had written policies!

METHODOLOGY

To learn more about the collection security policies and procedures of libraries in institutions similar to Georgia State University, in 1983 a survey of the library directors of member universities in the Association of Urban Universities was conducted (see Appendix A). Georgia State University is a member of the association. Because of their identities as urban institutions, these institutions share common concerns and problems. Among these concerns are location in highly populated areas and diversity of clientele, including persons unaffiliated with the university. Pamela J. Cravey, Carolyn L. Robison, and Ralph E. Russell reported on the findings of that survey (1984, 314–19). In 1986, a questionnaire, similar to that used in 1983, was mailed to the library directors of the 28 university libraries. Membership in the association had changed since 1983, with six universities dropping membership and eight different universities joining. Thus the findings of the 1986 survey may not necessarily indicate a change in institutional policies but, rather, a change in the overall makeup of the association.

Questions dealt with the use of electronic book theft detection systems, the employment of door guards or system monitors, the existence of written collection security policies, punitive actions taken against persons found attempting to steal library materials or found with mutilated library materials in their possession, and the outcomes of any legal actions taken against offenders. Complete responses were obtained from 22 of the 28, a response rate of 78.67 percent. As the data were nominal, frequency distributions were used in analysis of data.

FINDINGS

The first questions in the survey concerned the use of electronic book theft detection systems. Twenty-one of the 22 respondents, 96 percent, had such systems in use. This percentage indicated a high level of perceived need for collection security systems among association member libraries. Sixteen libraries had the 3-M Tattle-Tape system, three libraries had the Checkpoint system, and two had the Knogo system.[1]

The employment of staff specifically for library collection security purposes was more prevalent among libraries surveyed in 1986 than among those surveyed in 1983—an increase of 17 percent. The 1 library that did not use an electronic system also did not employ staff for security purposes. Of the 11 libraries that employed system monitors, 9 employed part-time staff. Position titles varied from student assistant to turnstile attendant, clerk, office assistant, and work-study student. The majority of these staff, 75 percent, reported directly to the head of the circulation department while 25 percent reported to other full-time circulation staff.

Only one respondent stated that library full-time staff were employed as system monitors. This employee was a circulation assistant reporting to the circulation department head. Three respondents indicated that campus security personnel served in this capacity and reported to either the director or assistant director of security. One library employed part-time staff in addition to security officers. One respondent stated that, while the library did not employ individuals as door checkers or system monitors, a security officer was assigned responsibility for monitoring the entrance only. Three respondents indicated that since the security system was adjacent to the circulation desk, staff at the desk monitored the system in addition to their other duties.

Pat Schindler indicated that the "image projected by security personnel cannot be overemphasized" (1978, 2). Of the 11 institutions that employed staff as system monitors, 5 required them to wear special clothing; 6 did not. Security-type uniforms, or dark trousers and a white or blue shirt, worn with a tie, were the special clothing of choice.

Seventeen responses were received to the question concerning the level of authority of those monitoring the security system, whether they were employed specifically for that purpose or they had that responsibility in addition to other duties. Of the 17 monitors, all had the authority to question, 10 had the authority to detain, 7 had authority to search, and 1 had authority to arrest. The one library with authority to arrest had security officers, paid and supervised by campus security, whose primary responsibility was to restrict individuals from entering the library.

Terri L. Pedersen indicated that the emphasis on "the success of the individual striving for personal gain no matter what the cost" coupled with the idea that it would be easy to take materials from the library, has contributed to the high rate of theft and mutilation of library materials (1990, 123, 128). Weiss's study of students in a large urban university indicated that most students who violated library rules did so because they perceived no danger of being caught (1981, 341–47). In the 1986 survey, only 8 of the 22 respondents, 36 percent, indicated that punitive actions were taken when uncharged library materials were detected on the person. In the 1983 survey, 10 of the 18 respondents, or 56 percent, took punitive actions. This percentage showed a decline in punitive actions taken of 20 percent over a period of three years. Curiously, only 3 of the 11 libraries that employed staff specifically as door checkers or system monitors took punitive action against violators. The punitive actions taken included handling the matter within the library, referral to the office of student affairs or student court, loss of borrowing privileges, giving a warning, calling the police and issuing a criminal trespass warning to nonstudent offenders, and retention of the student's identification card.

Fifty percent of the punitive actions taken involved campus police or security. Only 2 respondents indicated involvement by municipal police and the court system. Seven respondents, 32 percent, used the campus judicial system and 11 respondents, 50 percent, involved the office of the dean of students. Only 1 noted the involvement of the director of the library, and 1 noted involvement of the university attorney.

Responses to the question concerning which university officials were involved in the development of collection security procedures varied greatly. Eighteen percent of the procedures were developed by library personnel; 14 percent were developed by library personnel in concert with campus police and university administrators; 9 percent were developed by university administrators only; and another 9 percent were developed by campus police with university administrators. Other individual institutions involved campus police only and the senate advisory committee. Nine of the 22 institutions, 41 percent, either did not respond to the question or stated no one was involved in development of collection security policies. Only 4 of the respondents indicated that they had a written collection security policy. This is the same number as those who responded affirmatively to the 1983 survey.

One respondent did not answer the question concerning pursuing situations involving students, faculty, or staff differently from those involving nonaffiliated users. Of the 21 who did respond, 67 percent made no distinction. Of the 33 percent that did treat unaffiliated persons differently, university-affiliated persons were handled within the university and nonaffiliated persons were either banned from the library under criminal trespass warning or turned over to the city police.

In the majority of cases, 86 percent, the format of materials made no difference in the way the situation was handled. Of the two respondents that did pursue attempted theft or mutilation of materials differently based on format, one indicated the levying of heavy fines ($100), depending on amount and format (i.e., periodical, monograph, and so on). The second respondent provided no explanation of how the situation was handled. No further information was provided.

In response to the question concerning the number of prosecutions initiated for theft or mutilation of library materials, 16 respondents, 73 percent, stated that they had initiated none. One respondent indicated that it had initiated three to five prosecutions and that the outcomes were suspension or probation plus heavy fines. One respondent claimed to have initiated several prosecutions, all of which had been thrown out for various reasons. One respondent stated records of possible prosecutions were kept by the office of the dean of students. The rest of the institutions did not respond to the question.

Sixteen of the respondents, 73 percent, stated that they had never been sued or threatened by suit by a library patron. Only one respondent stated that it had been twice sued. One suit was for a charge of police brutality by campus police. After the judge heard all of the testimony from the witnesses, the university won the suit. The same institution also had a case pending in the courts based on a student's claim that his rights were violated when he was detained at the exit gate. Two additional respondents stated that they had not been sued but had been threatened by suit. One threat involved injury due to closing of the exit gate. The second involved a claim of false arrest.

In 1990 the survey was again replicated with the current membership of the Association of Urban Universities. Again, association composition had changed slightly, so response might reflect either real changes or changes in the membership. The 1990 survey had a response rate of 76 percent. Generally, emphasis on collection security seemed to have declined in the four-year period. Declines occurred in the use of electronic security systems (down 1 percent) and in the use of system monitors (down 19 percent). Declines were also seen in the ability of library personnel to detain and search suspects as well as in the use of municipal police and the court system. There were no prosecutions reported. To offset these declines, other changes occurred. For example, patrons were no longer treated differently based on the format of the materials. Further, a 5 percent increase occurred among the system monitors who were required to wear special clothing. Finally, the number of institutions taking punitive actions, which showed a 20 percent decline between 1983 and 1986, remained constant. There was, however, 27 percent increase if all types of punitive actions, including warnings, were considered. There was a slight increase in the number of institutions that had written collection security policies.

It appeared that there was a decline in activity that required a financial commitment from the institution (electronic systems, monitors, pursuit through the legal system) while there was an increase in activity that created the illusion of enhanced security (uniforms, more punitive actions). The two more serious issues remained largely unaddressed. These issues—the presence/absence of detailed collection security policies/procedures and the absence of a policy that specifically deals with the diverse clientele typical of an urban setting—were identified as critical issues in 1977. Thus, evidence from the 1990 survey supported the thesis that "unless libraries are willing to make a stronger commitment to preventing theft by first identifying the thief and then taking appropriate punitive action, loss of library materials will continue to be a serious threat to library collections" (Olsen and Ostler 1985, 67).

LEGAL ASPECTS OF A LIBRARY COLLECTION SECURITY SYSTEM

There are significant legal considerations that affect the day-to-day operation of any collection security program established by an academic library. It is important to be aware of the distinction between a public and a private institution. A private institution usually does not have to be concerned about violations of the constitutional rights of a particular individual. The courts generally have determined that a private institution and its students and employees do not come within the ambit of the Fourteenth Amendment. (See, e.g., *Greenya v. George Washington University*, 512 F.2d 556 [D.C. Cir 1975]; *Rendell-Baker v. Kohn*, 102 S.Ct. 2764 [1982].) The courts have used this amendment to apply the Bill of Rights protections to limit the actions of state and local governments. Thus, a private college or university can implement its collection security program with less fear of legal action. Private institutions, however, are not immune from possible litigation, because nonconstitutional legal remedies are available for certain types of wrongful actions.

A public institution, on the other hand, must be very circumspect in the way it conducts all of its activities. The courts have clearly stated that college students at public institutions do not forfeit their constitutional rights when they enter the institution (*Dixon v. Alabama State Board of Education*, 294 F.2d 150 [5th Cir. 1961]; *Goss v. Lopez*, 419 U.S. 565 [1975]). Thus, the activities of a library at a public institution are governed by the restrictions of the U.S. Constitution. That is, if a library employee conducted a search of an exiting library patron and if that search was in violation of the provisions of the Fourth Amendment to the Constitution, then a cause of action for damages could arise for this unconstitutional search under 42 U.S.C. 1983, which allows individuals redress against persons who deprive them of their civil rights while acting under color of state law. This would not only allow the individual to seek damages for any embarrassment or injury that might have been suffered as a part of that search but would also allow attorney's fees to be levied against the state employee. Accordingly, it is important to know what is a permissible search under the Fourth Amendment.

The Fourth Amendment states in general terms that no searches or seizures may occur unless there is a warrant and unless based on probable cause. The Supreme Court, however, has long established a number of exceptions to this requirement for a warrant, but the Court has consistently held that probable cause remains a prerequisite for any valid search. A search situation could arise when a patron of the library exited the library with a concealed book and set off an alarm system. If the library employee detained an individual as a result of the alarm, there is a question as to whether or not a search can be conducted to find and retrieve the materials. There is a paucity of case law on this specific situation; however, there are several analogous situations where courts have upheld searches, provided there was probable cause. Probably the best analogy may be the shoplifting situation, in which an alarm is set off by a detection device hidden in an article of clothing. The alarm system, if it is reliable and properly functioning, would furnish probable cause to conduct a limited search of an individual. In fact, some states have statutory provisions that state that the activation of an alarm device would constitute probable cause to detain a person to determine why the alarm was activated (See, e.g., Official Code of Georgia Annotated, Section 51–7–61; *Lindsey v. Sears, Roebuck, & Co.*, 389 So. 2f 902 [La. 1980]).

Another, similar situation would involve the use of narcotics-sniffing dogs to detect narcotics that might be hidden in suitcases or on someone's person. As long as the reliability of these dogs and their past successful performance could be demonstrated, there would be probable cause to conduct a search of an individual if the dog detected narcotics on the person or the person's property (*U.S. v. Place*, 462 U.S. 696 [1983]). Finally, a similar situation would exist with regard to airport searches. If an X-ray machine or metal detector reacted, then such reaction would constitute sufficient probable cause to justify a limited search of the person. If items such as drugs or weapons were found, such items could be seized, and the individual could be prosecuted (*U.S. v. Albardo*, 495 F.2d 799 [2d Cir. 1974]).

There are two other possible justifications for a search of a patron who activates an alarm upon exiting a library. First, one could argue that a patron has consented to the search. Courts are very rigid in their application of the rules regarding consenting to searches. Such consent must be voluntary and freely given (*Schneckloth v. Bustamonte*, 412 U.S. 218 [1973]). There is certainly some question as to whether or not persons who have been detained and asked to turn over their materials have truly consented to such a search. Thus, consent may be a weak justification for such a search. The second justification for a search could be the notion of "exigent circumstances." The law has developed so that a search without a warrant can be made under "exigent circumstances," that is, when evidence of a crime might be lost unless such a search took place. This situation is also a well-circumscribed exception to the search warrant requirement and would still require probable cause. In summary, an individual exiting the library who set off an alarm can probably be lawfully searched since you could argue that the alarm constituted probable cause and the exigent circumstances (risk of losing the material) necessitated the search without a warrant. The risk of loss would seem to be a fairly reliable way in which to justify such a search. Of course, any search of an individual would have to be reasonable. A strip search or a body cavity search would probably not be deemed reasonable by a court should it be contested.

As discussed above, an individual who is a victim of an illegal search could have a cause of action for a violation of constitutional rights if a search is improper. Furthermore, any evidence that might be seized by a university security officer or police as a result of this search might also be unavailable for use at a trial. Such a trial would, of course, be pursuant to the policy adopted by the library as to whether or not it wished to prosecute patrons who attempted to steal or mutilate its materials. If the library did have such a policy, then the exclusionary rule, which is a product of both the Fourth and Fifth amendments, could be used to prohibit the use of the stolen property and any discussion about the retrieval of such stolen property as evidence in any prosecution. Since the nature of the offense is the theft of that particular material, the application of the exclusionary rule would mean that it would be impossible to prosecute someone in this situation.

In addition to the constitutional proscriptions that have been discussed above, both private and public institutions have to worry about various common law and statutorily developed torts. If individuals are detained against their will without some justification, then they may have a cause of action for false imprisonment. Some states have recognized that there is a common law (recognized by most courts as a result of American and English legal tradition) right of a shopkeeper to detain an individual who is suspected of stealing from the shopkeeper. It would seem to be a reasonable analogy to claim that this sort of common law right should extend to a library worker if there is reasonable cause to believe that an individual was trying to steal materials belonging to the library; however, the length of time of the detention and the nature of the detention (e.g., handcuffing would certainly be inappropriate if the police had not arrived) could well have an impact on whether or not a false imprisonment action would be successful against a college or university employee who detained a library patron.

Some states also have statutory provisions that either directly or implicitly protect a library employee from liability when he or she stops a suspected thief. For example, the state of Virginia has a statutory provision that provides that a library employee will not have liability for false imprisonment, battery, slander, and a host of other causes of action if he or she detains a library patron when there is probable cause to believe that library materials are being concealed for purposes of removal from the library by that patron. The statute also provides that the activation of an electronic surveillance system would constitute probable cause to detain a patron, provided that there was notice posted in the library that an antitheft device was used (Code of Virginia, Section 42.1–73.1; compare this with O.C.G.A. Section 45–11–1, which protects a public officer or employee [who could be a library employee of a state institution] from civil liability for the detention of an individual provided there was probable cause to believe the person was committing an unlawful act. An unlawful act includes the willful removal of any book, document, record, or other property from any "public office," which would include a state library). It is important to be familiar with the difference in state laws in developing collection security plans.

If an institution brings criminal charges against a library patron who has stolen a book and is unsuccessful in bringing those charges, then the institution could be subject to a tort claim for false arrest. In almost every jurisdiction, such a claim requires at least two elements. First, the individual who is prosecuted must be successful in either having the case dismissed or getting a favorable verdict at a trial. A second essential element is that the arrest must have been without probable cause. Thus, if probable cause existed to search as described above, then it would probably also exist with regard to the arrest of an individual if library materials were found pursuant to a search.

CONCLUSIONS

Electronic security systems remain popular devices for stemming the theft and mutilation of library materials in the general collection. Written procedures for handling gate alarms not only provide handy reference for staff but may serve as legal protection for public and private libraries.

In adopting a collection security policy, there are legal concerns that should be considered other than the ones that have been mentioned. The policy and the procedures for the system should be written, and they should be consistent and equally applied. This need is important for several reasons. A written policy regarding the actions against students through the university disciplinary process may well become part of the contract of enrollment of that student. Accordingly, the institution should abide by such written policies and treat the student in a manner consistent with these policies. To do otherwise could well result in a claim of breach of contract by a student against the institution. Likewise, if an institution has a policy to prosecute certain individuals but not others, then there could be an equal protection claim filed against a state institution. The Fourteenth Amendment contains a due process and an equal protection clause. The equal protection clause basically requires that if a state institution treats groups of individuals differently from other groups of individuals, there must be either a rational basis for such treatment or some compelling state interest if a fundamental right or a protected class is involved. It is most likely that treating students differently from nonstudents would not be a protected classification. An institution, however, should be aware that an equal protection claim could be made, although the likelihood of success would be small. Urban academic libraries, by virtue of their locations, frequently serve nonaffiliated community patrons who have no campus borrowing privileges. The opportunities for gate alarms to represent real attempted thefts are many. Written policies and procedures are essential, but they must be developed to reflect the laws of the state in which the library is located.

APPENDIX A

Collection Security Survey

1. Do you have an electronic book theft detection system in use?
   YES _____ NO _____
   If yes, name the brand or briefly describe the system.

2. Do you employ individuals whose primary responsibilities are as door checkers or system monitors?
   YES _____ NO _____

3. If yes, what type of staff is used? (check all which apply)
   _____ Library part time
   At what pay level? (Give average hourly rate of pay.)_____
   What is the position title? _____

   _____
   To whom do they report? (Use position title.) _____
   _____ Library full time
   At what pay level? (Give approximate annual
   rate of pay.) _____
   What is the position title? _____

   _____
   To whom do they report? (Use position title.) _____
   _____ Campus security personnel
   At what pay level? (Give approximate annual rate of pay.)_____
   What is the position title? _____

   _____
   To whom do they report? (Use position title.) _____
   _____ Contracted other
   At what pay level? (Give approximate hourly
   rate of pay.) _____
   What is the position title? _____

   _____
   To whom do they report? (Use position title.) _____
   Briefly summarize the specifics of the contract. _____

4. Do these monitors wear special clothing?
   YES _____ NO _____
   If yes, please describe.

5. Which of the following levels of authority do the door monitors hold:
   Question?   YES _____   NO _____
   Detain?   YES _____   NO _____
   Search?   YES _____   NO _____
   Arrest?   YES _____   NO _____

6. Are punitive actions taken when uncharged library materials are detected on the person or in the unauthorized possession of someone exiting the library?

      YES _____ NO _____

If yes, please explain the type of actions taken.

7. Do any of these actions involve the:

Campus Police or Security?	YES _____	NO _____
Municipal Police?	YES _____	NO _____
Campus Judicial System?	YES _____	NO _____
Court System?	YES _____	NO _____
Dean of Students Office?	YES _____	NO _____

Other? Please identify. _____

_____

8. What university officials have been involved in the development of your collection security policies?

Please give titles of all positions.

9. Do you pursue situations involving university students, faculty or staff differently than those involving non-affiliated persons?

      YES _____ NO _____

If yes, describe.

10. Do you pursue the attempted theft or multilation of materials differently based on the format of the materials?

      YES _____ NO _____

If yes, explain.

11. Do you have a written collection security policy?

      YES _____ NO _____

If yes, we would appreciate your sharing a copy with us.

12. How many prosecutions have you initiated for theft or mutilation? _____

What were the outcomes?

13. Has your library been sued or threatened by suit by a library patron?

      YES _____ NO _____

If yes, please describe the bases of the suit or threat and the outcome.

NOTE

1. For further information on these systems, contact the following:

Checkpoint Systems, Inc.
550 Grove Road
P.O. Box 188
Thorofare, NJ 08086

Knogo
100 Tec Street
Hicksville, NY 11801

3M System
3M Center
St. Paul, MN 55144

REFERENCES

Bahr, Alice H. 1981. *Book theft and library security systems 1981–82*. White Plains, NY: Knowledge Industry.

———. 1989. Library security training: sources. *Library and Archival Security* 9:37–43.

Brand, Marvine. 1984. *Security for libraries*. Chicago: American Library Association.

Brawner, Lee B., and Nelson, Norman. 1984. Improving security and safety for libraries. *Public Library Quarterly* 5 (Spring):41–58.

Burns Security Institute. 1973. *National survey on library security*. Briarcliff Manor, NY: Burns Security Institute.

Cravey, Pamela J.; Robison, Carolyn L.; and Russell, Ralph E. 1984. The myth of collection security in urban university libraries. In *Proceedings of the ACRL Third National Conference*, Seattle, April 4–7. Chicago: Association of College and Research Libraries.

Edwards, John D. 1986. Book losses and mutilation in law school libraries. *Law Library Journal* 78 (Summer): 443–64.

Hendrick, Clyde, and Murfin, Marjorie E. 1974. Project library ripoff: A study of periodical mutilation in a university library. *College and Research Libraries* 35 (November):402–11.

Lincoln, Alan Jay. 1984. *Crime in the library*. New York: Bowker.

———. 1987. *Library crime and security: An international perspective*. Binghamton, NY: Haworth.

———. 1989. Vandalism: Causes, consequences and prevention. *Library and Archival Security* 9:37–61.

Mast, Sharon. 1983. Ripping off and ripping out: Book theft and mutilation from academic libraries. *Library and Archival Security* 5 (Winter):31–51.

Olsen, Randy J., and Ostler, Larry J. 1985. Get tough on theft: Electronic theft detection. *Library and Archival Security* 7:67–77.

Pedersen, Terri L. 1990. Theft and mutilation of library materials. *College and Research Libraries* 51 (March):120–28.

Pegg, M. A. 1981. Security systems in open-access libraries. *LIBER Bulletin* 16:49–54.

The protection of the library and archive: An international bibliography. 1983. *Library and Archival Security* 5 (Summer/Fall):1–183.

Rappaport, Philip. 1977. Installation of an electronic security system in a library. *Journal of the Hong Kong Library Association* 41:1–5.

Richards, James H., Jr. 1979. Missing inaction. *Journal of Academic Librarianship* 5:366–69.

Schindler, Pat. 1978. The use of security guards in libraries. *Library Security Newsletter* 2 (Summer):1–6.

Varner, Carroll. 1983. Journal mutilation in academic libraries. *Library and Archival Security* 5 (Winter):19–29.

Watstein, Sarah B. 1983. Book mutilation: An unwelcome by-product of electronic systems. *Library and Archival Security* 5 (Spring):11–33.

Weiss, Dana. 1981. Book theft and mutilation in a large urban university library. *College and Research Libraries* 5 (July):341–47.

17

Security and Safety of People in Urban Academic Libraries

Elizabeth Ader and Julie Pinnell

Urban academic libraries exist amidst all the elements that would lead one to hypothesize that they are high crime sites. Urban areas have higher rates of crime than rural areas (U.S. Department of Commerce 1989, 166), and there is growing concern on college campuses across the nation as the awareness of crime on campus increases (Greene 1989, A31-A32). Because libraries are public places that offer service until late at night and crimes happen most frequently at night (U.S. Department of Justice 1987, 7), they would seem a likely setting for criminal activity. When considering the subject of the safety and security of people in the urban university library, the authors wanted to know what safety and security problems urban academic libraries experienced and with what frequency. While crime in the urban academic library is what captured their imagination initially, there was also curiosity about what these libraries do in a more generic sense to assure the safety of their patrons and staff in terms of disaster planning.

METHODOLOGY

The authors decided to conduct a telephone survey of 20 urban university libraries. A pool of 25 libraries was selected, a number greater than the target to assure fulfilling that goal. Twenty-one of these contacts were successfully interviewed. The original pool of 25 libraries was chosen in a way to be representative of all geographic regions of the contiguous United States and to have a mix of public and private institutions. In addition, the criteria for selection included (1) location in a metropolitan statistical area with a population of at least 1 million and (2) collection size of 1 million or more volumes. These criteria, plus the institutions' willingness to participate, determined the final group of institutions.

The institutions interviewed included 8 institutions in the west, 4 in the northeast, 6 in the midwest and 3 in the south. There were 12 public institutions, 8 private, and one that was supported by both public and private institutions. All but 2 had collections of over 1 million volumes.

The libraries selected were first contacted by telephone to determine who in the organization was responsible for safety and security. This person was asked to participate in the survey. If the answer was affirmative, a telephone interview appointment was made. Participants were sent a copy of the interview questions to aid them in preparing for the interview. Those interviewed were from libraries at the institutions listed in Appendix A, and the questionnaire used appears in Appendix B. The responses presented here are not directly attributed to their source, because security is a sensitive issue and many of the respondents did not wish to be cited directly.

The telephone interviews lasted an average of 30 to 45 minutes. Information was collected on the main library and branches, but the information on branches was so inconsistent it will not be reported in this chapter.

LIBRARY HOURS

Academic libraries tend to be open well beyond normal business hours and are often accessible many more hours than other campus buildings. Monday through Thursday the libraries surveyed opened from 7 A.M. (earliest) to 9 A.M. (latest) and closed at 10 P.M. (earliest) to 2 A.M. (latest). On Fridays, the opening times remained between 7 A.M. and 9 A.M., but closing time varied from 5 P.M. (earliest) to 11 P.M. (latest). Saturday and Sunday hours varied greatly among the libraries: Saturday opening times ranged from 8 A.M. (earliest) to 10 A.M. (latest), and closing times from 5 P.M. (earliest) to midnight (latest); Sunday opening times were from 9 A.M. (earliest) to 1 P.M. (latest), and closing times from 5 P.M. (earliest) to 2 A.M. (latest). Only one library reported being available 24 hours a day.

STAFFING PATTERNS

Staffing patterns in the libraries before 5 P.M. and after 5 P.M. were compared. As might be expected, there was a substantial drop in the number of staff in the libraries after 5 P.M. Not all of the libraries reporting distinguished between staff in public services areas and staff in the technical services areas. For those libraries open until midnight or later the number of staff in the library varied from 5 to 50. Of the libraries surveyed, 3 did not give numbers of staff, and 2 gave total numbers but did not break down staff into the categories of professional, support, or student. One reported that staffing was flexible according to the demand. The number of professional staff on duty after 5 P.M. ranged from a high of 4 to a low of 1. Thirteen of the remaining 17 libraries had 1 to 2 professional staff on duty. The remaining 4 had 3 to 4 professionals on duty. The number of support staff on duty after 5 P.M. ranged from a high of 12 to a low of 1. Of the 16 libraries reporting support staff on duty after 5 p.m., 7 libraries had from 4 to 6 support staff on duty, 5 had from 10 to 12, and 5 had from 1 to 3. Student staff ranged from a high of 35 to a low of zero. Of the 16 reporting, 1 library reported the total figure for student staff but did not report the number working after 5 P.M., and 1 respondent did not know. Ten libraries reported having between 10 and zero students on duty after 5 P.M., 3 reported having from 11 to 25, and 1 reported having from 26 to 35.

STACK AREAS

All libraries reported that their main stack areas were open. If the library reported any closed areas, they were among the following: special collections, government documents, reserves, current periodicals, microforms, archives, and fine arts materials. None of the libraries reported having closed stacks for the security and safety of those using the library.

Sixteen of the 21 libraries surveyed had only 1 public entrance to the library. Five had 2 entrances. Twelve of the 21 reported having guards at the entrances; 9 reported that no guards were posted. Of the 12, 11 had guards all hours the library was open, and 1 had a guard for 40 hours of the total hours the library was open. Two of these 9 have security gates that are located close to the circulation desk, and 1 library reported having a student assistant available to assist if the security alarm was tripped.

The function of the guards varied. Their duties included checking patrons' parcels and materials at the time of exit, giving information, screening patrons' belongings for food and drink, responding to detection/security devices, and restricting entrance to the library. Four of the libraries surveyed reported restricting access to the library by actually checking identification cards. One library reported having signs on the doors advising those entering that use of the facility was restricted to those with university business; however, this restriction was not enforced by any other action. Another library reported that patrons entering the library were asked if they were affiliated with the university, but the patrons were not asked to produce any proof of affiliation.

Six libraries reported having full-time security personnel in the library or patrolling the library. In one instance, student police cadets patrolled the library hourly on their rounds. Another reported having security personnel on duty from 3:30 P.M. until one-half hour after closing time. These personnel were supervised by campus police. A third had security personnel on duty during evening hours for 37.5 hours out of a total of 100 hours the library was open. Another reported having a security guard 40 hours a week from 4:30 P.M. to 12:30 A.M. Tuesday through Saturday. Only two libraries reported having security in the building all hours the library was open. In one of these instances, there were a security supervisor, three support personnel, and two to three students. In the other instance, campus security had an Office of Public Safety in the library. This campus had two levels of security: the campus police, who carried firearms, and public safety personnel, who did not.

In those instances where security personnel did patrol the library building regularly, the following areas were included: rest rooms, study rooms, stack areas, and the reserve room if it was a separate room. Two libraries reported regular patrols in the parking area, and two others reported that these areas had their own attendants.

One library reported that campus police came into the library, but not on a regular basis; however, they did respond very quickly when needed, that is, in two minutes or less. Another library reported having patrols in the library during exam week only. The remaining libraries reported part-time security or no security personnel in the library. In the latter situation, security was provided by campus police on an as-needed basis.

CRIME LEVEL IN THE SURROUNDING AREA

Only two of the respondents rated the crime level in the area surrounding their library to be higher than average for the city. Of these, one said that it was higher than average for thefts and drugs only, but lower than average for violent crime. Both respondents that characterized the surrounding area as having a higher than average crime level had local statistics to support this claim. Eight of those interviewed rated the area as average in crime level, and seven rated their area as lower than average. Two respondents could not say how the campus crime rate compared to the local area. Fifteen of these responses could be directly supported with campus or local statistics. The levels of above average, average, and below average were consistently defined in terms of the respondent's home city.

Interestingly, of the three institutions reporting higher than average crime levels, none restricted access to their libraries. Only one had a security guard, and in this case the guard was only a three-quarter-time staff person.

SAFETY OF PATRONS AND STAFF

When respondents were asked if they perceived a problem regarding the safety of patrons or staff in the library, 18 of the 21 replied no. One of these qualified that answer to say there was no problem before 9 P.M., but from 9 P.M. to midnight the respondent perceived there was a threat due to a lack of staff present in the building.

Of those who did perceive a safety problem, one said that there was a problem sometimes and it usually consisted of theft of personal property and "peepers or suspicious lurkers." The other two simply said that they believed there were threats to the safety of people in their libraries but did not specify the nature of the threat.

One of the latter had local statistics that placed the area surrounding the library at an above average crime level and had had an assault in the library within the past year. The other library had placed the area surrounding the library in the average to below average crime level and had not had any violent incidents in the library that year, although there had been two notable violent crimes in previous years.

Four of those interviewed indicated that they did not perceive a problem with the safety and security of people in their library but noted that staff and/or patrons did. One of these said that he probably was not as sensitive to the staff's concern because he was an administrator and worked only during the day, whereas many of the staff worked at night. The influence of this factor on the survey results is unclear. In each case the person contacted was in charge of overseeing the safety and security in the library, and all were administrative staff or faculty. Two of the respondents said that staff were afraid to close at night, and another mentioned that staff had fears that the library cash box located in their office would attract robbers. One mentioned that there was pressure on campus to extend library hours, but staff were afraid to work any later than they already did.

One of those interviewed noted that although staff and patrons were concerned, he felt their fears were out of proportion with reality because, although surrounded by a high crime area, the campus was secure. The safety office on this campus published a pamphlet citing statistics that showed campus crime to be at a lower level than the suburbs, which are popularly considered safe.

CRIMES OCCURRING IN THE LIBRARY

Those contacted were also asked if they had experienced any situations in the library in the past year that endangered patrons or staff. Twelve of the respondents noted crimes of opportunity as a problem (stolen books and purses and, in one case, a computer), and five mentioned acts of perversion (voyeurs, exhibitionists). Most felt these types of incidents were disturbing rather than threatening. One respondent referred to these incidents as "routine." Another noted that 75 percent of reported thefts happened after 6 P.M.

Two libraries reported single incidents of assaults on patrons, and another listed two separate occurrences of patrons verbally threatening staff. One library representative said it had not had any incidents but in an aside said that the library had received a bomb threat for which the building was cleared. The interviewee did not consider this threat to be a valid "incident" because it happened during finals week, a time of extreme stress, and because no bomb was found. A scuffle occurred at another library when a staff person opening the library tried to prevent an armed intruder who had spent the night in the library from fleeing.

One library had not had any threatening incidents in five years. Another said it had experienced only what it would define as "routine" incidents but nothing threatening for the last five years.

Five institutions mentioned the presence of vagrants or street people in their libraries. Only two linked this group with criminal or problem behavior (assault in one and theft and exhibitionism in the other). In two libraries street people were cited as being frightening to the staff. One of these reported that staff members were afraid to check closely at closing time for fear of confrontations with the vagrants.

Four of the libraries noted problems with sexual activity in men's restrooms. The methods for dealing with this problem varied. In one case the men's restroom on a floor that was not staffed in the evening was locked at 7 P.M. In another library a men's room was locked, with no plans for reopening. On another campus where this problem is perceived as campuswide, undercover security agents staked out the men's restrooms on campus, including the library's.

The results appear to be consistent in that most respondents reported average to lower than average crime levels. Only five reported incidents that threatened the physical safety of people within the last year, and the overwhelming majority stated that they did not perceive a problem with security in their library.

ESCORT SERVICES

Campus escort services that provide some measure of safety for faculty, students, or staff when leaving the library were provided in a majority of cases. Seventeen of the 21 libraries surveyed reported some sort of escort service. In addition, 1 library reported that a service had been discussed and a short trial run had been completed. The librarian reporting did not know how successful the experiment had been or if a full-fledged service would be offered sometime in the future. In some cases, the service was not well organized and operated sporadically. Two campuses reported that the student government tried to provide such a service, but because of lack of funding it could not be depended upon. In several instances, it was reported that campus security would escort staff or patrons to their cars if called upon to do so. One campus reported having a transportation service to take staff or students to their cars on campus; however, this service was very shorthanded and lacked enough cars to provide adequate service. Of the campuses reporting escort services, most were provided by campus student personnel. One campus provided both a night shuttle service that could respond in about 10 minutes and parking safety officers who escorted students and staff to their cars in the library parking lot. On another campus these services were provided by students who worked for the Department of Public Safety as community service officers. One campus had a tram service that operated to points both on and off campus, this service had a regular stop at the library. One campus reported that its student personnel are screened and trained by the campus human resources department. In another instance, campus security employed students to escort staff and students on campus to their cars, those requesting the service walked to their cars while the students rode nearby on scooters. Some services were offered by different groups at different times on the same campus. For example, before 11 P.M. students provided the escort service, and after 11 P.M. it was provided by campus security officers. Relative to escort services, several respondents noted that library staff frequently left the library together at closing time.

SAFETY EQUIPMENT

In response to the inquiry about safety equipment none of the libraries surveyed had metal detectors. In this instance, metal detector was intended to be understood as the type of device used in airports to detect weapons. Eight respondents listed 3M, Checkpoint, and NoGo book security systems under this category, but since these are used for property protection rather than for the safety and security of people, these responses were disregarded.

Two of the libraries had security camera systems, 10 had public address systems, all had fire extinguishers, 19 had first aid kits, 11 had emergency telephones, and 17 had special safety lighting. All but 4 of the reporting institutions indicated that they had paid special attention to lighting. Two libraries had backup generators for lighting, and 1 had a battery backup available for when the electricity failed. In addition, the following were used in some libraries: flashlights that plugged into the wall, portable radios for weather emergencies, and walkie-talkies. Two libraries reported having motion detection systems.

SAFETY AND DISASTER PROCEDURES

The inquiry about written disaster procedures resulted in the following affirmative answers: 17 of the 21 had procedures for fire, 12 had them for severe weather, 6 for earthquakes, 14 for floods, and 12 for tornado or hurricane conditions. One mentioned procedures for volcano eruptions. When asked whether they had written procedures to guide staff in handling violent behavior of patrons or staff members, 14 reported having written procedures and 1 other respondent said that the institution was working on a set of written instructions that had not been completed. Two of those queried replied that they did not have written emergency procedures. Four others said they gave only verbal instructions, which directed the staff member to call the police immediately. Twenty of those surveyed believed that their safety and security policies and procedures were consistent with local law. One of those interviewed was not sure.

Only seven of those questioned had regular cycles of review of their safety and security policies for effectiveness. These cycles ranged from weekly to every

10 years. One of these had its policies reviewed by the state attorney general. Seven characterized review of their policies as irregular or periodic. These responses ranged from reviews conducted whenever incidents occurred to reviews every few years. Five of those interviewed regularly reviewed their safety and security policies for consistency with local law.

Sixteen of the institutions made some provision for training their staff in security and emergency procedures. Four institutions offered workshops conducted by campus police. Three relied on supervisors to include this information when training staff. One library coordinated this training with its campus Office of Health and Safety. Other methods of training were annual fire and safety instruction and fire drills, workshops, meetings, staff newspaper articles, written procedures, and calls to campus police when problems arose. One of the five that did not provide training for staff was developing a training program.

CONCLUSION

The authors were interested in two major areas: the safety of people in the event of emergencies and disaster situations and the security of people in the event of threats to personal safety related to criminal acts.

Because safety of people is jeopardized in the event of fire, severe weather, and so on, the authors questioned the participants regarding planning and procedures for these events. The majority of respondents had written procedures and provided training for staff in these areas.

Threats to safety related to criminal acts were the other area of interest. A recent survey reported in the *Chronicle of Higher Education* discussed crime statistics from 368 academic institutions. The findings revealed "that colleges and universities mirrored their surrounding communities [*sic*]. Although criminal incidents occur less frequently on college campuses than in the surrounding community, the types of crime perpetuated are similar" (Greene 1989, A32). The institutions surveyed for this chapter were chosen on the basis of their location in urban areas. Statistically, these areas have higher rates of crime. The authors hypothesized that the security and safety of people in urban academic libraries would reflect the high crime statistics of the surrounding areas.

With the survey of these libraries revealed was different from what was expected. Eighteen of 21 institutions surveyed reported that patrons and staff were perceived to be safe while in their libraries. In the current atmosphere of increased awareness and concern regarding campus crime, it was interesting to discover that the majority of libraries surveyed were unequivocal about the safety of staff and patrons in their libraries. These libraries were remarkably free of incidents of crime that they would have considered a threat. Due to the small number of libraries surveyed and the unexpected results related to crime and personal safety, the authors see a need for a larger survey to explore this issue further.

APPENDIX A

Institutions Included in the Survey

Arizona State University—Tempe, Arizona
Auraria—Denver, Colorado
Boston University—Boston, Massachusetts
Columbia University—New York, New York
Georgia State University—Atlanta, Georgia
San Francisco State University—San Francisco, California
Tulane University of Louisiana—New Orleans, Louisiana
University of Arizona—Tucson, Arizona
University of Cincinnati—Cincinnati, Ohio
University of Denver—Denver, Colorado
University of Houston-Central—Houston, Texas
University of Illinois-Chicago—Chicago, Illinois
University of Miami—Coral Gables, Florida
University of Minnesota—Minneapolis, Minnesota
University of Missouri-Kansas City—Kansas City, Missouri
University of Pennsylvania—Philadelphia, Pennsylvania
University of Pittsburgh—Pittsburgh, Pennsylvania
University of Southern California—Los Angeles, California
University of Washington—Seattle, Washington
Washington University—St. Louis, Missouri
Wayne State University—Detroit, Michigan

APPENDIX B

Questionnaire: Security and Safety of People in the Urban University/College Library

University/Library:

Name/Title of person being interviewed:

Name/Title of Interviewer:

Date/Time of interview:

What are the library hours?
  Main branch
  Other branches

Do they vary with the academic year? If so, how and when do they vary?
  Main branch
  Other branches

How many staff in the following categories are on duty during daytime hours:

Main branch
  Professional
  Support
  Student

Other branches
  Professional
  Support
  Student

How many staff in the following categories are on duty during the hours after 5:00 P.M.:

Main branch
  Professional
  Support
  Student

Other branches
  Professional
  Support
  Student

How many levels or floors does your library have?
Branches?

Are the stacks in your library open to the patrons or closed? Branches?

If some are open, some closed, please designate and explain.

Which floors and functions are staffed? Please give hours, number of staff, and category of staff (professional, support and/or student):

	Main Branch	Other Branches
Circulation		
Reference		
Periodicals		
Reserves		
Interlibrary Loan		
Copy Services		
Other		

How many entrances and exits are there in your library? Branches?

Where are they located in your library? Branches?

Are guards posted at the entrances?   Exits?   Both?

If so, how many hours a day? Branches?

What category of staff (professional, support, student)? Employed by the library?

Provided by some other campus unit such as Campus Security?

What is the function of the guards?

Is access to your library restricted? Branches? If so, by what means?

What would you say is the crime level in the area surrounding your library:

	Main Branch	Other Branches
Higher than average		
Average		
Lower than average		

Are there campus or local statistics to support this statement?

Do you perceive that there is a problem regarding the safety of patrons or staff in your library? Branches?

In the past year did any situations occur in the library or the library area which endangered patrons or staff? Branches?

Are there full-time security personnel in the library? If so, are they:

	Main Branch	Other Branches
Library personnel (title/position)		
campus security		
local or city police		

Do the security personnel patrol the building regularly throughout the hours the library is open? Branches?

Do the security personnel include the following in their pattern:

	Main Branch	Other Branches
rest rooms		
study rooms		
all stack areas		
reserve room (if separate)		
parking lot		

Is security provided on an as-needed basis? If so, is it provided by:

	Main Branch	Other Branches
library personnel (title/position)		
campus security		
city or local police		

Are escort services provided? Branches? If so, are they provided by:

library personnel: student or non-student

campus personnel: student or non-student

non-campus personnel: (please give title of position)

What security equipment is used in the library, in areas surrounding the library, or in the parking areas:

	Main Branch	Other Branches
metal detectors		
security cameras		
public address system		
fire extinguisher		
first aid		
emergency phones		
lighting		
other		

Do you have written emergency procedures for any of the following:

	Main Branch	Other Branches
fire		
weather		
earthquake		
flood		
tornado		
violent behavior (patron and/or staff member)		

Are your safety and security policies and procedures consistent with local law?

How often are your safety and security policies and procedures reviewed for:

effectiveness

consistency with local law

Do you have any provision for training staff in security and emergency procedures? Branches? If so, describe briefly.

Would you be willing to share your policies and procedures with us?

REFERENCES

Greene, Elizabeth. 1989. Many college officials are found to be ignorant of crime on their campuses. *Chronicle of Higher Education* 35, no. 20:A31-A32.

U.S. Department of Commerce, Bureau of the Census. 1989. *Statistical abstract of the United States*, 109th ed. Washington, DC: Government Printing Office.

U.S. Department of Justice, Office of Bureau of Justice Statistics. 1987. *Criminal victimization in the United States 1987*. Washington, DC: Government Printing Office.

18

Preservation and Environmental Control Issues in the Urban/Metropolitan Academic Library

James E. Gwin

Environmental control is the single most important aspect of preservation in libraries. Most academic libraries collect information in a variety of formats (books, microforms, nonprint materials, manuscripts, and so on), each with a different physical composition. All of these are organic materials and deteriorate. The rate at which they deteriorate depends on the chemical and physical stability of the composite materials and the environment in which they are stored. The importance of the storage environment for these materials can scarcely be overestimated.

The atmosphere, especially in our industrialized urban areas, contains a host of pollutants. In Chicago, the "windy city," for instance, dirt carrying the contaminants of urban air settles on library materials, abrades the surface, provides nutrients for mold growth, and promotes acid deterioration of paper (Morrow 1983, 9–10).

These pollutants are widespread because the United States has become almost completely urbanized. The problem of the permanence of library materials is made more serious since the largest collections of libraries tend to be concentrated in urban areas where they serve the greatest concentrations of people.

Four important environmental factors that relate to the atmosphere and contribute to the deterioration of books and materials will be discussed in this chapter: temperature, humidity, air pollution, and light. Each is related to the other, and when conditions in the library are poor, they can work together to cause serious damage. When they are controlled, the slow decay of materials can be greatly retarded.

HUMIDITY AND TEMPERATURE

The humidity and temperature in a library facility need to be considered together, working to either preserve or destroy library materials. A temperature of 65° F plus or minus 5° F or even colder is recommended for book storage spaces. The relative position of open stacks and reading rooms in libraries makes it difficult to maintain an ideal stacks temperature (Association of Research Libraries 1982, 40–42). For most library materials lower temperatures are better but uncomfortable for humans and may not be energy-efficient.

The speed of chemical reaction depends in large part on temperature; on the average the speed doubles with each 18° F rise (conversely halving with each 18° F drop) in temperature. The actual rate varies considerably in different kinds of materials undergoing different reactions. Typically, for library materials, the rate deterioration resulting from degradation reactions may double, or even triple, with every 18° F increase, with most paper deteriorating at a higher rate.

Humidity control is generally shown as relative humidity (RH), which indicates the amount of moisture in the air at a given temperature at a particular instant. A reading of 45 percent with a plus of 5 percent is recommended in the ARL manual (Association of Research Libraries 1982, 40–42). Raising the temperature will lower the RH, while lowering the temperature will raise the RH. Mold is likely to grow at 60–65 percent RH or higher.

The library climate needs to be kept as close to constant as possible. Systems controlling humidity are as important as those controlling temperature. It is also important that changes in temperature and relative humidity be held to less than plus/minus 5° and plus/minus 6 percent RH, respectively (Association of Research Libraries 1982, 40–42).

It is highly desirable that libraries have an environmental control system to regulate both temperature and humidity. Air-conditioning systems usually control only the temperature. The free movement and regular replacement of air can reduce pockets of high relative humidities and decrease the likelihood of mold. Good air movement is very important where environmental control systems are lacking or inadequate. If air ducts are cleaned regularly or their filters changed often, dust or soot buildup will be avoided (Metcalf 1986, 573–74).

AIR POLLUTION

In addition to changes in temperatures and humidity, library collections are vulnerable to the hazards of air pollution and smog. The atmosphere contains a host of various pollutants, especially in industrialized urban areas.

Most pollutants occur in very small concentrations in comparison with the normal atmospheric constituents, yet some occur in high enough concentrations to have adverse effects on library materials. Regarding the dimensions of air pollution, the emissions of the principal pollutants into the atmosphere in the United States have been estimated by the National Research Council of the National Academy of Sciences to be between 125 to 300 million tons per year ("Pollution" 1969, 47).

Pollutants representing the greatest known hazard to library materials are, for the most part, either acidic or oxidizing. Notable deleterious substances to library materials are sulfur dioxide (SO_2), the oxides of nitrogen, and ozone. These substances play roles in a rather complicated system of photochemical air pollution that is seriously damaging to man, animals, vegetation, and materials.

Sulfur dioxide, or at least SO_2-containing pollutants from coal burning, has been recognized since the thirteenth century as a damaging pollutant in the atmosphere. But photochemical air pollution is a fairly recently recognized phenomenon, first noticed about 35 years ago because of its effect in causing the cracking of rubber products and damage to plant species. Therefore it is not surprising that it does considerable damage to library materials.

Sulfur dioxide is readily absorbed on surfaces; fortunately, the concentration indoors is only one-half of what it is outdoors. In urban areas, however, that one-half is still a significant concentration. Sulfur dioxide quickly combines with more oxygen to form sulfur trioxide (SO_3), which combines with omnipresent moisture in the air to form sulfuric acid (H_2SO_4). Sulfuric acid is a strong, corrosive chemical that degrades surfaces. The most obvious effect in libraries is leather deterioration—a powdery, weakened condition termed "red hot" (Morrow 1983, 15).

Sulfur dioxide is also a danger to cellulose materials (cloth and paper). The oxidation of sulfur dioxide to sulfuric acid is aided by impurities in the materials, such as traces of iron, alum sizing, and residual lignin. The impurities act as catalysts to form a chemical reaction. The most familiar effect in libraries is brown, brittle edges of books caused by sulfur dioxide's penetrating the pages and reacting with the impurities to form sulfuric acid.

In addition to the acidic effects of sulfur dioxide present in urban areas, photochemical oxidants such as ozone are strong deteriorative agents. The ozone gaseous layer in the atmosphere helps to filter out harmful radiation from the sun. But ozone also acts as a powerful destroyer of organic materials by breaking the double bonds on carbon chains. The ozone problem, which was first identified in the giant urban center of Los Angeles, has spread to all urban areas. This is a particular problem in the area of the country known as the Sunbelt (Morrow 1983, 15).

Dust or particulate matter is perhaps a more superficial problem than the oxidizing and reducing gases. Still, all dust has sharp edges and, together with perspiration and skin oils, will cause disfiguring damage to all types of library materials over time. Maintenance costs for dusting shelves and books can be reduced with proper filtration of the air.

Some form of air filtration system should be considered in most libraries for both preservation and maintenance. Although there is a considerable variety of types of filters available, the most common include fabric, cyclone, electrostatic, alkaline water sprays, and activated carbon. Electrostatic filtering is not recommended because electrostatic precipitators or filters add the pollutant ozone to the air as they filter particulate matter. For instance, the Library of Congress does not permit the use of oil or viscous impingement filters because of the by-product production of polluting aerosols. Except for "scrubbers," or the washing of air, dry filters are recommended. In specifying a level of filtering efficiency, it should be noted that the more complete the filtering process, the higher the cost because it requires larger fan systems to pull the air through the filters and thus consumes more energy. The more efficient filter will require more frequent servicing or replacement, as the particulate matter will accumulate more rapidly. The Library of Congress recommends a minimum filtration efficiency of 95 percent for air filtration systems (Metcalf 1986, 118–19).

A water wash where the pH is kept at 8.5 to 9.0 is recommended for reducing gases such as sulphur dioxide. Special technical advice needs to be sought when installing a system that will handle gases because of the technical problems relating to corrosion and scaling in the system. Both the Library of Congress and the Folger Library have such systems in place.

Activated carbon is recommended for the removal of oxidants. It should be noted that the cost of installing systems that are capable of handling the removal of dust, ozone, nitrogen oxides, and sulfur dioxide is fairly high. There are examples of such comprehensive systems in Hartford, Connecticut, at Yale University's Beinecke Library and at the Winterthur Museum and Library in Delaware (Metcalf 1986, 119).

LIGHTING

All light degrades or fades library materials, especially the high-energy, short wavelengths of light in the ultraviolet (UV) and blue end of the light spectrum.

Sunlight is the greatest source of UV radiation. Light from the sky (blue light) is higher in UV than light from the sun (yellow light). Reflected daylight is lower in UV than direct daylight since no surface, except perhaps snow, reflects UV. UV is most intense when it comes straight downward from a light source. Direct sunlight and skylights should be avoided since they permit so much UV radiation.

Incandescent lamps or fluorescent lamps emit little or no UV. There is a difference in UV output between cool white and warm white fluorescent lamps. Warm whites have less UV, and the difference is significant. Even warm white fluorescent lamps need to be filtered. The best lamps are those that emit no measurable UV at all, but these are much more expensive than standard tubes.

These lamps are color-balanced so that they represent colors accurately. UV is so destructive that, especially for valuable collections in rare book rooms and display cases, the added costs may be justified.

The perceived brightness of light is, in part, a psychological function of the color of the light. Warm and cool white fluorescent lamps give off the same measured brightness. Warm whites are perceived as dimmer because of their warmer color. To feel comfortable, people often want bright light to be cool in color, and they want dim lights to be warm. One way to handle the problem of perceived brightness would be to use filtered cool whites in reading rooms and work areas and filtered warm whites in stack and storage areas (Southeastern Library Network 1985, 5).

Light level sources should provide 30–50 footcandles (300–500 lux) with a maximum of 75 microwatts lumen (measure of UV radiation) (Association of Research Libraries 1982, 42).

It is important to exclude UV radiation of 400 millimicrons and lower through the use of filters or other means. At higher wavelengths, intensities should be maintained at the minimum level required for visual discrimination (Research Libraries Group 1983, 60).

The filtering out of UV radiation is not a complicated procedure. Curtains or blinds can be used for windows that allow direct sunlight to reach library materials. UV filter sleeves and sheets are available to fit over fluorescent tubes and window surfaces. Automatic light turn-off switches can be installed in stack areas. The central library at the University of South Carolina in Columbia installed a lighting control system that switches off some 28,000 lights when they are not needed (*Library Journal* 1984, 619). A similar system was installed in the Boatwright Library at the University of Richmond in 1988 and provided substantial energy savings and improved preservation for library materials.

MONITORING DEVICES AND SYSTEMS

It is usually not possible for the average library to acquire a large and expensive system of instrumentation that will monitor all aspects of the environment. The Canadian Conservation Institute (Lafontaine 1978, 15–17) suggests that libraries desiring to monitor their own environments purchase relatively inexpensive pieces of equipment (environment recording kits) to check relative humidity, temperature, and light.

A device used to record the humidity and temperature of a room is a hygro-thermograph. It is commonly used in book stack areas to monitor heating, ventilation, and air-conditioning systems for periods of a week to 30 days.

Devices that measure light intensity levels include photometers, luxmeters, and footcandle meters. Any device purchased should be able to measure light levels as low as 25 to 50 lux with a reasonable degree of accuracy (10 percent or better) and should be able to measure either in lux or in footcandles (one foot candle equals 10.76 lux).

Laboratory analysis of air samples from various locations inside an urban library will give accurate data on the degree and amount of pollution penetrating the building. This information is desirable, but the cost can be very expensive. A simple, inexpensive alternative is to place sulphur dioxide test strips in selected areas throughout the library. These, by a change in color, will indicate the presence of sulphur dioxide and, by the degree of change of color, give an approximate indication of the relative amount of penetration into the various areas.

A source list of companies that provide equipment and services to libraries for environmental control activities is included in Appendix A. It was compiled from comprehensive conservation/preservation supply lists developed over several years by the Southeastern Library Network's (SOLINET) preservation program.

SUMMARY

The basic idea in preventive conservation for libraries is to create an environment in which the enemies of library materials cannot exist. This chapter has presented some evidence of the environmental factors that directly affect the deterioration of library materials, as well as some generally accepted recommendations for storage conditions for most library materials that can help to retard deterioration. If certain steps are taken, such as using the inexpensive instruments suggested for recording conditions, it is possible to implement a local action program to prevent damage resulting from humidity that is too high or low, from extreme temperatures, from intense light, and from air that contains a high degree of pollutants.

The National Information Standards Organization (NISO) is currently developing a comprehensive national standard for environmental control for library and archives collections. This standard, combined with strategies for demonstrating the loss accrued through inadequate environments, will help provide librarians the information they need to argue for improved environmental controls.

APPENDIX A

Source List of Library Preservation and Environmental Control Equipment and Supplies

Abbeon Cal, Inc.
123 Gray Avenue
Santa Barbara, CA 93101
805-966-0810
 Equipment

Absorene Manufacturing Co.
1609 North 14th Street
St. Louis, MO 63106
314-231-6355
 Surface cleaning materials

Applied Science Laboratory
2216 Hull Street
Richmond, VA 23224
804-231-9386
 Barrow paper test kit

Beckman Instruments
2500 Harbor Blvd., North
Fullerton, CA 92635
714-871-4848
 Environmental monitoring equipment

Bendix Corporation
National Environment Instruments Div.
P.O. Box 520, Pilgrim Station
Warwick, RI 02888
 Gas detector kits

The Dickson Company
930 South Westwood Drive
Addison, IL 60101
800-323-2448, 312-543-3747
 Environmental monitoring equipment

Environmental Tectonics Corp.
County Line Industrial Park
Southhampton, PA 18966
800-523-6079, 215-355-9100
 Environmental monitoring equipment

Fisher Scientific Company
711 Forbes Avenue
Pittsburgh, PA 15219
412-562-8300
 Environmental monitoring equipment

Science Associates
Qualimetric, Inc.
P. O. Box 239
Princeton, NJ 08542
609-924-4470, 800-247-7234
 Environmental monitoring equipment

Solomat Corporation
Glenbrook Industrial Park
652 Glenbrook Road
Stamford, CT 06906
800-932-4500
 Environmental monitoring equipment

TCA-Taylor
Consumer Products Division
Sybron Corporation
95 Glenn Bridge Road
Arden, NC 28704
704-684-5178, 800-438-6045

Thomas Scientific
P. O. Box 99
99 High Hill Road
Swedesboro, NJ 08085
215-988-0533, 800-345-2100
 Environmental monitoring equipment,
 laboratory supplies

VL Service Lighting
200 Franklin Square
Somerset, NJ 08873
201-563-3800
 Low-UV fluorescent tubes

Source: SOLINET Preservation Program

REFERENCES

Association of Research Libraries. 1982. *Preservation planning manual.* Washington, DC: Association of Research Libraries.
Lafontaine, R. H. 1978. *Recommended environmental monitors for museums, archives and art galleries.* Ottawa, Canada: Canadian Conservation Institute.
Library Journal. 1984. 109 (April):619.

Metcalf, Keyes D. 1986. *Planning academic and research library buildings*, 2d ed. by
    Philip D. Leighton and David C. Weber. Chicago: American Library Association.
Morrow, Carolyn Clark. 1983. *The preservation challenge: A guide to conserving library
    materials*. White Plains, NY: Knowledge Industry.
Pollution: Causes, costs, controls. 1969. *Chemical Engineering News* 47 (June 9):33–
    68.
Research Libraries Group. 1983. *RLG preservation manual*. Stanford, CA: Research
    Libraries Group.
Southeastern Library Network. 1985. Environmental specifications for the storage of
    library and archival materials. *SOLINET preservation program leaflet* 1: 3–5.

PART VI

Managerial Perspectives

19

Personnel Management in the Urban Academic Library

James R. Coffey

What is unique to the urban academic library, in managing human resources, is its work force: confrontational, often articulate, sometimes facile in its approach to complex problems, and demanding of the knowledge and abilities of the manager. It is seldom boring. In this chapter consideration is given to three areas of personnel management—hiring, training, and personal dynamics—which in the urban library can require special recognition and responses. Hiring will receive the greatest attention because it demands the most strenuous effort of the manager and allows only a small amount of time for making a long-term decision.

BASICS

The most basic principle for a manager is to want to build a unique team that takes pride in its work and wants to be the best. To accomplish this goal requires self-discipline as well as vision, but the vision is not so hard to actualize if some of the following elements of discipline are given careful attention:

1. Know the accepted framework of operation; know what is binding on the employee and owing to the employee.
2. Build effective working relationships. Keep people in mind first and foremost—not objects, not statistics, and not work flow goals.

3. Keep morale high by cultivating productive work relationships and terminating mismatched ones.

4. Communicate with the departmental staff, the administration, and the user. Bring all three together whenever possible.

5. Include people in deliberations, either in formal meetings or off-the-cuff. This procedure makes people aware of the fact that they are needed.

6. Share information about changes or long-range plans. This procedure conveys a sense of trust and respect and makes people feel that this library is going somewhere.

7. Hire and train people slowly and carefully; this procedure communicates a respect for who we are and what we do.

8. Be open to a fair and candid dialogue with the union representative or the staff association. This procedure conveys a sense of working cooperatively.

Can all of these procedures be followed by the average library manager? Yes, but not overnight and often with fear and trembling. Library managers are developed, not necessarily born. With perseverance, the experience becomes increasingly more positive—and there is nothing like success in personnel administration to make one feel self-confident and in charge.

At the end of this chapter, there is an outline of bases to cover for someone who is new to managing a department or who is not new but feeling not fully in control (Appendix A). I have used it as a checklist over the years, and I offer it to the reader as something that might be useful. It is worth the time and effort to go over such a checklist and to develop a plan for staff development and for the direction the department should take. Once past this planning and preparation process, the daily work of management is not so overwhelming as it seems. It becomes easy to switch priorities or reschedule work because the plan enables the manager to keep goals and means in mind when making short-term decisions.

The approach in this chapter is practical and "how to." It assumes a problem-solving mind-set and a sensitivity to people. It assumes a recognition that library management is going to demand that a person be ready for stress and for change and also ready for the thrill of positive interaction with different personalities. There is a certain exciting dynamic to supervision, especially if habits of productive confrontation are developed and cultivated.

THE HIRING PROCESS

If the hiring process is done carefully and thoroughly and given all the time it requires, then there is a 95 percent chance that the rest of the working relationship is going to be satisfactory. It takes effort, it takes the ability to listen attentively, and it takes more than one person to do it right. While some factors in the process present problems more likely to be encountered in the urban library, it is important to keep in mind that good people are out there. The recruitment effort should keep going until the right match of employee to library is found.

In hiring, the major elements are reviewing applications or résumés and interviewing. It is important to be painstaking in this effort.

Reviewing Résumés and Applications

People present a picture of themselves in the résumé. By looking carefully at what they say and what they have done, you can decide whether you want to interview them, whether they may be literate and mature, and whether they give evidence of being able to make good judgments. Libraries need reasonably literate employees who can make sensible connections between the purposes the library serves and how the employees can contribute to those purposes. Employers should be looking for evidence of these basic requirements in the applications submitted. In the urban library situation, the administrator reviewing job applications is likely to encounter a broad spectrum of abilities and work habits. Some of the striking, regularly recurring negative factors are tendency to change jobs frequently (sometimes at progressively lower salaries), failure to answer what was asked on the application form, poor spelling, insufficient schooling, not understanding the questions, gaps in schooling or employment history, poor or inconsistent reasons for wanting a job at a library, and the inability to express oneself in writing. These factors are important signals to a library employer. To work in a library, the applicant should be reasonably well educated through the secondary level and should be able to react like an adult in an environment with other adults. Deficiencies in these areas are sometimes apparent from the résumé or application, and the administrator ought to think about them when considering people for an interview; let us review some of these factors.

1. The drifter who goes frequently from job to job may be someone who gets bored easily, who cannot get along with people, or who is terminated because of inability to do the work. The tendency to change jobs frequently should raise doubts. Will the person leave the library soon if hired? If so, then a great deal of time and money will have been wasted in hiring and training.

2. Failure to answer what was asked on the application. This failure raises questions such as, Did the person understand what was read? Did the person not want to take the time to give it serious consideration? If the applicant did not understand the questions on a simple application form, would he or she have problems later reading procedures or written directions? The application should present the potential interviewee as serious and able to do the job—not as someone who might not be able to function independently.

3. Poor spelling, insufficient schooling, the inability to express oneself in writing. Libraries often depend on the literal accuracy of information. The library worker has to be able to make clear, discriminating judgments from both written and verbal communication and to realize that, especially with automation, there is only one way: the right way. If the applicant does not spell correctly or cannot express himself or herself well, then the potential employer has to consider the implications for data entry to an

automated system, for alphabetizing, or for being able to respond competently to needs expressed by the user.

4. Gaps in schooling or employment. The person reviewing the application should look carefully for work or school history not accounted for. If all other areas are satisfactory, then the applicant should be asked to give an account of any gaps during the interview. Gaps may indicate a tendency to drop out periodically; they may indicate an inability to stay with a job; they may suggest a history of personal problems that could potentially entail putting the library staff at risk. They also may raise questions as to how steady and productive the individual may be. Some people, on the other hand, have good reasons for the gaps but do not feel at ease explaining them on an impersonal application form. Some opportunity for bringing these reasons out in the open should be provided in order to be fair to the applicant and to respect a person's need for privacy.

5. Poor or inconsistent reasons for wanting to work in a library. People do not usually know how to answer the question of why they want a job. Often, not knowing what an academic library does, they find it hard to use the right buzz words to light up the librarian. People say that they have always liked books or that they think it would be an interesting job, but seldom do they go beyond this explanation. In the end, saying, "I need a job, I think I'm qualified, and I'll work hard and deal fairly with you," in short, being honest, will probably count for more in giving the interviewer insight on whom to consider seriously. If, in the interview, the applicant listens thoughtfully to what libraries do and what is expected and if that interview gives both parties the chance to evaluate objectively a potential working relationship, then that experience will be more helpful than hearing contrived reasons. At other times, a person might say that she did not like her earlier job as a welder and thought she would switch and get a different view of life. Changing careers may be a good decision, but switching to a library is not necessarily the logical change. The main problem to avoid in this respect is employing the person who is in transition and wants a place to get a paycheck while looking for another job or another direction.

6. The "don't care" attitude. Some people, on their résumés or in an interview, exhibit a "don't care" attitude. They do not express a great deal of curiosity, they show little evidence of having accomplished anything, they do not seem to have a vision of the future, and they do not seem to connect their day-to-day existence with any purpose in life. How such people engage in dialogue with interviewers reveals much about what they might do in the work situation. Someone whose life experience shows that they care and have been cared about is likely to relate to work with enthusiasm. Someone who waits for someone else to do things, who is passive, who does not have plans to be self-reliant is not likely to take the initiative. He or she will expect some support and coddling at work. Having been expected to be or to do nothing in the past, these people will expect to have few demands made on them in the future. They usually do not work until someone lights a fire under them. This kind of employee will not take the initiative in starting work. If hired, he or she will require the supervisor to make all the decisions necessary to get a job done. The supervisor has to consider whether the time and mental energies to deal with this situation are available and whether it is in the library's interest to direct managerial energy this way.

Interviewing

Interviewing can take place once the applications are screened for potentially suitable candidates. It is important to listen to the applicant and to encourage him or her to talk about qualifications. It is also important to acquaint the person with the supervisor so both can try to judge how well they can work together. Having a clear idea of what one wants from the person doing the job gives one the ability to evaluate the interview accurately.

Cultural Diversity

The labor force is changing. Census predictions indicate that the people coming into the work force will bring with them a wider variety of backgrounds than was formerly the case. We should be ready for this opportunity and open to its possibilities. Therefore, one of the factors to work into an overall policy view on hiring will be diversity. People who are culturally different will be facing each other more and more in the interview process. To smooth the transition, the interviewer has to be open to taking advantage of the talent presented. Both the interviewer and the interviewee will bring to the hiring process cultural attitudes and assumptions that have to be accounted for and respected. Recognizing these phenomena as different, not as right or wrong, can help the interviewer to keep the process professional and objective.

The interview serves the purpose of admitting to the work group those people who will serve best the aims of the institution while fitting in harmoniously with an already existing, productive staff. If the staff is not already productive, then one way to change that situation is to hire new people carefully. The aim is to hire more good people to be on this unique team. In order to do this, the one involved in hiring will deal objectively with cultural diversity and recognize what factors can acceptably be different and what factors necessarily have to be common to the group.

Employee Pool

Urban libraries tend to attract a geographically local group of employees who often do not share the interests of the administrative staff. They tend to have completed their educational experience with high school and to be from lower- to middle-income brackets. Sometimes the people employed are faculty spouses. In addition, many urban libraries may scare off potential employees from outlying areas because of their locations in neighborhoods viewed as unsafe. Local people often have a better grasp of the extent to which this view is or is not true. Therefore, they may know more about how and when to be cautious; they may also not see themselves as having many choices in the first place.

Along with the economic differences there may be a difference in educational and social outlook that can cause administrative staff to fail to appreciate the abilities of potentially good employees. In addition, to relate intimately to the personal encounter would be a big mistake in the interview because the personal reactions of the interviewer or interviewee do not bear as importantly on the process as much as do the questions: Will this person fit in with the team and can he or she do (to a high degree of accuracy) what we need done? The salty-tongued mail deliverer can strike up a good working relationship with the library director. The question does not need to asked whether they could meet comfortably at a social register garden party. But such encounters may, in the interview, threaten either or both parties and prevent the benefits of hiring someone from outweighing the perceived disadvantages. The interviewer has to face difference in a positive light, not just because it is the polite thing to do. It has to be recognized that the work force is not homogeneous, that diversity, especially in the urban setting, is here to stay, and that good people, whatever their experience of life, are the ones for whom we are looking. It is also helpful to recognize that diverse outlooks contribute productively to the overall organization.

Preconceptions

Another situation to be faced is what the newcomer knows about libraries, about this library in particular, and about the functioning of the particular department for which he or she is being considered. Many people entering the library work force take the opportunity to reflect on these questions only if and when asked by the interviewer. Ignorance of libraries is probably excusable—at least, it seems to be almost universal—but what is important is that this lack of understanding of a library often leads people to the conclusion that it is a soft, quiet, contemplative haven away from the realities of life. In contrast, the urban academic library is busy, often pressured, and possibly, the larger it is, the host to at least one representative of every conceivable social misfortune; so people who cannot deal calmly with the real world will have a hard time adjusting to library work. Such people range from those who are "shocked by what is going on," to those who are "going on," to those who think that a library job is what they need to help them to handle their psychological stress. People who are better able to take in stride the realities of life and whose attitudes are balanced can be more useful to the library; nevertheless, they often come to the interview with a view of libraries as something less than businesslike. The interviewer has to get people talking about what they think a library is and help to bring their notion, if different, around to a clearer picture of what is the real case.

Once the purposes and functioning of the library have been communicated clearly, the interviewee should be given a picture of where this particular library stands with respect to its goals. It is not necessary for the interviewer to hide real problems in regard to productivity or interpersonal conflicts, but it is important to make distinctions between the goals to be aimed for by the new person as opposed to "what's going on now." Otherwise, the new employee is not prepared for what is coming, and the transition may be made more difficult. It is not to be expected that the applicant "has always wanted to work in a library."

Applicants often think a librarian is anyone who works in a library, and they do not necessarily come to the interview with a commitment to information services. Many people recognize that working in a library involves checking out books and trying to help people. They are often intrigued in an interview by the explanation of how a library works and what it does, but they are not necessarily converted immediately to its mission. They need not be. They do need to be willing to work productively to support those goals and to realize that they will be compensated for their work.

Harmonizing Goals

The applicant generally has pretty predictable, reasonable goals to pursue: a salary, benefits, a job that fits in conveniently with family responsibilities, tuition benefits for their dependents, or a job that can be left at quitting time and not taken home. It is unrealistic for the interviewer to expect the applicant to bring a much more encompassing perspective to the interview. No applicant should be hired, however, if the person does not show that he or she intends to harmonize personal goals with those of the library and of the particular department. The job is to be offered for the doing, not as a convenience to the employee. If you cannot feel sure that the person will give as well as get, then you are bringing frustration on yourself and costly personnel problems on the library. The aims of the applicant and the aims of the employer can be different without harm to the library; however, they should be reconciled if there is to be a harmonious work relationship.

The assumption that an applicant's stated aim would lead him or her to be a supportive, productive employee is not a safe one. People can give an interviewer the feeling that they will work out well because they are going to library school (or want to) and therefore will work hard and show dedication. Not so! An interviewer may decide that, because an applicant suddenly needs an income to support the family, he or she will do everything possible to do a good job and maintain job security. While people often have good reasons for working well, they often fail to connect these reasons to their actual effort in the workplace. An interviewer must probe carefully to detect this kind of discrepancy, which often does not surface until the person is hired and has gone through the probationary period. Some library employees see no contradiction between putting forth their best efforts during the probationary period and coasting forever after, once their jobs are seen to be secure. If there are such differences in the perspectives between the administrator and the employee, then the interviewer should take great pains to have them come out in the interview dialogue.

Expectations

Having dealt with the interviewee's need for a clear explanation of what the library is about, how it functions, and what it needs, the interviewer next needs to be able to state clearly and unequivocally what is expected of the applicant. Each point or desired behavior needs to be gone over in sufficient detail to enable the interviewee to judge whether he or she is up to handling the requirements. The applicant needs to justify why the requirements can be met. The interviewer in turn has to be able to make this same judgment independently of assurances on the part of the applicant. It is essential to get clearly to the point and not to place on the applicant the burden of "getting the message." When the employer wants the applicant to be dedicated to the mission of the institution, to be ladylike in deportment, to be a few minutes early for work each day, or to ask for a change in schedule no more than once a year, then this expectation must be stated clearly in the interview; otherwise, one cannot complain about it afterward. An applicant has no way of knowing the atmosphere of the place, the tone to be set, and the expectations if they are not made clear at the beginning. It is understandable that a new employee could be offended for being censured for wearing inappropriate clothing or taking a casual attitude about promptness if not given notice ahead of time. The work rules should be discussed in the interview; the reality of diversity makes it imperative that the interview process head off misunderstandings before they arise. Nothing that could become an issue should be assumed or left to the discretion of the applicant.

Work Ethic

Not everybody shares the reverence for activity that characterizes the traditional work ethic. As long as the work gets done accurately and in sufficient quantity, the motivational philosophy does not need to be that of the manager. In some cultures work is not viewed as self-affirming or as something that gets rewarded. Such ideas are contrary to the life experience of some people, and expecting them to doubt the evidence of their own experience is asking them to take big leaps—certainly bigger than we would be willing to take ourselves. If the individual, regardless of cultural attitude, can give reasonable assurances that he or she can grasp fully the requirements of the job and also put forth the expected productive effort, then the fact that his or her feelings about work are different may not matter. The interviewer needs to make the determination that the employee and supervisor can function harmoniously and productively—not always to think alike. The emphasis should be on respecting the difference, not on feeling threatened by it. The interview process will screen out too many productive people with vitally different and important perspectives if interviewers look only for people like themselves who share their values. But one should not be fooled into thinking that people who show no evidence of being able to work reliably should be hired anyway and given a chance. Conversely, sometimes interviewers revel in difference for its own sake and hire only because the applicant is different and not with any regard to ability, aptitude, or attitude of wanting to contribute.

Sexism

Facile assumptions about the contributions of men and women are damaging in the workplace. Giving a man what he wants and not taking seriously an idea that comes from a woman are common attitudes among library staff. These attitudes are often accepted unconsciously at face value. If a woman constantly receives the message that her contribution need not be taken seriously, she learns to assume that she need not have a sense of responsibility about her work. A man, on the other hand, who is misled into believing that we go by his decisions because, being a man, he knows best what to do is likely to make shortsighted decisions that often lead to nothing but waste. There often goes along with this belief a reluctance or failure even to recognize his own ineptitude. The basic danger to the functioning of the library is that some contributions will have excessive support and others will not get the attention they deserve. This attitude can be very unproductive. The hiring administrator should try to detect the extent to which potential employees are open to constructive contributions from anyone and the extent to which they are closed to the ideas and leadership of others.

When hiring for library positions, the interviewer needs to be on the lookout for attitudes that give an idea of whether the interviewee respects the thoughts, opinions, and feelings of others (one does not need to share them, just to respect them) and whether he or she recognizes the value of perspectives that take the total picture into account.

The Intellectual Candidate

The larger academic libraries often have available to them candidates who are highly literate and well educated and who are usually graduates of their own institutions. Since library jobs often require a high degree of literacy and education, these candidates can be a temptation to the interviewer and the supervisor. It is possible with these candidates to make assumptions about their suitability based purely on the excellence of their educational opportunities. An interviewer has to give these candidates the same rigorous review as any other applicant and is well advised to make sure the process is thorough. While it is helpful and productive to have such people on the library staff, they can present problems. There is often a noticeable disparity in education and upbringing between these employees and other staff not so well educated. The difference often becomes an obstacle to good workplace relationships and ultimately to productivity.

The Innovator and the Adaptor

Every library can use people who have the instincts of the innovator or of the adaptor. Libraries often do not have enough innovators: risk takers, people who look for novel approaches or who keep up with the latest trends. When such people do get hired, they are often viewed as interfering nuisances, especially if they are support staff. The trick for the interviewer is to make distinctions between the candidate who is able to contribute the innovator's outlook and the chronic malcontent who finds fault but cannot come up with anything better. Of course, if this innovative talent is expected of the candidate, the interviewer has to make it clear that the applicant is expected to use it and to be sure there is scope for it in the library. The innovator needs the scope and the satisfaction of having his or her contribution utilized and not frustrated. An innovative mentality is not necessarily a product of a good education. The innovator's ideas are sometimes ignored because the originator does not have the education that someone in management thinks is requisite.

The adaptor has the ability to invest novel ideas with reality. This kind of person will consider the idea, find out if and how it can be implemented, and take the time to harness the idea to a routine so that its benefits can accrue to the library. The adaptor gives structure to ideas and tends to enjoy seeing the ideas put into practice. The interviewer has to watch out to hire an adaptor and not just someone who will adapt uncritically to the system. The real adaptor is open to new ideas; the acceptor is threatened by them.

TRAINING

In the training part of the process, the new employee has the opportunity to experience firsthand the extent to which the manager takes seriously the work to be done. Careful teaching and careful attention to the way the new employee learns convey the attitude of respect for what gets done in the job.

Explaining the Library's Operations

In the interview, the newcomer to the staff may have been given a picture of what the library is there for and how it goes about achieving its goals. In the course of training, the purpose and goals of the library need to be reiterated and absorbed by the new employee to get the new person acclimated to the job so that it is performed in line with those goals. The new person has to "take on the philosophy" and become an agent for effecting those purposes. New workers in the urban academic library are often out of tune with the role of information in society and what the library is supposed to do with it. If the new worker is to play his or her role effectively, then a clear understanding of why we are doing something has to be conveyed—and especially the part the particular department plays. Technical services puts the book on the shelf; public services helps the user to get it off the shelf. The why and the what have to be clear to any worker, but, in the urban library, unfamiliarity with libraries is common to newcomers. The person doing the training, then, has to make clear the functioning of the various departments and be sure the employee has assimilated it.

Training someone to do the job requires care and attention in any library, so the urban library is not unique in that respect. It is especially important, however, to convey to the new urban library employee that the work is taken seriously and that we intend to do it right and to offer the best service to our user group. At the same time it is equally important to be sensitive to the need for making the new employee feel welcome and to indicate respect and enthusiasm for his or her ability to be part of a team. If one feels sure of a new employee's ability and willingness, it is easy to relax and let him or her perform and gain a sense of ease and confidence. It is important for the manager to recognize that some people do not feel familiar with or at ease in a library at first. For some it represents a totally new environment, and it invites unfavorable comparisons with other environments in which they are more relaxed. Some people need time to make the cultural transition and should be left alone to come along more gradually and get used to working here. Other people need to have more assurances about their welcome.

Stress

The new library employee may not be prepared for the extent to which the workplace can be stressful. Shrinking resources often put on the library a greater demand for productivity; therefore maximum productivity is a top priority goal for the library manager. New employees are unlikely to be expecting stress, so how to deal with periods of peak activity should be discussed. Too often people become threatened or discouraged by the enormity of a task during busy times. The goal of getting the work done and done right remains, but the emphasis should be on the feelings of the employee. Some new employees in the urban library feel or project a judgmental attitude on the part of their employers or coworkers, and this perception adds to their anxiety. Most of the time employees adjust by surviving one or two cycles of activity, but securing the valuable contribution of a good employee requires attention to the personal factor, especially by helping him or her get a healthy perspective on dealing with demanding situations.

Monitoring Performance

New employees in the urban library should not be put on their own too quickly. The supervisor, by way of conveying the importance of high-quality and accurate work, should have all the work submitted for review. Any inaccuracies should be pointed out and explained. It is important that the errors be understood by the employee, with special reference to the impact on the work of others and, most important, on the service the library offers.

Positive feedback and encouragement are extremely important at this stage. If possible, they help to get people talking about how they feel they are doing and what concerns they have. A special effort should be made to find out if the new person is at ease and feels welcome.

The foregoing ideas are intended to convey an attitude of respect for what gets done in a library and a consequent desire to contribute one's best effort to that end. However casual a library environment may be—and it can be comfortably casual at times—the importance of feeling that we put out a good product is paramount, and this is conveyed not only verbally but by example. If the supervisor is equivocal or ambivalent, the new employee is going to pick up that attitude and take the same attitude toward the work. The employee in the urban environment is often accustomed to direct, confrontational communication and generally deals easily with it. Clear, consistent communication works best in the urban setting. This can be handled with dignity and grace, but it takes a little getting used to. By the same token, direct and unequivocal responses should not be misinterpreted as challenges to one's authority so much as the expression of a need for clarification. A healthy exchange of ideas, sometimes an animated exchange, is not uncommon in the urban library. The supervisor has to recognize the difference between heightened feelings and negative feelings. The former are productive as long as there are real communication, respect for one another's point of view, and a desire for the process that will make best use of people's talents and lead to the most effective product.

PERSONAL DYNAMICS

Once the urban employee is established in the job and performing competently, the business of maintaining a pleasant, effective working relationship goes on. However demanding the efforts expended in hiring and training may be, this area is the one in which the real art of personnel management is practiced.

Confrontational Skills

In my personal experience, the urban library employee is confrontational. He or she communicates attitudes, emotions, and ideas directly. This communication may not always be verbal, but when the need to be heard is felt, the supervisor is left in no doubt about it. In many cases it will be the job of the supervisor to recognize this need, provide the outlet for it, and encourage its expression. This job requires real skill and determination but it rarely fails to clear the air and make for a better working relationship. It can also accomplish the sorting out of feelings from facts and the redirection of energies toward productivity. The new supervisor is going to be either transformed or defeated by this skill because the context within which it is learned can be personally threatening. Many people in authority avoid confrontation because they cannot sort out all the factors in the interpersonal dynamic and do not feel on solid ground when they discuss problems with employees. It can be made more difficult for the new supervisor when the situation is one in which the employee expects the manager to know everything about the job, including the details of how things are done in one's own particular library.

Resolving Conflict

In the first place, all dynamic relationships require confrontation and problem solving for growth. One does this work in developing intimate relationships; one has to do it in developing workplace relationships, even though the emotional commitment may be lacking. What complicates the development of working relationships is first, that supervisors do not always recognize that the emotional commitment need not be there for an effective working relationship and second, that they view the problem-solving process in a right/wrong, I'm OK you're not OK context. In any problem, all individuals can be right and wrong, OK and not OK without anyone's losing face or authority. Above all, talk! Get to the bottom of the problem no matter how long it takes to talk about it.

Egalitarianism/Authority

The urban employee respects authoritative direction and expects it as a minimum from a supervisor or a manager. He or she, however, is not generally intimidated by it or submissive to it. If the directive "makes sense," the employee will follow it; if not, he or she speaks out, expecting an equal hearing and respect from the supervisor. The urban employee is sensitive to messages of perceived superiority/inferiority and demands equal recognition. Getting respect does not mean they will not follow directions, but feelings of not being accepted personally on an equal footing can be severely detrimental to productivity and often lead to irretrievably adversarial situations.

Problem Solving

However well expended the effort in hiring and training, there will be the downside of spending time with anyone for 40 hours a week. Problems develop with even the best of employees, and a conference between employee and supervisor will be called for. In such cases, in urban situations, two principles apply: (1) a word to the wise is usually not sufficient; the problem as the supervisor sees it has to be stated directly and unequivocally and (2) the supervisor should be prepared to see where he or she is at fault and be willing to change what needs to be changed.

Most people do not like to hear of, or be reminded about, what they do wrong, but most people are reasonable about dealing with it if they are not pushed too fast and if they have time to consider both sides of the story. It is not necessary to resolve everything in one meeting; it is best to schedule another one so that calmer feelings can be brought to bear on the problem. A supervisor should not become disturbed by an initially anxious or hostile reaction; people are usually not prepared for what they hear in such a conference.

Staff Unions

Dealing with the union strikes terror into many academic librarians to whom contractual confrontations conjure up visions of emotional scenes and personal stress. In fact, while we are occasionally treated to the excitement of such scenes, most contractual confrontations are quiet growth experiences for both the manager and the employee. The union contract can serve the purpose of giving a librarian the discipline of a well-defined modus vivendi for managing labor relations. It can also catch up short those people who erroneously believe that unionization or having a contract has the sole purpose of justifying every gratification of which they imagine themselves in need. Some employees violate terms of the contract because they do not know that they are terms of the contract or because they think having a contract entitles them to arrive late, take extended breaks, slow down in work, and so on. Most of the time, however, people are in the office to do a job and to do it reasonably well.

If a contract has been signed, then both contracting parties are obligated to live up to the terms of the agreement. It is useful to bring out that point anytime there is a casual discussion in the office about labor relations and to say that if people want changes made, they should get in touch with their executive committee. In implementing the library's part of the agreement, it helps the librarian to have a supportive administration. Read the contract, and if there are any terms you have agreed to, live up to them; do not gripe about what is in the agreement; renegotiate at the next set of talks.

The history of academic library unions shows that they tend to weaken over a period of time. If the administration and the unionized staff have kept up a spirit of respect and cooperation, employees feel that they achieve their aims in other ways and do not rely as much on unionized support. History also suggests that managerial incompetence can revive the union quickly. There is a real advantage to having a union contract to regulate labor relations. For one thing, it makes clear the responsibilities of all concerned. For another, it prevents the ego from obscuring the issues. Having negotiated a contract with the library staff, management should do what it can to make it work. Feelings or frustrations should not be allowed to interfere with progress in establishing working relationships. Egos can wreck the chances for progress, but it should be kept in mind that emotional or ego gratification is not so important as a functioning working relationship for productivity. The union person or librarian you are mad at today is going to be the person you need to cooperate with tomorrow, so do not make any unnecessary enemies. Rarely is the adversarial attitude a personal one.

Develop communication skills. Find a way to let people know informally what you are thinking so that when you address issues formally people know what is on your mind. They can deal more easily with the known and work out a reasonable response. If they have an inkling ahead of time, they can either adjust to realities or work out negotiable alternatives.

Handling Problems

When dealing with the urban academic employee in a disciplinary situation, the best advice is to come to the point. Use whatever style you are comfortable with, but get to the point and do so without making the person feel attacked personally. Do not be personally judgmental; focus on the problem, be ready to listen, and outline the timetable for change. Do not expect immediate progress and get back to the discussion at reasonable intervals. If you are in a situation and an issue or question comes up that you are not familiar with or do not feel qualified to answer, say so; do not pretend you know; say you will check and get back to them. Do not make any moves you are not sure of. People respect you for admitting what you are not sure of; they do not trust people who make up answers as they go along. It looks as if they are not sincere and as if they care more about saving face than being fair to their employees.

If the idea of personnel management in the urban academic library was to be summed up in one word, the word would be "involvement." Urban employees seem to stress the need for more interaction between employee and employer. To be successful, the manager has to make sure the barriers are down and the doors are open. Ivory tower management just does not work.

CONCLUSION

There are many common elements in library supervision or management with regard to the type of library or the geographical location. Among these are teamwork, scope for working creatively, trust of one's ability, and good communication. The urban academic library tends to be unique in terms of its work force: personal and confrontational. It demands an interactive style of the manager. It demands the ability to listen and to talk back. It takes thoughtful attention to find the right people to work there, and it takes active dialogue to develop and channel productive energies. Putting together a first-rate team out of very diverse cultural backgrounds is going to be both a fact of life for the future and a challenge to look forward to.

APPENDIX A

CHECKLIST FOR THE NEW MANAGER

Becoming Familiar

1. Go around the library and meet the people who work there.
2. Understand the organization chart.
3. Establish the habit of communication with the support staff.
4. Understand departmental responsibilities and the work flow.
5. Know the technology in use and what you want from it.
6. Look over procedures and arrange to have them written if they are not yet in written form.

Labor-Management Relations

1. Read the contract.
2. Know the salary and benefits package.
3. Know the work rules.

Staff Development

1. Become acquainted with the strengths of each staff person.
2. Have a plan for staff growth/job development.
3. Have a plan for future changes in job description.

Hiring

1. Assess the needs: review the job description, state the requirements, make any changes necessary, think through expectations.
2. Be aware of the affirmative action plan and how it is to be implemented.
3. Advertise position.
4. Review applications.

Interviewing

1. Have a list of questions ready.
2. Have another person with you in the interview.
3. Encourage the interviewee to talk.
4. Concentrate on getting to know the person.
5. Settle only for the best candidate; readvertise if necessary.

Training

1. Have a goal for each training session.
2. Have a time frame.
3. Understand how the individual learns best.
4. Give the person a chance to operate alone.
5. Meet constantly; check work; provide feedback.
6. Give the person a written procedure to work with.

Personal Interactions

1. Take time to talk to everyone each day if possible.
2. Confront problems tactfully and at an appropriate time.
3. Share information; ask advice.
4. Be available.

REFERENCES

Half, Robert. 1985. *Robert Half on hiring*. New York: Crown.
Kusack, James M. 1986. *Unions for academic library support staff*. New York: Greenwood Press.
Levin-Epstein, Michael D. 1987. *Primer of equal employment opportunity*, 4th ed. Washington, DC: Bureau of National Affairs.
Pounian, Charles. 1989. Trends in human resource management. In *Trends in urban library management*, ed. Mohammed M. Aman and Donald J. Sager, asst. ed. Kathleen Reed. Metuchen, NJ: Scarecrow Press.
Young, Richard A. 1969. *Recruiting and hiring minority employees*. New York: American Management Association.

20

Acculturation of the International Student Employee in Urban University Libraries

Harriett M. Pastor and Lia S. Hemphill

The international student population in the United States has been increasing steadily since the 1970s. "In academic year 1988/89 the number of foreign students studying at accredited U.S. colleges and universities was 366,354" (Institute of International Education 1989, 1). This represents an increase of 2.9 percent over the year before. These students represent every country in the world. According to *Open Doors* (Institute of International Education 1989), the majority of students study in the following urban areas: Boston, New York, Miami, Austin, Los Angeles, Philadelphia, and Phoenix. The large urban centers have attracted the greater majority of these students because the areas are more likely to have other foreign students, relatives, ethnic restaurants, social clubs, and a general cultural diversity. The cost of living in these areas is presently estimated to be $750 per month, excluding tuition, books, travel, or dependents.

The number of international students, especially in the urban academic university, will continue to increase and be a major factor in higher education, and therefore the urban university library will be affected by this large international student population. This chapter will address the acculturation/acclimation process of this important student population and show how the library at the urban university is in a unique position to aid these students in the acculturation process. The terms *international* and *foreign* will be used interchangeably, as will *acculturation* and *acclimation*.

Foreign students are a special user group who bring to the urban academic library unique problems, expectations, and behaviors, as well as a richness of culture and tradition. "Historically . . . libraries and librarians have not been directly involved in the cultural and educational adjustment process of the foreign student" (MacDonald and Sarkodie-Mensah 1988, 425). In a recent reading of the literature, however, it was found that librarians are indeed addressing the needs of the international student, as well as the need for sensitivity training for the library staff.

International students share common characteristics relating to communication, language competency, listening skills, body language, learning styles, expectations of the library, cultural habits, and insecurity about their academic success. At the same time problems arise for the library staff in dealing with international students and their unique needs and cultural differences. "Effective communication between library staff and international students is essential not only to the students' success in the academic environment but in furthering the good will of the library staff in their interaction with foreign students" (Greenfield, Johnston, and Williams 1986, 227).

Many university libraries have created staff development programs to assist the library staff in communicating with the foreign students. "Librarians must learn to be more sensitive to communication problems and contrasting learning styles" (Wayman 1984, 339). Other libraries in conjunction with their ESL (English as a Second Language) programs have developed bibliographic instruction and library orientation programs for foreign students. Yet many university libraries have neither adequate staffing nor funding to develop significant programs relating to the interaction between the foreign student and the academic library.

The acculturation process can be a stressful period for many international students as they come in contact with the host society. To many of these students, the academic library is as foreign as their surroundings. Many of the students come from countries that do not have research libraries, and if they do, the material is either locked up or too old to be of any use to them. Self-sufficiency in primary research, alphabetizing, interlibrary loan service, the use of government documents, and reference service and instruction from librarians—to name a few library skills and services—are often mysteries to the foreign student.

Some foreign students have difficulty in asking questions of the librarians, and if they do ask, they often have neither the listening skills nor language competency to interact successfully. Yet international students repeatedly cite library research skills as essential to their academic success. The attitudes about the library and librarians are of the utmost importance to the overall success of the foreign student in the academic library.

Many foreign students enter the United States on an F1 visa, which allows the foreign student to study full-time at an American university and then return home. Unless students are financially secure before arriving, they will need employment to supplement their income as they struggle to meet living expenses in the urban area. The F1 visa allows the student to work 20 hours a week for the university, and in exceptional cases the student may be allowed to work 20 hours off campus. The library often is an attractive place of employment for many international students.

It has been observed that the acculturation process and academic success of foreign students have been greatly aided by their employment in the library. In a search of the literature much information on sensitivity training for library staff dealing with the international student was found, as well as bibliographic instruction and orientation for the foreign student. Literature on how the acculturation process of the international student is positively affected by being employed in a university library was, however, not available.

Questionnaires were used with two separate population groups, librarians and international students. An informal telephone poll consisting of a series of questions was conducted of librarians who work in university libraries in the United States with large concentrations of international students. This group of librarians was actively supervising international students. At the same time a written survey was done of foreign students who, as students, had worked or were presently working in academic libraries. The purpose of the survey of students was to compare personal experiences of the acculturation process with foreign students who had library work experience. The students were asked whether working in the library helped or hindered their assimilation into American culture. The lack of control groups and the statistical inexperience of the authors necessarily limited these surveys. Therefore it was decided that the purpose would be to gather impressions.

According to the surveys, libraries hire students in the reference, acquisition, ILL, circulation, serials, security, and government documents departments. Of the librarians surveyed, all but one said their library employed foreign students. Most libraries placed the students in the circulation department, but all library departments had employed foreign students at one time or another. As the international student became knowledgeable about the operation of the urban academic library, the student felt comfortable bringing in friends and other foreign students for research assistance. For the foreign student whose language skills are adequate and research skills non-existent, the library becomes a learning center.

Since the majority of students were supervised by females, the survey queried if any particular culture had trouble accepting female supervision. The conclusion was that in the rare incidents it did occur, it was primarily observed in students from Southwest Asia. All students answering the survey stated that they benefited from the close interaction between themselves and the librarian as supervisor. The working relationship between librarian and foreign student helps in the acculturation process. Colleagues who were polled noted that foreign students are good workers, dependable, eager, and learn the job quickly.

Most universities require foreign students to pass the TOEFL (Teaching of English as a Foreign Language) exam before being accepted into an accredited program of study. The test is designed to determine the international students' comprehension of English. The survey asked how the library supervisors judged language competencies. All those surveyed used the oral interview as their criterion.

Most of the students had never worked in a library before, and all felt that their academic careers benefited by their working at the university library. The students developed a good working relationship with the library staff and felt that the staff helped them in acclimating to the United States. A few libraries had in-house sensitivity training programs for the staff, and it was felt that university libraries with a population of international students could benefit from adding training programs for staff. Most libraries, either alone or in conjunction with the ESL program, offered library tours and orientations for this special user group. Very few libraries made special efforts to purchase materials from the home country of the international students.

Many of the unique problems, fears, expectations, and behaviors that foreign students bring to the setting of the university library can be lessened by the foreign students' employment in the library. Communication, which is the most pressing problem, can be enhanced by the daily exchange of directions between supervisor and worker. The foreign student, being paid to do a job, is required to listen to directions and ask questions and thereby becomes acclimated to the American learning style and means of communication. Slang and the use of humor, which can be a problem for the international student, become more familiar in the working situation. Other American working students and library staff members are readily available to explain the idiosyncracies of the English language.

Cultural differences in foreign students can be tempered. International students may learn from the employment experience that being punctual is important and that Americans do not necessarily defer to men or people of status. A firm handshake and direct eye contact are considered assets and not overly familiar in American society. A smile is usually an expression of pleasure or a common greeting. By having working contact with the university library staff, the foreign student learns that Americans are verbal, learn by question and answer, and value individual success, attention to detail, and independent work.

As international students become more comfortable in the work situation, barriers to communication are lowered by asking questions of librarians and library staff. Their new knowledge can greatly benefit their research efforts and academic success. "Once a librarian is recognized as a person who is able and willing to help, foreign students will not hesitate to ask for assistance. A positive or negative experience with one librarian may influence a student perception of an entire staff" (Ball and Mahony 1987, 161).

Hands-on experience in the academic library is mentioned repeatedly in the literature as the means by which foreign students learn best. Certainly the library work training gives them this experience. Whether foreign students work in the circulation department or the ILL department, they become familiar with the structure, management, special services, role of librarians, and the rich rewards of academic success that can be found in the university library. Working international students themselves help other foreign students because of their new-found knowledge of the university library system.

Librarians of the host country may not learn the languages or visit the countries of the foreign students, but they stand to benefit from learning about foreign visitors' different cultures and backgrounds. By playing a positive role in the lives of these international students, who may someday be leaders in their home countries, library personnel have many opportunities to promote international cooperation and goodwill. The urban academic library offers a viable mutual opportunity for a cultural exchange as well as a great impact on the acculturation process of this important group of students.

REFERENCES

Ball, Mary Alice, and Mahony, Molly. 1987. Foreign students, libraries, and culture. *College and Research Libraries* 48 (March):160–66.

Cope, Johnnye, and Black, Evelyn. 1985. New library orientation for international students. *College Teaching* 33 no. 4:159–62.

Greenfield, Louise; Johnston, Susan; and Williams, Karen. 1986. Educating the world: Training library staff to communicate effectively with international students. *Journal of Academic Librarianship* 12 no. 4:227–31.

Hull, W. Frank. 1978. *Foreign students in the United States of America*. New York: Praeger.

Institute of International Education. 1989. *Open doors 1988/89*. New York: Institute of International Education.

Kline, Laura S., and Rod, Catherine M. 1984. Library orientation programs for foreign students: A survey. *RQ* 24 (Winter):210–13.

Koehler, Boyd, and Swanson, Kathryn. 1988. ESL students and bibliographic instruction: Learning yet another language. *Research Strategies* 6 no. 4:148–60.

MacDonald, Gina, and Sarkodie-Mensah, Elizabeth. 1988. ESL students and American libraries. *College and Research Libraries* 49 (September):425–31.

Mood, Terry Ann. 1982. Foreign students and the academic library. *RQ* 22 (Winter): 175–80.

Moorhead, Wendy. 1986. Ignorance was our excuse. *College and Research Library News* 47 (October):585–87.

Ormondroyd, Joan. 1989. The international student and course-integrated instruction: The librarian's perspective. *Research Strategies* 7 (Fall):148–58.

Sarkodie-Mensah, Kwasi. 1986. In the words of a foreigner. *Research Strategies* 4 (Winter):30–31.

Wayman, Sally G. 1984. The international student in the academic library. *Journal of Academic Librarianship* 9 no. 6: 336–41.

21

Space: The Physical Environment of the Urban Academic Library

Ruth J. Person and Joan G. Rapp

One of the issues that distinguishes the urban academic library from its more suburban or rural counterparts is that of physical environment and space. All academic libraries function in at least three primary ways that significantly affect space considerations: (1) as repositories and dissemination points for scholarly information resources, (2) as gathering places for members of the campus community, particularly students, and (3) as study and research facilities. In *Library Space Planning* Ruth Fraley and Carol Anderson list the three key factors affecting library operations that warrant space planning and/or reorganization as "lack of collection-growth space, lack of space for people, and a change in the direction or mission of the organization or community served by the library" (1985, 1). Richard Boss devotes a full monograph to planning for a fourth factor, information technologies. Noting that "libraries and information centers are changing significantly," he finds it "imperative that facilities planning provide for these technologies and for the increasing role that they will play in the future" (1987, 1).

While many academic libraries, no matter what their location, have space problems related to the incorporation of new technology, the growth of collections to accompany the growth in scholarly publishing, the expansion of user populations, and sometimes a change in institutional mission, urban libraries have additional special concerns about physical environment that relate to these four areas and to others as well.

Any comprehensive discussion of space issues must address both interior and

exterior dimensions of the physical environment. One of the most critical concerns of today's urban academic library relates to the use and arrangement of
interior space for maximum utility, given the special needs of the urban location
and the constituency of the urban university. On the other hand, the aesthetic
and practical considerations related to exterior library space, urban design, and
the library's physical presence in an urban environment are also important issues
for academic master planning, overall campus development, and library architecture. It is often difficult to separate these interior and exterior dimensions
clearly. While some problems and concerns are specific to either interior or
exterior design, configuration, and use, many issues cross the boundaries between
these areas and have both interior and exterior ramifications.

While the authors generalize about the characteristics of the urban environment
and urban academic libraries, there are many variations in the actual physical
setting of urban campuses. Unlike their rural counterparts, urban campuses are
often (but not always) notable for their lack of definable visual boundaries, that
is, it is often difficult on an urban campus to know when one is actually "on
campus," so mixed are the uses of space in some areas or so physically indistinguishable are the buildings from their office or retail neighbors. Yet other
urban campuses manage to maintain a distinct visual separation in spite of density.
Topography, landscape features, and neighborhood characteristics also lend in-
dividuality to campuses. To note the many differences in individual campuses,
one has only to contrast the University of Missouri (UM)-St. Louis (built on the
rolling hills of a former golf course outside the high-density downtown region
of St. Louis) with George Washington University, located in the very midst of
high-density development in Washington, DC, or view Virginia Commonwealth
University, also out of the central downtown area of Richmond, like UM-
St. Louis but, in contrast, lacking in expansive "green space."

This chapter will address a variety of space considerations for the academic
library as they specifically relate to the urban campus environment. These include
the place of the library in the physical environment of the campus and the
relationship of the library to general principles of urban design. Factors relating
to the urban environment such as special needs for security (both personal and
property), the general unavailability (and/or extraordinary cost) of land for expansion, and the very nature of the campus user community are also important
considerations. Likewise, more general issues such as the planning process and
the role of information technology have special meaning for urban academic
libraries.

All of these concerns may also be used as a springboard for questioning how
well urban academic libraries are designed for their unique mission and identifying suggestions for future efforts to enhance design. The chapter is thus intended to pose questions and identify characteristics unique to the urban setting
rather than to suggest technical solutions. A number of developments, particularly
in the technological area, represent challenges for nearly all academic libraries;
these developments will be addressed here principally if they have special sig-

nificance to an urban location. Also, while the discussion will focus on the two major avenues for changes in the physical environment—new building projects and extensive remodeling—readers can use the issues addressed here as a means of examining even a stable situation with an eye to small but critical changes that could enhance spatial arrangements and physical characteristics of an existing urban library building.

THE URBAN ENVIRONMENT

The Academic Library as a Catalyst in the Urban Setting: An Overarching Vision

While the urban academic library has a particular campus function, it is also part of the larger physical context of the campus and of the city in which it is located. As we move through the decade of the 1990s into the twenty-first century, we find a renewed critical interest in the efforts of architects and planners to shape the context of the urban environment. Publicized in part by the interest of the Prince of Wales, this movement calls attention to the inadequate efforts (in some views) of architects and planners to speak to human considerations in the urban design context and suggests a new look at urban architecture. Because they are a part of the larger urban fabric, urban academic libraries should be a part of this reexamination.

Before a major library building or remodeling project is undertaken, an urban campus has a unique opportunity to examine the library's place in the overall campus master plan and to determine what particular kinds of design elements in a new building or addition or what significant alterations in an existing structure can move the overall design of the whole campus forward. This kind of examination, however, requires a new way of thinking about the library for all of the partners in the planning and design process.

Within the campus environment, the library is the one physical facility in which every part of the campus constituency has a stake. On many campuses, because of its central function, the library may often be a highly visible focus of the physical environment (as well as a not-insignificant part of the larger city environment). Thus, the library may be in the unique position of serving as an "urban catalyst" for change both on the campus and in the larger urban environment if a new building or extensive remodeling is planned.

As described by Wayne Attoe and Donn Logan in *American Urban Architecture: Catalysts in the Design of Cities*, urban catalysis is a "sequence of limited, achievable visions, each with the power to kindle and condition other achievable visions" (1989, 45). These authors share the belief that, to date, the metaphors that have been used to guide urban design theory are inadequate. An urban catalyst, they believe, "has a greater purpose than to solve a functional problem . . . or provide an amenity. A catalyst is an urban element that is shaped by the city . . . and then, in turn, shapes its context" (1989, 45). In this view the new or remodeled urban library building could then serve as a catalyst for guiding the subsequent development of the urban campus, because "the potential of a building to lead other buildings is enormous" (1989, 46). Since the library building is a central partner in the academic mission of the campus because of its functions and central to the physical heart of the campus because of its relative size, it has great potential to provide a driving force for the future design elements of the campus.

To enable the library to serve as a catalyst for the campus and the urban environment, however, planners need to take a somewhat different, proactive stance. As architect Robert E. Oringdulph notes, "Historically, library design has been reactive, shaped by what the library has been, rather than proactive, which considers what the library may be and designs toward that goal" (1990, 73). The vision of the urban academic library as a catalyst requires an essential shift in the focus of all parties in the general campus master planning effort as well as in any efforts related to specific library construction/addition/remodeling.

Eric Rockwell's succinct reminder in his recent "The Seven Deadly Sins of Architects" tells us: "The architects' vocabulary is full of words like *statement*, and *integrity*, and *look*. Not that there's anything wrong with such concepts; but if you hear a lot of such talk, beware. Architects like to look at the macro level. They don't sweat micro issues, such as circulation desk function. What really excites them is a four-page, color spread in *Architectural Forum*" (1989, 341). Architects must realize that a library building is much more than just aesthetics; they must be able to look at the building on all levels, particularly on a functional one.

Indeed, however, while architects may focus on the "macro level" of design of a particular building, they may in fact need to take an even broader view of the library as an integral and catalytic part of the urban campus (while also paying greater attention to more of the "micro" issues identified later that can significantly affect an urban library). In other words, they need to consider the library as more than just a self-contained, single building on the campus. The library building should not be viewed as a "single end product but an element that impels and guides subsequent development" (Attoe and Logan 1989, 45). At the same time, library planners and staff, who often are more concerned with functional aspects, have an equal responsibility to shift their thinking. They also need to conceptualize the library as a more important visual catalyst in the overall design of the campus. Balancing the functional, the aesthetic, and the catalytic in the creation of the urban library is clearly no small task but one that, if undertaken successfully, can make an impact far beyond the contribution of a merely functional and attractive building on campus.

Attoe and Logan suggest a number of elements, rephrased here as questions, to be considered in creating an urban catalyst. Participants in library space planning should ask themselves:

1. If the (new) library (or addition or alteration) is viewed as the introduction of a new element on campus, what modification of existing elements on the campus might take place as a result of this introduction?

2. What about the library design will enhance or transform existing campus elements in a positive way?

3. How can the impact of the library as catalyst be channeled so that it does not damage its context?

4. How can the uniqueness of the campus be understood?

5. What strategic process can be designed to ensure influence on future urban form in a step-by-step manner (understanding that every situation and every catalytic reaction are unique)?

6. How can a product be created that is better than the sum of the ingredients?

7. How can the individual identity of the catalyst remain intact in this process? (1989, 46–47).

The Library as "Home Base": Addressing User Needs

Characteristics of both the urban location and urban students and employees have a great impact on library space planning, whether minor changes—such as expanding stack space by removing patron seating—or major new additions, renovations, or buildings are contemplated. Many urban campuses are hardly bucolic in nature and do not lend themselves to the informal outdoor gathering more characteristic of their rural counterparts. Furthermore, since residence facilities are often either nonexistent or minimal—or are geographically decentralized in the off-campus community—these typical indoor gathering spots for students are often not as prevalent on the urban campus. The urban campus may also not be as self-contained; that is, while a rural campus generally must provide most of the goods, services, and facilities that students (and staff) need, there is typically much greater reliance on a surrounding urban community to serve the needs of the campus for food, entertainment, retail sales, and the like. The probability of consistent student (or staff) contact is reduced in such an environment. Students more typically then may turn to the library as the one place available for gathering, whether for social or group study reasons. The urban library may be one of the few places on campus that students find to interact informally with other students; it may also be one of the few places for students to work on group assignments or presentations.

On the other hand, the library may be one of the few places where adequate seating and space are available for quiet study and research in an environment that is often crowded, noisy, and hectic—not a setting conducive to thought and concentration. Particularly for commuting students, quiet study space is important because they have no residence facility to utilize for study purposes. These individual "people spaces" in libraries are seemingly even more important on an urban campus as lounges and similar areas are taken up for other uses.

Commuting students who arrive on the urban campus for the day or evening have often traveled considerable distance and cannot come and go in the ways students using nearby residence halls might do in the rural environment. These students must often move about campus encumbered by books, study materials, and sometimes even food needed for the day; they may arrive at the library encumbered with a day's worth of "baggage." Not only is there a problem in carrying this baggage into and around the library, but it is also very difficult to use indexes and search for library materials while trying to juggle backpacks or carryalls. Because of the typically higher crime rates in urban areas, leaving valuables in study carrels or on tables is also more of a security risk. Thus these commuting students are likely to need some kind of storage space for the "baggage" they must bring daily.

Given the needs for gathering, for quiet space, for storage, and the like, the library can and does function as a kind of a "home base" for many students on the urban campus. That "home base" notion is sometimes expanded to accommodate other needs of the campus for small conferences, classes, computer labs, even certain social or ceremonial events and makes the library a more central focus of the campus in terms of overall interaction of the campus community. In many ways, such a focus follows the long-standing tradition of the public library as a focal point for community action. If the academic library functions as this home base for students, accommodations for gathering and for solitary work are necessary; if it functions in such a way for the larger campus community, then adaptations to public traffic patterns for meetings and other events must be considered.

Urban Constraints

As noted above, urban campuses typically must be far more concerned than their rural or suburban counterparts about the physical security of property and persons. Statistics from the 1989 *Uniform Crime Reports* indicate that the aggravated assault rate per 100,000 inhabitants in metropolitan statistical areas is about three times that of rural areas; the ratio is worse for robbery, which occurs about 19 times as frequently in these metropolitan areas (1989, 49). Additional security problems are often posed on urban campuses by the geographic dispersal of facilities. Because urban land is typically so expensive and space for new buildings may be unavailable, growing campuses have frequently expanded into surrounding office buildings. These buildings may be interspersed with other noncampus office buildings, warehouses, and retail facilities and make control by campus security personnel much more difficult.

The increased security risk in the urban environment extends to the personal safety of staff and patrons. In planning layouts and space changes, the interior of the urban library must be rigorously examined for possible areas that might encourage crime (i.e., isolated spaces that are not immediately visible to staff and security personnel, poorly lit areas, and any areas that expose personal property, institutional property, and/or individuals to unnecessary risk). The "solitary nooks" suggested by Oringdulph (1990, 72) as part of the varied configuration of study space that should be incorporated into library design may thus often present critical security problems if not designed so as to allow

visibility for staff to monitor. Likewise, the development of closed or unob-
servable group study spaces, areas utilizing valuable equipment, or carrels may
be problematic for security reasons.

As Robert Rohlf notes, library lighting has been and remains one of the major
challenges facing library architects and designers. In the case of the urban library,
lighting becomes an important security issue. "Failing to locate light switches
in appropriate places, to provide night lights, and to allow staff members to exit
and enter buildings in other than darkness" (1986, 103) can be serious security
problems in the urban library. If switches are located where they are accessible
to unauthorized users (who may turn them off and create security risks) or far
from entrances and exits, serious security risks may exist for staff. The security
of the library at night is a particular necessity because of the increasing number
of nighttime students and faculty teaching classes who may be able to use the
library only immediately before or after class. Lighting may also be a design
issue because in some cases building density restricts the amount of outdoor
light that reaches the interior if one building blocks another's natural light source.

One of the important but sometimes overlooked characteristics of the urban
environment that affects the library is noise. Greater population density, con-
gested traffic patterns, airport and freeway noise, and street maintenance all
become amplified when combined in an urban setting. Thus, creating the quiet
space so much needed by urban library patrons can become a significant design
problem.

It is only realistic to note that space needs deriving in part from consideration
of the urban community, the urban physical environment, and the campus's
urban clientele will likely run up against another aspect of the urban environment
that makes planning even more difficult: the value and scarcity of space itself.
Land is more likely to be scarce and expensive in a urban community. Land use
may be further affected by zoning of various kinds, which may restrict height,
overall size, design (e.g., in an historic preservation district), or building density
on campus. Entrances suitable for commercial loading and unloading might also
be severely restricted because of traffic patterns and regulations. A plan that
meets the ideal aesthetic and functional requirements of the campus, the librarian,
and the architect might well be infeasible, given these restrictions, high cost, or
the simple unavailability of land. Trade-offs among all the factors we have
considered are more likely to be needed in planning library space on an urban
campus. Lack of available space and the difficulty of first choosing an ideal site
on the campus and then designing to take advantage of the natural setting will
make compromise among aesthetic, structural, and functional considerations a
necessity.

Urban Partnerships

The urban situation brings many positive influences as well as problems.
Library space planning—as a function of resource planning—is far more likely

to reflect the much greater availability of information resources in the surrounding community of an urban campus. Consortia or other mutually beneficial informal cooperative arrangements—often with a courier service for library materials—are likely to exist among many urban colleges and universities and sometimes with other nonacademic urban libraries. The existence of these linkages, in addition to allowing relatively easy access of patrons to other local academic, public, and special libraries, must often be factored into the final equation yielding an overall space needs projection.

In addition, the library's relationship to its nonacademic community users must be considered. Seating needs might directly reflect the existence of a government documents depository collection heavily used by public offices or by businesses. Staff working space might need to reflect an existing proposal to provide for-profit search services and document delivery to local business and industry. For example, at Cleveland State University, the library now provides services for the research facility of General Electric. Of particular importance to many public urban colleges and universities is the campus library's role in support of the urban institution's growing awareness of its community responsibility. What Director Hannelore Rader notes of Cleveland State University is increasingly true of other campuses: "New relationships and services are being developed with the urban community to help the campus with recruitment and retention of minorities. Library internship for high school students and an innovative reference assistant program are but the beginnings of that endeavor. The library will play a more active role in supporting such campus concerns" (1987, 455). These concerns may generate space needs of their own in the library, particularly in terms of additional staff work space for special projects and services.

THE PLANNING PROCESS

Once a critical library space need has been identified, many factors come into play in deciding how to solve the problem. In reality, availability of funds is usually the major factor in determining the solution. Typically the least expensive solution is internal rearrangement of movable furnishings and equipment, that is, a reallocation of space to different functions, coupled with a variety of space-saving options, such as compact storage, use of microforms, remote storage, a shift to more cooperative access arrangements, or electronic transmission of documents. Ralph Ellsworth concisely addresses these options in "The ABC's of Remodeling/Enlarging an Academic Library Building" (1982, 334–43) and notes that the degree to which these options will be available to various libraries and in what combinations will vary considerably. For example, substitution of microform for bound volumes presents an array of problems more complex than space requirements, because of high initial costs for reader-printers, ongoing service costs, differing processing costs, and user reactions. Though there will be space savings in microform use, just how much will depend on the extent of its use, the size of the volumes in question, and the reader space that must be added to accommodate the equipment.

If small changes or internal rearrangement cannot solve space problems, then a new building, addition, or major alteration may be in order. There are almost as many prescriptions for the steps in the library building and/or renovation process as there are writers on the topic. Regardless of prescriptions, one pitfall seems clear: locking oneself into a notion that the process will be clear-cut and sequential. Designs will have to be rethought; the architects, consultants (if any), and librarian will—in the best situation—be in constant communication and make compromises through the entire process. The worst scenario has the librarian out of the communication loop; an almost equally bad situation is one in which the architect decides that he or she is the only professional whose judgment matters. If the circulation desk is to be far enough from an electronic security system to prevent interference, if adequate lighting for nighttime study is desired in a beautiful atrium, if comfortable chairs are needed—the librarian should work from the outset to become a partner with the architect and campus planners so that these or other issues (as well as overall design considerations) may be adequately addressed. In any case, the librarian should be prepared to be flexible, to make rational, well-documented cases for professional concerns, and to be prepared to win a few and to lose a few—even big ones! Likewise, architects and campus planners need to be prepared to understand the special needs of urban libraries.

The Systems Approach

Need for both quiet study space and informal meeting places, for increased security in an inviting atmosphere, for more space in an already crowded setting, for a secure campus environment with easy physical access, for creature comforts such as lounges and even vending machines, and for preservation of the collection and the interior of the building—all these conflicting needs may make most steps of space planning in an urban academic library significantly more difficult than in other settings. The potential difficulties reinforce the importance of an overall "systems approach" to planning, which should take place prior to any space rearrangement considerations. What may in the future be "manageable" mistakes in a setting with room to expand or grow may be permanently costly mistakes in the urban environment, where so many external concerns and restrictions already impinge on space planning. Why things are as they are must come before how they can be made better.

Before developing a building program or even a plan for reallocation of existing space, staff must determine whether and to what extent the current building imposes on the current organizational structure, procedures, and even the service philosophy of the library. Do multiple service desks exist because of space constraints on the lobby floor? Is there an in-house "departmental" library because there is no room for the science reference sources to be housed with social sciences and humanities material? Is the government publications department a separate administrative entity because it has to be housed in a hard-to-get-to wing? Answering questions about existing services and constraints and actively analyzing what should be offered prior to even thinking about a specific new space plan not only are highly desirable but also lengthen the time before serious space issues surface again.

By the time a decision is reached that the library has used all other desirable or feasible options and that renovation or new construction is necessary, the library should have rigorously determined why new space is needed. The obvious answer is not always the right one. For example, complaints about lack of study space at the University of Missouri-St. Louis's Thomas Jefferson Library in the mid-1980s actually reflected several years of removing student seating to accommodate rapid collection growth. By the time a new addition was begun in 1988, a library built for about .25 million volumes was in fact housing over .5 million monographs, 1 million microforms, and an extensive depository collection from the Government Printing Office. To solve the real problem (collection space), rather than the apparent one (study space), the new plan called for much of the new assignable square footage to be stacks rather than study space.

For all the reasons previously discussed, initiating close communication from the outset and maintaining it throughout the project are probably more important for the urban academic library than for many others—hence the special importance and role of the library space planner. In a small library, the director usually assumes this role. In larger libraries, a designated staff member may be the library's liaison from library staff to campus planners, architects, contractors, consultants, and interior designers. The space planner must be someone who can find his or her way through the institution, preferably someone who has or can develop good informal contacts with other campus units. The planner must have excellent communication skills to ensure that all parties who need to be involved are heard and that library jargon is not misinterpreted by the architects. For example, "circulation" is likely to mean patterns of people-movement to nonlibrary personnel, as opposed to its library definition of loaning of materials.

Above all, the space planner must be extremely well organized in the midst of chaos, delays, confusion, and conflicting demands in the complex environment of the urban setting. In the already confined spaces of an urban campus, the space planner must ensure through careful coordination with architects and contractors that the library remains open, materials are accessible, services are provided, and security is maintained. Particularly during a major renovation or building addition, this need to preserve an orderly operation may require detailed planning for project phasing and multiple moves of service points and offices.

INFORMATION TECHNOLOGY IN THE URBAN SETTING

If we consider the many possible influences of the urban setting, confirm our organizational structure and service thrust, and determine which factor—or combination of factors—affecting library operations is creating a critical space need, there is yet another issue on which some agreement must be reached before a space plan can actually be implemented. Given the number of books and journals being published on the one hand and the rapid development of new information storage and retrieval technologies on the other, with what degree of certainty can the need for space or type of facility actually be predicted? The current professional literature is filled with discussions of the "electronic" or "paperless" library and predictions of the demise of the book as we know it. Perhaps a more realistic expectation is that echoed by Boss in 1987:

It may take several more years before a substantial percentage of the information libraries and information centers seek to collect is in machine-readable form. A scenario more plausible than a paperless, disembodied library or information center is one with a combination of hard-copy and electronic information. A library or information center's collection typically grows at a rate of 5 percent per year. Were an organization to commit half of its acquisitions budget to information in electronic form, it would still have some three-quarters of its collection in hard copy after two decades (25).

The scenario will vary from library to library, and institutional, systemwide, or state planning formulas that govern space allocation for stacks, reader stations, and staff may be slow in changing to reflect changing library needs. Librarians and their consultants will have to continue to monitor the latest technologies and determine which are the most promising and how quickly these can be adopted into the library's development. Ironically, even where there is little hope for increased funding for collections—and even less for new technologies—space planning will require concern with new technologies. As libraries fall further behind in their ability to purchase a stable percentage of the world's publishing output, "access" will become increasingly important for a larger number of libraries. The key to the quick access demanded by faculty and students is precisely new technologies: electronic publishing, electronic interlibrary loan networks, and telefacsimile transmission. Such technologies have special relevance in the urban setting but at the same time may require a shift in campus culture and attitude concerning access.

Urban academic libraries are more likely to be able to share resources and even to engage in cooperative collection development because of the ease of direct use of other library facilities more often available in an urban environment, speed of courier service, and speed and low cost of telefacsimile transmission. For urban libraries in cooperative groups or consortia, the pricing structure of local telefacsimile transmission typically makes resource sharing (at least for articles) a very low-cost option, once the initial capital investment has been made. This kind of access development, however, while financially advantageous, requires a new way of thinking about the quality of library collections. As Helen Gater identifies in discussing the development of an entirely new library facility for the Arizona State University West Campus in Phoenix:

The inherent danger of an academic library de-emphasizing the collection is that the library will be perceived by administrators, faculty and even other librarians as "second rate." Traditional measures of academic library excellence are, after all, the collection and the book budget. The potential budget implications of such a perception were serious. Not only are operating budgets typically related to acquisitions rate and collection size, a program viewed as second rate by nature is not likely to obtain the funding to become first rate. Additionally, there was a very real danger that a literal and extreme interpretation of non-duplication of library materials would prevail—an interpretation that would have proved disastrous to both campuses (1989, 41).

These choices about access not only demand acceptance of a different view of the importance of "collections" but may have space implications as well. While the library's size may not be increased to accommodate a growing collection, different kinds of space may be required to maintain a full-service telefacsimile service, rapid courier service, and the like.

CONCLUSION

While all academic libraries may share common problems related to space and the physical environment, urban academic libraries have more specific problems related to their location. The complexity of managing space in this setting seems likely to continue as long as urban problems such as security, overcrowding, scarcity of land, and land use restrictions remain. In many ways, most of these problems can be expected to increase with the next decade and to make the necessity of careful planning for library alteration and building projects even more critical.

In particular, however, the renewed focus on the design of cities gives librarians, campus planners, and architects a unique opportunity to make a special contribution to the revitalization of urban design. Visionary planners can use the occasion of library building or remodeling as a catalytic force to shape the future campus and its surrounding urban space by looking at the library as a building designed to lead rather than follow.

NOTE

The authors would like to acknowledge the assistance of William A. Bowersox, FAIA, St. Louis, Missouri, in the preparation of this chapter.

REFERENCES

Attoe, Wayne, and Logan, Donn. 1989. *American urban architecture: Catalysts in the design of cities.* Berkeley: University of California.

Boss, Richard W. 1987. *Information technologies and space planning for libraries and information centers.* Boston: G. K. Hall.

Ellsworth, Ralph E. 1982. ABCs of remodeling/enlarging an academic library building: A personal statement. *Journal of Academic Librarianship* 7 (January):334–43.

Fraley, Ruth, and Anderson, Carol Lee. 1985. *Library space planning: How to access, allocate, and reorganize collections, resources, and physical facilities.* New York: Neal-Schuman.

Gater, Helen. 1989. Creation of an academic library: Lessons from an empty slate. *Journal of Library Administration* 10, no. 2–3: 39–48.

Oringdulph, Robert E. 1990. Thoughts on library buildings and their parts. *Library Administration and Management* 4, no. 2 (Spring):71–76.

Rader, Hannelore B. 1987. Creativity in an urban university library. *College and Research Libraries News* no. 8 (Sept.):445.

Rockwell, Eric [pseud.]. 1989. The seven deadly sins of architects; Gluttony and lust aren't on the list—but ignorance and myopia in library design are. *American Libraries* 20 (April):307.

Rohlf, Robert H. 1986. Library design: What not to do: Successful library building programs avoid these common pitfalls. *American Libraries* 17 (February):100.

U.S. Department of Justice, Federal Bureau of Investigation. 1989. *Uniform Crime Reports for the United States.* Washington, DC: FBI.

22

The Future Results of Using New Technology

John W. Head

This chapter considers some of the likely results of the continued application of current technology as well as some of the possible results of further advances in technology in the near future. It is traditional in chapters of this type to discuss the difficulties of predicting the future. Steven P. Schnaars' *Megamistakes: Forecasting and the Myth of Rapid Technological Change* (1989) is a good source for anyone interested in that topic.

Libraries have moved from very low to fairly high technology in a remarkable short period of time. The resulting changes have been expensive, often difficult, and have begun to change dramatically what libraries are, how they are perceived, and how librarians work. In the span of 1960 to 1985 we have gone from technology essentially limited to the telephone, the typewriter, microfilm, some audiovisual materials, and possibly a teletype to the application of computers, telecommunications, electronic theft detection systems, compact disc-read only memory (CD-ROM) drives, facsimile machines, and television equipment. Of course, in its day, the photocopier was a dramatic piece of technology, and it remains one of the most heavily used machines. While technology has changed greatly, it does not seem likely that the paperless office, much less the paperless library, is just around the corner. Indeed, one of the first things generally done with electronic text is to print it on paper. Paper is convenient, cheap, and portable. We can browse at our time and place of preference and need only enough light to see comfortably. We can make it our own with marginal notes and comments as readers have done for centuries. Still, we all know that this situation is changing, for more and more, text is accessed from computers both local and remote and a certain amount of mail is sent electronically. Computerized interlibrary loan systems have brought electronic mail to libraries large and small. Despite all of the changes and our concern with them, for most academic libraries the book, the journal, and the reference librarian are still primary. We may expect to see a greater shift to depending on technologies fancier than print, but for some time the newer technologies will supplement rather than replace the older. If a reference question can be answered from the *World Almanac* or another common reference source, it can be done both more quickly and cheaply than from searching an online database. The great book and periodical collections of our research libraries are largely available only in the printed form in which they are now held. Conversion of older texts to computer-readable form is not progressing rapidly, nor does this seem a likely short-term prospect. The addition of full-text files to the major online systems, such as DIALOG, is impressive and highly useful, but it still represents only a tiny fraction of all current publications. Nor does it seem likely that all machine-readable texts—and that is what most texts published in the advanced nations are today—will soon be loaded onto some online computer system or recorded on magnetic disks or optical discs; the texts are in electronic form only because computers have taken over most preparation for printing. Nevertheless, the Sony corporation in mid-May 1990 announced a hand-held "Data Discman" player designed for displaying books from three-inch compact discs on a built-in screen. The discs were reported to be capable of holding 100,000 pages of text, and the $380 machine was announced to be ready for the Japanese market by July 1990, with overseas sales to follow in less than a year. The Sony spokesman was quoted as saying that Sony hoped to create a "new culture" and a new approach to information. No mention was made of what types of books would become available on these discs, but one advantage mentioned was that the machines would eliminate the need for people to go to libraries.

THE BIBLIOGRAPHIC UTILITIES

The term *bibliographic utilities* seems to have taken a firm place in library science, even though it is an awkward and not entirely accurate bit of jargon. Trends for the three great bibliographic utilities in the United States—the Online Computer Library Center (OCLC), the Research Libraries Information Network (RLIN), and the Western Library Network (WLN)—are perhaps even less predictable than trends for academic libraries in general, for they will be influenced by changes in their member libraries, changes in the whole society, and changes in technology and its applications. These organizations have become virtually indispensable to the day-to-day operations of academic libraries for the services that they provide, such as supplying access to bibliographic records online for cataloging and verification, providing interlibrary loan systems, and assisting member libraries with the creation of computerized cataloging files for local holdings. Each of these three organizations also provides various other services. Some of the difficulties in projecting trends for them include:

1. Competition from corporate sources for new and conversion data on both CD-ROMs and batch conversion of shelf lists into Machine Readable Cataloging (MARC) format records. OCLC is itself producing CD-ROM files of catalog records, some of which could be used in place of online cataloging on the OCLC system.

2. Competing interlibrary loan systems have been created in some states because many small libraries cannot afford the membership and use charges of the utilities. In some cases these state systems heavily subsidize the costs of interlibrary loans.

3. There are substantial concerns over the governance and operation of the utilities. The three utilities are all nonprofit organizations presumably devoted to serving the participating libraries, but in some instances they seem to have behaved like corporations dealing with customers, and not all of the customers are happy. OCLC probably has the greatest problem because its membership is so large and diverse. Obviously, not all members will support the same priorities; some members emphasize complete, high-quality records while others might give up some detail and even quality control in order to lower costs. Of course, OCLC's large membership is also a great strength and the reason why OCLC's database of bibliographic records is so extensive.

Early 1990 was notable for OCLC because of two major changes: OCLC added subject access with its EPIC service, and it sold its entire LS/2000 local systems division and departed from the turnkey (packaged) automation business.

Meanwhile the three utilities and the Library of Congress have cooperated on building communications links between the four systems, and there has also been cooperation in building an authoritative file of serial records. Where will all these changes take libraries and the utilities? Probably until the year 2000 most of the current relationships will remain intact. Bibliographic utilities are likely to remain major providers of cataloging information and interloan services for midsize and large academic libraries, while some smaller college libraries and some junior college libraries may try to hold cataloging costs down by using CD-ROM files of MARC records and alternative interloan arrangements where they exist or are developed. Bibliographic utilities will continue to provide assistance to libraries in building local databases and to branch out into other areas such as OCLC's CD-ROM databases and WLN's sale of system software. Each of the three utilities has gone through some type of crisis. Should this happen again, the result could be a major reorganization, a merger, or even sale of the system to a for-profit corporation, as has already happened in OCLC's sale of its local systems division. The utilities are probably so important to their members that outright distintegration would be averted by the members if at all possible. Another possibility, no doubt remote, is the merger of two or all three of the utilities. The utilities have surprised some of their members/customers before and may well do so again. At the present moment any changes that do come about seem likely to be driven by finance, management, and the complex set of relationships involved rather than by any change in technology.

LOCAL SYSTEMS AND UPGRADES

Local automation systems have been achieved by developing the systems through campus resources, by borrowing or buying systems from other libraries, and by purchasing turnkey systems. Many of the early systems automated only a single function. There were both many successes and many failures. A number of lessons have been drawn from these experiences. Successful avoidance of failure can be helped by developing staff expertise and staying within the limits of staff competencies and by selecting (or developing) reliable software and selecting reliable computer equipment.

The history of automation developments tends to be different for the large urban universities and the small liberal arts or specialized colleges in urban areas. A great many of the larger libraries had some type of automation program earlier and may now be on their second, third, or even fourth system. This fact does not mean that all the large libraries had all major functions automated early on; neither is it true that all smaller academic libraries were latecomers. Nevertheless, the high costs, the experimental nature of the early developments, the lack of library expertise, and the lack of access to a major computer center certainly caused many smaller academic libraries to wait. What has brought automation to the smaller academic libraries is the well-developed turnkey system that was priced low enough and that required only modest computer expertise from the staff.

During the 1980s there was a very large increase in the number of academic libraries with at least some of the major functions automated. Joseph R. Matthews's report in *Library Journal*, for example, shows the cumulative number of installed automation systems in all types of libraries climbing from 168 systems in 1979 to 1,109 systems in 1985 (1986, 26). Multi-function, "integrated" systems proved to be very popular with both academic and public libraries. Many of the midsize and smaller academic libraries either are on their first system or started in the mid-1970s to early-1980s with a turnkey circulation system, which has recently been replaced (or soon will be) with an integrated system that automates the major functions of circulation, the catalog, acquisitions records, and serials records. Most integrated systems also produce reports that can be valuable for general management and for collections development. Of course, some smaller academic libraries also automated other functions through local development in the 1970s (or even in the 1960s), usually through the campus computer center. Not all of these projects survived when other demands on the computer center increased or when the computer center switched to a new computer system. During the 1970s many librarians got their first experiences using automation without any local computer; they used OCLC, and they searched the files of online search systems like DIALOG, MEDLINE, ORBIT, and BRS.

Automating this way could be done using computer terminals and leased or dial-up telephone lines, and it served to acquaint many librarians with computing on sophisticated online systems, which were frequently more advanced than anything else being done with computer language processing on the same campuses. Of course, the early 1980s brought the democratization of computing through microcomputers, and librarians, like everyone else, used them for word processing, spreadsheets, small local databases, and many other uses, including automating major library functions, although the latter could usually be done at first only in the largest libraries because of the limitations of the early microcomputers.

A particularly interesting and candid account of what libraries have gone through as they have switched and upgraded systems is given in *The Academic Library in Transition: Planning for the 1990s*, edited by Beverly P. Lynch (1989). Four authors contributed sections to the chapter "Technology and Automation," which in some 50 pages covers the history of automation at the University of Illinois at Chicago (UIC) from the planning in the early 1960s to nearly the present. In the early 1960s UIC set out to develop an integrated library automation system. Considerable planning was done, including flowcharting, programming, and testing of some modules. For various reasons this project was not completed. In the mid–1970s the library decided to acquire a CLSI (CL Systems Inc.) turnkey circulation and acquisitions system. Work on this approach ran afoul of both the central University of Illinois Administrative Data Processing Center (ADP) and the local computer center at UIC. ADP began developing a competing system, while the library continued to insist on the CLSI system. CLSI was finally selected for circulation, but ADP was given a major oversight role, which it used, at least in the eyes of the librarians, mainly to destroy permanently any hopes of a good working relationship between the library and CLSI.

Meanwhile the University of Illinois at Urbana decided to select Ohio State University's Library Control System (LCS) for use as a circulation system. By 1979 both the Urbana campus of the university and the Medical Center campus began to use LCS. Chicago decided to follow suit and converted in 1980 to be able to link systems easily, even though this change required data conversion to the brief, non-MARC records used by LCS and a switch to keying in reader and book identification numbers instead of using bar-code readers, as they had with CLSI. UIC had by this time done data conversion to two different non-MARC formats. LCS proved successful as the basis for a statewide resource-sharing system, but UIC librarians never deemed it an adequate local circulation system. The library again began looking for a new local system, especially a system that could meet the original goal of an integrated system. Eventually, NOTIS, the system developed at Northwestern University, was selected, and by 1984 the software had been installed and tested. Data conversion for the new system was complex, involving both the Southeastern Library Network (SOLINET, an OCLC area service provider in the south that also provides many other services) and Blackwell North America (which has expanded beyond book jobbing to providing database conversion services). To add key word and boolean searching, BRS software was added to the system.

All of these changes were complicated over the years by a move of the entire campus, a merger, and great growth in the number of students and faculty and in the size of the library. Many of the developments seem to have been strongly influenced by forces outside the library, and some battles were essentially for power and turf. Both CLSI and LCS were essentially stopgaps accepted as temporary solutions. Only in the later 1980s did UIC finally obtain an integrated system, the goal it had begun to seek in the early 1960s.

Switching systems is not easy. It entails evaluation, selection, acquisition, training, data conversion, loading of records, testing, and implementation. If the new system is from a vendor other than the current one, all of the manuals and procedures will be different. Usually little from the old system can be salvaged to work with the new system, and the monetary value of the old system is likely to be much less than original cost, if it is worth more than scrap.

Turnkey vendors are attempting to upgrade their systems to keep customers who want new features or need more powerful or flexible systems. Despite the efforts of vendors and the difficulties of changing systems, many libraries are likely to change systems during the 1990s. Librarians will want new and better systems as these become available. They will want to leave orphaned systems. It will be interesting to see how many current LS/2000 libraries will stay with that system now that OCLC has sold its local systems division and turned support over to Ameritec, which is one of the "Baby Bell" companies. Since the early 1970s several companies have entered and left the library automation marketplace, and some of the current vendors have apparently come very close to failure. One of the major pressures on vendors has been technology, especially trying to move software technology too fast with inadequate capital for expensive developmental costs.

LINKING LOCAL SYSTEMS

Remote, computerized access to bibliographic information was first made possible through the bibliographic utilities. It is now also possible through dial-up access to online catalogs serving local libraries, through statewide systems and, with less current information, through CD-ROM union catalogs and holdings lists. The CD-ROM union catalogs have the same problem as book catalogs: as soon as they are produced, they begin to become out of date. It is also possible to interconnect online catalogs so that searchers in one library may "seamlessly" and "transparently" search other catalogs via their local library's terminals. A number of such links have already been established, and it seems likely that these communication links will be one of the technological applications to be most widely adopted. Some work has been done on establishing standards for linking local systems, but it also seems likely that there will be many ad hoc and temporary links established on a bi- or tri-library basis. Many of these will be established through campus area networks managed by campus computer centers that will already be linked to both the online catalog and to the neighboring academic campus networks. Eventually, the methods for interconnecting libraries will be sorted out and regularized. In the meantime, catalog searchers will be faced with some strange and confusing screen displays and operating conventions. In many cases the links will be anything but transparent or seamless. Instead the searcher will simply become an indirect user of another library's online catalog and will be forced to learn how to search from whatever help screens and prompts are available. We already know that many catalog searchers are having problems using just a single local system, even though that local system is popular and heavily used. Won't the confusion be severely compounded when our patrons have access to several catalogs of other libraries through the same terminals that they used for the local catalog? Won't we have many searchers who lose track of which catalog that call number, now jotted on a slip of paper or printed on a terminal printer, actually came from? We think we have problems explaining computer searching on one catalog, but it is bound to get even more interesting with widespread linking of catalogs, for all the benefits that it can provide.

At a minimum we probably need to try to add a message line to the display and remind users which catalog they are searching. If we have printers with our terminals, we should try to arrange to have the library's name displayed with entries that are printed, particularly for those entries that are from other libraries. Linking systems could be a way to minimize the disadvantages of rural universities and colleges as compared to their urban counterparts, but it is more likely in the short run to increase the advantages of the urban libraries. Bibliographic access followed by prompt physical access is much harder for the more isolated library. In urban areas faculty and students often use libraries of more than one university, while for those in rural locations not only are the distance and time in travel likely to be longer, but in addition there probably will be no public transportation. Propinquity wins all the time. It is also harder to work out interloan delivery systems that must span wide areas. The greatest advantage of academic personnel in urban areas, however, is simply the opportunity to develop good working relationships because of the chance to meet in person and frequently. It also helps urban libraries that in most urban areas at least one of the local universities will have sufficiently strong computer and telecommunications resources and expertise to see a complex linking project through to realization and to maintain it and keep it functioning.

ACCESS TO ONLINE SEARCH SYSTEMS

The use of online search systems such as DIALOG, BRS, and MEDLINE is well documented, and this use and its growth in the 1970s and 1980s constitute a continuing major change in academic libraries. The most serious and intractable problem is cost. The systems are wonderful, the multiplication in numbers or files rapid, the addition of full-text files a major advance that provides the actual content—not just a citation to a paper that might be useful—if you could get it. The cost of providing extensive service to faculty and students, however, is very high for academic libraries. Thus, a great many libraries have chosen one of two paths. Some libraries have chosen to charge fees to recover at least part of the costs of searches. Other libraries do not charge but cover search costs out of the library budget. In this second instance, budgets for searches are usually limited, and an online search becomes a last resort that is offered only after the print sources have been checked and found wanting. Whichever choice librarians make—charge or free—the number of searches run for faculty and students may be less than one per person in a given year. Thus, most faculty and most students do not get any online searches or get one only rarely. Our major problem is not technology but cost and the best policies to select in apportioning limited resources.

CD-ROM DATABASES

Compact read-only discs are optical discs that appeared on the library scene in the mid-1980s and quickly became a major library resource, competing with and supplementing print, microform, and online information sources. Much of the initial reaction was devoted to two aspects of the CD-ROM. The first was techno-babble about this wonderful new technology, which could store so much information on such a tiny surface. The second was a flood of worries about standards (or, rather, the lack of adequate standards) that would make CD-ROMs practical tools. Then, libraries were full of CD-ROMs. Perhaps only the photocopier gained such rapid and broad acceptance and widespread adoption in libraries. Academic librarians quickly decided that CD-ROM databases were the ones that we could afford to search extensively and provide for direct student searching. CD-ROMs cover many types of files, including full-text files, but it is probably the standard bibliographic file (just as it was with online systems) that are most widely used by libraries. In some cases the same file or a similar file is available from two or more vendors. This availability has helped to reduce prices, and the relatively modest cost for creating a disc means that potential competition may also reduce the temptation of vendors to increase fees rapidly.

Of course, optical discs were not new, but the so-called High Sierra standards provided just the minimum level of confidence to reassure both librarians and database producers that they could safely invest in the new technology without fear of choosing a technology that would soon become obsolete and orphaned.

While other optical disc formats will be added to supplement CD-ROMs, the investment in CD-ROM equipment both for manufacturing and for reading seems substantial enough to protect it as a major technology for several years. Nevertheless, we will probably see some types of optical discs produced with larger capacities and faster access times. Many popular databases already require two or more discs, and to accommodate them we must switch discs or buy enough drives to hold all of the database. Optical discs, especially the CD-ROMs, have brought interactive database searching out of the reference office and into the hands of the patrons who are seeking information. Our role as librarians is not any the less for this development, although this has been the third concern about CD-ROMs. We will still have plenty to do in selecting the best files, providing training and assistance, and assisting searchers to choose and use other resources, including, among others, both reference books and online searches.

EXPANDING THE ONLINE CATALOG

The June 1989 issue of *Information Technology and Libraries* was a special issue devoted to "Locally Loaded Databases in Online Library Systems." Ever since the Project MAC/INTREX work in the late 1960s at Massachusetts Institute of Technology, local computer access to databases has been a goal for libraries, although for most of that time not a very practical goal. Many nineteenth-century library catalogs contained selected entries for periodical articles as well as for books, but when periodical indexes became commonplace, this indexing effort was discarded and university catalogs still grew to thousands of drawers of cards without including any entries for the indexing of journal contents. Once indexes to journals and other materials became available on magnetic tape, a few universities loaded them onto some campus computer and made them available for local searching. Thus, locally loaded databases were sometimes available before the library had an automated catalog, but now online catalogs are becoming the standard, and some library automation systems are flexible enough to allow the addition of journal indexes. There are numerous remaining problems, such as the record format and indexing for journal articles. There are standard formats for most types of materials cataloged and loaded onto local library computer systems, but there is no MARC format for journal articles, and magnetic tapes produced by different indexing services also do not all follow any standard format.

In many cases the periodical and report indexes may be loaded onto a computer other than the dedicated library computer. These computer systems may then be linked so that any of the databases can be searched from any terminal on campus. Most large universities have an academic, campuswide computer network in place, while many smaller universities and colleges may not have a local network available for academic purposes, although some of the same institutions have administrative networks. While most CD-ROM units are based on microcomputers and are single-user units or have tiny in-room "networks," the "locally loaded" databases that are being accessed by library or campus computers are based on minicomputers or mainframes that can be searched from terminals all over campus as well as in the library.

Along with CD-ROMs, locally loaded databases are one of the most exciting technological applications that libraries are participating in, and like CD-ROMs, their use seems likely to spread substantially through the rest of the century. Of course, locally loaded databases provide essentially the same applications as CD-ROMs and online search systems. Thus, during the current decade we can probably expect some shifting and jostling among these three approaches to accessing outside databases, but none seems likely totally to displace any other. Another major expansion of CD-ROM access is likely to occur as CD-ROMs are tied into either library or campus computer systems with access over the campus network. The major problem here is working out pricing with CD-ROM vendors for libraries providing access over a network as opposed to access through a dedicated microcomputer. It may become necessary to block some files from off-campus users, especially searchers from other colleges or universities, who otherwise have free access to neighboring catalogs.

The public access catalog of the Colorado Alliance of Research Libraries (CARL) supports online catalogs for its member libraries as well as a number of other databases. The most interesting of these is called UnCover, a table-of-contents index to about 10,000 journals. This could be a revolutionary development that would supplement and possibly rival online search services and CD-ROM databases; however, it is too early to be certain how successful the project will be. This kind of effort has an appeal akin to DIALOG or BRS for academic libraries, especially if such projects could expand in both contributions and governance. If the alliance's service does not expand very rapidly, it seems likely that other regional networks may put forward similar services. An interesting scenario runs something like this: academic libraries cooperatively index journals, use optical scanners for contents page input, and then share the data through some type of computer networking. Thus, academic libraries could provide very fast access to indexing, and they could also benefit from a share of ownership in the database that they had helped create. Any of the bibliographic utilities might be able to put together the resources for such a project.

EXTENDING BIBLIOGRAPHIC ACCESS AND INTERLIBRARY LOAN

Extending bibliographic access commonly increases requests for interlibrary loan as searchers find references to materials their campus library does not own. A few libraries loading journal indexes onto local systems have loaded only those records for journals that they hold. An alternative would be to have the computer search locally held records first but allow access to all records if they are needed. This alternative would also be a useful feature on CD-ROM systems since it seems likely that some interloan requests would be answered satisfactorily by a source in the local library that was retrieved by the same search but was simply a couple of citations down the list.

One of the greatest successes of automation to date has to be the interlibrary loan systems of the bibliographic utilities. Other networks for resource sharing have been created, very often on a state level, primarily for the benefit of the small libraries that cannot afford membership or service costs in the bibliographic utilities. These systems may cover resources only within the state, and they may be less sophisticated, but they have also increased interloan requests greatly as service has improved, and many academic libraries participate, even though in these networks they are very likely to be primarily lenders. Some of the systems have held costs down by relying on CD-ROM rather than online union catalogs. In some cases the system costs, including costs of loaning materials, are at least partially covered by state assistance. But all of these successes provide us with a problem.

Improved tools for resource sharing may tempt us to cut local resources, but even with improved interlibrary loan request and delivery systems there is usually a delay of several days before receipt of the materials. Far more important than the delay is the problem that many of the materials loaned may be of no use to the borrower. Bibliographic records and citations in bibliographies typically contain scant information on subject content, point of view, level of coverage, or specific topics that might be covered within a book or journal article—with a given title and set of subject terms assigned. I suspect that librarians and library technicians who handle interloan requests know that many requests are a shot in the dark. The borrower is simply hoping that some needed, specific information will be in one of the works requested. In many cases borrowers have enough information to know just what they want, and they order only those items. But in many cases we are simply speeding up getting the wrong things. Local re- sources can usually be consulted much more quickly and evaluated on the spot by the patron. Remote access to full text gets us around this problem to the degree it is available and affordable. It seems likely that remote access to full text will increase greatly during the current decade but very unlikely that it will replace the need for strong local collections.

COMPUTER CENTERS AND LIBRARIES

A particularly useful source here is *Libraries & Computing Centers: Issues of Mutual Concern*, which appeared as an insert in the *Journal of Academic Librarianship* from March 1987 to May 1989. Many of the articles are obviously targeted at those folks in the computer center rather than librarians, but they still provide a good overview of the issues. During this period there was some flirtation with the idea of merging the two facilities under a vice president for information resources or some such title. A merger along these lines at Columbia University attracted considerable attention.

Now it seems more likely that cooperation, rather than merger, will be the most likely outcome, just as the series mentioned above concluded (Dougherty 1989). Libraries can, and have, linked their online catalogs to the campus network that is managed by the computer center and thus provide campuswide access. The computer center may also have the computer power to store other databases and the retrieval software to access them. In fact they commonly have loaded databases for various academic departments for years; the key change here is that the resources are selected for wider appeal and become general services available to all students and faculty. Many of the library turnkey systems do not have the computing capacity or the storage capability to handle large files in addition to the files needed for the library automation system. Of course, power conflicts will come into play, and cooperation may be complicated by competition for computing resources and domination over policy, but that situation is hardly new in academia.

CONCLUSION

The core issue facing academic librarians is the nature of the academic library. A role long accepted is now open to question, and, just possibly, we have entered a realm of revolutionary change in which prediction and planning both become nearly impossible. There is a fear that the academic library—that all libraries— will be bypassed and replaced by direct end-user access to computerized information systems. In this scenario the library remains for a time as an archive, perhaps haunted by a few senile humanists who are too far gone to master computers.

There is also, of course, a host of more immediate concerns. Costs of library materials have increased even as the volume of published materials has increased. Other costs have also increased dramatically. This development leaves us with the funds to purchase an ever diminishing portion of the materials that are available. A useful source concerning this problem is Martin Cummings's *The Economics of Research Libraries* (1986), which points out that current technology costs academic libraries a substantial amount from budgets already strained by rapid increases in the costs of serials, books, and other materials, as well as increases for salaries, wages, and fringe benefits. This book concludes that automation may have many benefits, but reduced costs are seldom among them (the same conclusion is supported by many other sources). In his final chapter Cummings concludes, "Since it is unlikely that personnel costs in libraries can be reduced, and since prices of periodicals and books continue to rise, librarians will be required to depend more heavily on interlibrary borrowing, more selective acquisitions, and cooperative collection development" (129).

In an appendix to Cummings's book, "Economic Issues and Trends in Academic Libraries," Michael D. Cooper writes, "The average price of a U.S. hardcover book in 1982 was $25.48 and a U.S. periodical subscription was $73.89. Given the estimated 1982 lending costs, about 1.9 requests for a book and 5.4 requests for a periodical would cover the direct purchase cost" (1986, 151).

The possible areas for cost reductions are few: we can stop or reduce collecting in certain subject areas; we can replace librarians with technicians; we can postpone automation projects or building expansions.

Thomas Ballard, while his reference point is public rather than academic libraries, has forcefully stated the case for limitations on resource sharing, already suggested in the quote from Cooper. Again, Ballard is talking about public libraries, but surely some of the same limitations hold for at least undergraduate use of academic libraries. Interlibrary loans make up a small part of library use in general because most patrons prefer to see a book before they borrow it. (1986, 97–98).

Ballard, Theodore Roszak (1986), and Richard Saul Wurman (1989) all warn against allowing ourselves to be convinced that we—or anyone else—need instant access to all the information there is. What people can actually make use of is information that is meaningful and interesting to them, and this is always a tiny fraction of the recorded information in the world. The information explosion is real enough, but the data glut is just as real, and sorting through it has become the greatest barrier to locating relevant information. Collection building and access to remote information sources have been our traditional concerns. Perhaps selectivity and quality control will become our new goals, as difficult as they are to achieve and as limited as are the tools available.

To provide the best services, we need strong, accessible local collections and access to computerized information sources. But we also need to build other links. We know that most people, private citizens and professionals alike, go first to other people for information. Urban academic libraries exist in an environment filled with experts "who know the answer." Academic libraries should build a strong and extensive network of contacts with the living experts in the surrounding city. People in government agencies, businesses, societies, museums, orchestras, theaters, and the universities can be reached with a local phone call. A great many would be not only willing but pleased to share their expertise occasionally. We do not know who many of them are, but if we did, they would be an online resource more powerful than any we currently use.

We need to use technology to reach students, faculty, administrators, and researchers by making each technology a valuable resource that is easy to use— easy to use because a capable librarian has helped them learn how to use it. For this to succeed we need a substantial professional staff both good at interacting with our clientele and with the time they need to do that. If academic librarians are persons primarily occupied with internal administration rather than professionals working with clientele, the secret of their professional abilities will remain locked within the library as securely as any chained book.

REFERENCES

Ballard, Thomas H. 1986. *The failure of resource sharing in public libraries and alternative strategies for service*. Chicago: American Library Association.

Cooper, Michael D. 1986. Economic issues and trends in academic libraries. Appendix A in *The Economics of Research Libraries*. Washington, DC: Council on Library Resources.

Cummings, Martin M. 1986. *The economics of research libraries*. Washington, DC: Council on Library Resources.

Dougherty, Richard M. 1989. What happened to the merger debate? *Libraries & Computing Centers*. (Published as an insert in the May 1989 issue of *Journal of Academic Librarianship* 15 (May 1989) n.p.

Locally landed databases in online library systems. *Information Technology and Libraries* 8 (June 1989):99–185.

Lynch, Beverly P. ed. 1989. *The academic library in transition: Planning for the 1990s.* New York: Neal-Schuman.

Matthews, Joseph R. 1986. Growth & consolidation: The 1985 automated library system marketplace. *Library Journal* 111 (April 1):25–35.

Roszak, Theodore. 1986. *The cult of information: The folklore of computers and the true art of thinking.* New York: Pantheon.

Schnaars, Steven P. 1989. *Megamistakes: Forecasting and the myth of rapid technological change.* New York: Free Press.

Wurman, Richard Saul. 1989. *Information anxiety is produced by the ever-widening gap between what we understand and what we think we should understand. It is the black hole between data and knowledge, and it happens when information doesn't tell us what we want or need to know.* New York: Doubleday.

Index

About the Editor
and Contributors

GERARD B. McCABE is director of libraries at Clarion University of Pennsylvania. He is editor of *The Smaller Academic Library* (Greenwood Press, 1988) and *Operations Handbook for the Small Academic Library* (Greenwood Press, 1989).

ELIZABETH ADER is the head of access services at the Miller Nichols Library at the University of Missouri-Kansas City.

SUSAN ANDERSON is director of libraries at St. Petersburg Junior College, Florida.

CHRISTINA E. CARLSON is currently working on a doctorate in political science at Emory University. She is the senior editorial consultant at Georgia State University's Office of Institutional Research.

JAMES R. COFFEY is technical services librarian at the Camden, New Jersey, library of Rutgers University.

PAMELA J. CRAVEY is head of the circulation department, Pullen Library,

Georgia State University, Atlanta. Her research interests include occupational studies of role identity and image and management issues such as retreats, schedules, and space utilization. Dr. Cravey has received two Council on Library Resources grants and is active in the ACRL.

CATHERINE M. DWYER began her professional career as the government documents librarian at the Troy, N.Y., Public Library. She is currently the government documents librarian at the State University of New York, Albany.

EDWARD D. GARTEN is director of university libraries and associate professor at the University of Dayton. He holds the Ph.D. in higher education administration and for many years has been actively involved as a consultant/evaluator for both the North Central and Southern Associations of Colleges and Schools.

JAMES E. GWIN is director of technical services at the University of Richmond. He received a B.A. degree in history from the University of Chattanooga, an M.Ln. from Emory University, and an M.P.A. from Virginia Commonwealth University. He has been involved in the construction and renovation programs of four libraries since 1971.

E. RAY HALL is head reference librarian at the University of Tennessee, Chattanooga.

FLOYD C. HARDY is director of library services at North Carolina Central University. Previously, he was library director at Cheyney University of Pennsylvania, and held positions at New York University and Rutgers University. He received an A.M.L.S. degree from the University of Michigan and a Ph.D. degree in higher education administration from New York University.

JOHN W. HEAD has worked in public and academic libraries. He is a member of the American Library Association and the American Society for Information Science. Since 1973 he has been a faculty member at Clarion University of Pennsylvania, and specializes in courses in information retrieval, library automation, and research methods.

FRED HEATH is director of libraries at Texas Christian University. He is editor of *Library Administration and Management*.

LIA S. HEMPHILL earned a B.A. in history from Rosemont College in Rosemont, Pennsylvania, as well as an M.L.S. from Simmons College and an M.B.A. degree from Nova University, Ft. Lauderdale. Ms. Hemphill joined the Nova University Library staff in 1984 and is presently the acquisitions/serials librarian at the Einstein Library of Nova University.

RASHELLE S. KARP is an associate professor of Library Science at Clarion University of Pennsylvania.

DONNA R. LEONE received her M.L.S. degree in 1971. She also has a Ph.D. in communication/education. She currently works at the University of South Florida Media Center as the director. She is active in promoting the use and understanding of media in the university environment.

JAY R. McNAMARA is reference and government documents librarian at the University of Alabama, Huntsville.

JOHN D. MARSHALL, JR., is an attorney at Georgia State University (GSU), currently holding the title of assistant vice president for legal affairs. He is on the board of directors of the National Association of College and University Attorneys and a member of the state bar of Georgia. He also teaches law and higher education courses at GSU.

EUGENE S. MITCHELL is associate director for collection management at William Paterson College, New Jersey.

ADELE OLDENBURG holds an M.L.S. degree and a Ph.D. in educational leadership from Florida State University. After 21 years in community college librarianship, she retired in 1990. She is listed in *Who's Who in American Women* (10th edition) and active in the National Oral History Society.

HARRIETT M. PASTOR earned a bachelor's degree in biology from Cedar Crest College, Allentown, Pennsylvania, as well as an M.L.S. from the University of South Florida, Tampa. After working in microbiological research in the Washington area, Ms. Pastor relocated to Ft. Lauderdale and joined the library staff at Nova University. Ms. Pastor is currently the associate director of libraries at Nova.

RUTH J. PERSON, associate vice chancellor for academic affairs, University of Missouri-St. Louis, was previously a dean at Clarion University and associate dean/faculty member at Catholic University. A Ph.D., A.M.L.S. (University of Michigan), M.S.A. (George Washington University), and Institute for Educational Management (Harvard) graduate, she is a 1990/1991 American Council on Education fellow.

MARY JOYCE PICKETT, who is currently the director of library services at Illinois Benedictine College, previously held positions at Illinois Institute of Technology, Northwestern University, and Augustana College, Illinois. She served as chair of both the ACRL Extended Campus Library Services Discussion

Group (1985–1987) and the ACRL Task Force to Review the Guidelines for Extended Campus Library Services (1987–1989).

JULIE PINNELL is reference coordinator and social sciences reference librarian at the Miller Nichols Library at the University of Missouri-Kansas City.

JAMES E. PRATHER is the acting director of the office of institutional research at Georgia State University. He is also an assistant professor of political science at the school's College of Arts and Sciences.

YVONNE L. RALSTON is campus executive officer of the University of South Florida at Lakeland, Polk County, Florida. She holds a master's degree in library science and doctoral degree in administration. She has consulted at more than 50 colleges and universities in the United States and Puerto Rico on innovative instructional systems.

JOAN G. RAPP has been director of libraries at the University of Missouri-St. Louis since 1987. Previously, she held positions at San Diego State University and Temple University. She received an M.L.S. from Rutgers University, M.A. from the University of Washington, and M.B.A. from Southern Illinois University-Edwardsville.

CAROLYN L. ROBISON is associate university librarian, Pullen Library, Georgia State University, Atlanta. Her research interests include academic library administration, automation, personnel, and accreditation issues. Dr. Robison is active in the Association of College and Research Libraries and the Library Administration and Management Association of ALA.

RALPH E. RUSSELL has worked in libraries in New York City, Los Angeles, Jacksonville, Athens, Greenville, and Atlanta. The focus of his research and publication is library administration. He is currently a member of the OCLC Board of Trustees.

CAROLYN A. SHEEHY is director of Oesterle Library at North Central College, Naperville, Illinois. Formerly, she was assistant professor/reference librarian (head of department) at the University of Illinois, Chicago, and prior to that, administrative curator of special collections at the Newberry Library, Chicago. She holds graduate degrees from Mills College and Northern Illinois University.

LINDA KEIR SIMONS is coordinator of information services and associate professor in the University Libraries at the University of Dayton. In addition to the M.L.S. she holds an M.B.A. and has been actively involved in the provision of information services to business and industry.

KATHLEEN TILLER is a reference librarian at the University of Dayton, Dayton, Ohio, and a former high school English teacher.

DELMUS E. WILLIAMS is the director of the library at the University of Alabama, Huntsville.